Hijacking the Historical Jesus

Answering Recent Attacks on the Jesus of the Bible

By Phil Fernandes & Kyle Larson
with Matthew J. Coombe

IBD Press
Bremerton, WA

"Hijacking the Historical Jesus" will certainly bring to your remembrance the events of 9/11. Unlike those nineteen hijackers on that dreadful day, Dr. Fernandes and Kyle Larson deal with over two millennia of hijackers who have attempted to take over the historical Jesus. Their work has compiled the most complete list of hijackers past and present I have ever seen in one book; from the attacks that started with early Christian heresies, to the cults and religions of the world; to the philosophers and liberal theologians all the way up to the modern day hijacker's like Bart Ehrman and the Jesus Seminar.

In this day of compliance and compromise in order to not be ridiculed or ostracized among mainstream scholars, it is refreshing to read an uncompromised examination of the historical Jesus. I highly recommend this book.
Eric Urabe, President, Java Bible Fellowship

"The first thing that I noted about this book was the exhaustive list of topics in the table of contents, all of which looked like candy to this lover of the Bible and the Lord Jesus Christ. I wanted to jump in and devour it. However, I soon discovered that this book is no light fare. The authors have done their homework, and, it appears, the homework of many others as well. With the logic of scholars, the authors walk the reader through many issues regarding Jesus that have been debated for years as well as confronting more recent issues within Christology. This book should be required reading of all those who study Christology in academic settings and by all Christians who simply love Jesus and want to know the truth about who He is and how that truth affects them as believers."
Dr. Rick Walston, President of Columbia Evangelical Seminary

"Dr. Fernandes explicates the competing views against the historical Jesus of the New Testament identifying fact, fallacy, and fiction. He calls upon those investigating this matter to adopt neutral presuppositions so as to avail the investigator the most open minded and least biased path to the truth. Dr. Fernandes offers one of the most comprehensive works on the topic demonstrating that the Jesus of the New Testament represents the Jesus of the first century."
David W. Howard, Apologist and Conference Speaker

"Unlike liberal scholarship, *Hijacking the Historical Jesus* honestly approaches the biblical text. This book is a fresh breeze in conservative scholarship. If you want to defend the historicity of the Bible, this book is a must read."
Gary Tronson, MA in Theology (Liberty University)

The Historical Jesus may be the most popular New Testament area of study at present. Viewed from different perspectives in the press and elsewhere, many concerned persons may not know who can be trusted on these absolutely crucial questions. Some have no doubt even concluded that the biblical Jesus has been "hijacked" by the critics. I have known both Phil Fernandes and Kyle Larson for a couple of decades. Both have researched the relevant questions and their treatment here covers a wide variety of topics, criticisms, and responses. Besides, both of these fellows are great guys, too!
Gary R. Habermas, Distinguished Research Professor, Liberty University & Theological Seminary

Hijacking the Historical Jesus:
A Christian Response to Recent Attacks on the Historical Jesus
by Phil Fernandes and Kyle Larson

Printed in the United States of America

First printing 2012 by IBD Press, Bremerton, WA.

ISBN 13: 978-1478212522
ISBN 10: 1478212527

IBD Press
Institute of Biblical Defense
P. O. Box 3264
Bremerton, WA 98310
(360) 698-7382
instituteofbiblicaldefense.com
philfernandes.org
phil@biblicaldefense.org

Dedication

Phil dedicates this book to his beloved wife Cathy (his best friend next to Jesus), his daughter Melissa, son-in-law Tim, and Phil's grandson Nathan. May all who read this book love and serve the true Jesus of the Bible.

Table of Contents

Chapter One
The True Jesus of the Bible

On September 11th, 2001, Islamic extremists hijacked American commercial airplanes and flew them into the twin towers and the Pentagon. Another hijacked plane crashed in a field in Pennsylvania. Many commentators claimed that these terrorists had "hijacked" the Islamic faith. In reality, these Muslim terrorists seemed to take the violent commands of the Koran very seriously. They had not hijacked the Islamic faith; instead, they passionately obeyed the unethical commands uttered by Muhammad in the Koran.

However, the past few generations have witnessed a real hijacking: the hijacking of the historical Jesus. The historically reliable New Testament protrait of Jesus has been replaced with varieties of a politically-correct Jesus, New Age Christs, and other false Christs. In most cases, these false Christs were created in the image of the people who promote them.

Was Jesus married to Mary Magdalene and did He appoint her to lead His church? Or, was Jesus merely a man who never claimed to be God? Maybe Jesus was merely a legend or myth—He never really existed? In short, is traditional, biblical Christianity a perversion of first century Christianity? Today the traditional view of Jesus has been replaced by a myriad of false conceptions of Christ that look nothing like the true Jesus of the Bible. The traditional view of Jesus has been hijacked, and the Christian church needs to respond. We need to defend the true Jesus of history—the true Jesus of the Bible.

Today, two of the leading false pictures of Jesus in the Western world are being proclaimed by Dan Brown, author of the best-selling novel *The DaVinci Code*, and by the radical left-wing scholars who comprise the Jesus Seminar—a think tank dedicated to presenting an alternative, politically correct Jesus to the world. The next two chapters will examine their work and refute the false Jesuses they promote. Other false portraits of Jesus will be refuted as well.

In this chapter, we will examine ancient Christological heresies (i.e., ancient false views of Jesus), the liberal "Christian" view of Jesus, the cultic views of Jesus, and the mistaken views of Jesus found in the world religions as well as in postmodern circles. We will then briefly discuss the true biblical view of Jesus. In later chapters, after refuting the work of the DaVinci Code, the Jesus Seminar, and other recent attacks on the historical Jesus, we will build a strong case that the true Jesus of the Bible is identical with the real Jesus of history. The Bible clearly teaches that Jesus is fully God and fully man. He always existed as God the second Person of the Trinity, but at a point in time He added a human nature. Throughout the history of the church there have been those who have rejected this biblical view of Jesus and have instead promoted false Christs who cannot save.

Ancient Christological Heresies

In the first few hundred years of the history of the church, numerous false views of Jesus were taught (Erickson, *Word Became Flesh* 41-86). The early church fathers had to refute these false Christs, thus forcing the church fathers to systematize the biblical teachings about Jesus. Their work has gone a long way to help us discover the real Jesus found on the pages of the Bible. Before looking at the four key doctrines formulated by the early church fathers, we will examine the false views concerning Jesus proclaimed in ancient, modern, and postmodern times.

Docetism was an ancient heresy that acknowledged Jesus to be God, but denied His humanity. Docetists taught that Jesus only appeared to be a man, but was not genuinely human; He only pretended to be human. This false view of Jesus was taught by the ancient Gnostics. Gnostics believed that salvation came through secret knowledge that only the initiated few could receive. They taught that the realm of the flesh was totally evil; hence, God, who was from the totally pure realm of the spirit, could not truly become a man and partake in the evil realm of the flesh. By denying Jesus' humanity, Docetists rejected the true Jesus of the Bible.

Ebionism, another ancient heresy, taught that Jesus was not God. Ebionites accepted Christ's full humanity, but rejected His deity. Ebionites could accept Jesus as a prophet or a great holy man, but they refused to worship Jesus as God.

Arianism was the ancient heresy that denied Jesus' full deity, teaching that Jesus was a lesser god—He was not equal or one in nature with the Father. Arius, the founder of this heresy, taught that Jesus was the first being God the Father created. Once created, Jesus then created everything else. Arianism was condemned by the early church fathers at the council of Nicea in 325 AD. Today's Jehovah's Witnesses are modern Arians.

The ancient heresy called **Apollinarianism** denied Jesus' full humanity. Apollinarians accepted Jesus' full deity and acknowledged that He manifested Himself in a real human body. However, they denied that Jesus had a human spirit; rather, His human body was animated by His divine spirit. Hence, in their view, Jesus was not fully human.

Nestorianism was the ancient false doctrine which viewed Jesus as two distinct persons—a human Jesus and a divine Jesus. The early church fathers rejected this view since, if Jesus was two persons, then only the human Jesus died for our sins. If God did not die for our sins, then we are still in our sins—we remain lost. The one Person Jesus must be fully God to be the worthy sacrifice for our sins, yet He must be fully man to be able to die as our sacrifice. Just as it is a heresey to deny either Jesus' humanity or His deity, it is also heresy to divide Jesus into two persons. Jesus is one Person with two distinct natures.

The ancient mistaken notion of Jesus called **Eutychianism** taught that Jesus had only one blended nature—His deity and His humanity blended to form a unique hybrid nature. In essence, Eutychians taught that Jesus was not fully God and fully man; rather He was half man and half God. But, if this is the case, then Jesus would not be fully God. Since the Bible clearly teaches that Jesus is fully God, Eutychianism was condemned by the early church.

Adoptionism denied Jesus' deity by declaring Him to be merely a righteous, sinless man upon whom God's wisdom and power descended. In this false view, Jesus was not literally God but could be spoken of as God since God poured His wisdom and power upon Him.

Sabellianism was the heresy that taught that God is only one Person. Sabellius, the founder of this heretical movement, believed that the Father, Son, and Holy Spirit are all the same Person. At times, God would reveal Himself as the Father; at others times as the Son or the Spirit. But, according to Sabelllius, they are all the same Person. The early church condemned this view since the New Testament clearly teaches that the one true God is three distinct but equal and eternal Persons—the Father, Son, and Holy Spirit.

The Liberal "Christian" View of Jesus

Unfortunately, false views of Jesus did not disappear in ancient times. To the present day, there are heresies about the Person of Christ that the church must oppose. Even many who call themselves "Christians" deny the true Jesus of the Bible and proclaim a watered-down, politically correct Jesus. Liberal "Christians" are not open to the possibility of miracles. Therefore, they deny that God could become a man or rise from the dead. Liberal "Christians" believe Jesus to be a very wise man, but not God become a man. Liberal "Christians" cannot even accept Jesus as a prophet, for prophets miraculously proclaim God's truth, but liberal "Christians" reject the possibility of miracles. Therefore, they consider Jesus to be merely a wise teacher, but not the incarnate God.

The Cultic Views of Jesus

Pseudo-Christian cults claim to be Christian, but, in reality, they deny the essentials of the Christian Faith. They teach a false Jesus, a false Gospel, and a false way of salvation. They deny that Jesus is fully God and fully man, and they reject the biblical teaching that salvation is by God's grace alone, through faith alone, in the true Jesus of the Bible alone. We will look at a few pseudo-Christian cults to show how these cults proclaim a false Jesus—a Jesus vastly different from the true Jesus of the Bible.

The Latter-Day Saints, also known as the **Mormons**, teach that the Father, Son, and Holy Spirit are three separate gods, and that there are innumerable gods besides them (McConkie, 576-577). Mormons teach that Jesus is one of many gods and that He was not always god. He was once a man on this planet, but eventually attained godhood. Throughout all eternity He is progressing (i.e., getting better) in His godhood. Certainly, this is a far cry from the Jesus presented in the Bible. It should also be noted that Mormonism teaches that Mormon males can become gods someday. This is the Mormon doctrine called "eternal progression" (Ludlow, 71-79).

The Jehovah's Witnesses are modern-day Arians. They deny Jesus' full deity, teaching that He is a lesser god, the first being that God the Father created. Jehovah's Witnesses believe that after Jesus was created, He then created everything else that exists. Jesus is not equal to the Father; He is a lesser god. In fact, Jehovah's Witnesses teach that Jesus is Michael the Archangel become a man.

Christian Science and the **Unity School of Christianity** purport themselves to be Christian churches, but, in actuality, they have more in common with the false religion of Hinduism than with biblical Christianity. These cults are very similar in their thought. Christian Scientists are pantheists—they teach that God is the universe. He did not create the universe, but is identical to it. God is non-personal; He is not a personal God who can love us and give us moral commands. Instead, He is a non-personal force, an "it." Adherents of the Unity cult are panentheists—they believe that the universe is God's body. God is the soul of the universe. Whereas the Christian Scientist believes that God is everything, the Unity cultist believes that God is in everything. Whatever the case, in both of these cults, man is not separate from God—man is God. All people have the Christ or God consciousness within them. Jesus, in these cults, is demoted to being a mere man who exercised His God consciousness better than anyone else. Jesus is not the Christ; He just displayed His Christ consciousness to a greater degree than anyone else in history. The Christ within Jesus is the same Christ wihtin us. It is our job, according to these two mind science cults, to follow Jesus' example and unleash the Christ wihtin us.

Unitarian Universalism is a pseudo-Christian cult that teaches that everyone already is or will be saved. We do not need to look to Jesus for salvation. They also believe that God is only one Person, and that Jesus is not God. The Unitarian Universalist perspective of Jesus is similar to the liberal "Christian" view: Jesus is merely a wise man and a great teacher.

The Unification Church was founded by Reverend Sun Myung Moon. The Unification Church demotes Jesus to being Moon's forerunner. Jesus announced the future coming of the Lord of the Second Advent (i.e., Reverend Moon). Jesus, though He provided spiritual salvation for mankind, failed to physically redeem mankind. He failed to produce children and pass on His sinless nature to His offspring. Reverend Moon believes that he himself is sinless and that it is his job to physically redeem mankind. Therefore, the Unification

Church does great damage to the deity of Christ and greatly diminishes salvation through Him alone.

Scientology is a non-Christian cult that has grown in popularity over the years. It was founded by the late science-fiction author L. Ron Hubbard. Scientologists believe that humans were, in the distant past, gods called thetans who resided on other planets. The thetans seeded the planet earth with potential life, and eventually mankind evolved into existence. Scientology teaches that we can overcome our mental problems by recognizing our inner divinity—that we are actually gods from other planets. In this cult, Jesus is demoted to being just one of many gods. He is not qualitatively better than anyone else. He may have acknowledged His divine identity better than most people. Still, Jesus is not uniquely divine. In the teaching of Scientology, all humans are divine.

The Views of the World Religions Concerning Jesus

Not only do the cults misrepresent and pervert the true Jesus of the Bible, but the world's non-Christian religions do so as well. Though many Jews throughout the ages have accepted Jesus as God, Savior, and Messiah, most Jews have rejected Him. **Judaism**, in its present state, denies the deity of Christ. Though some members of the Jewish faith are willing to accept Jesus as a great teacher and maybe even a great prophet, Judaism today rejects Jesus as God, Savior, and Messiah (the anointed one who will rescue Israel from her enemies). Though the day will come when all Israel accepts Jesus as their Messiah and Lord (Romans 11:25-27), presently Judaism teaches that Jesus is merely a man, at best, a great teacher.

Islam honors Jesus as being a great prohet, but rejects Jesus' deity and salvation through His death on a cross. Muslims deny Jesus actually died on the cross. Though Jesus is viewed as a great prophet, Muhammad is considered to be the greatest prophet of Allah (the

Muslim name for God). In Muslim thought, it is blasphemous to say that God became a man.

Hinduism generally teaches pantheism—the idea that God is the universe and that, therefore, man is God. Jesus is not uniquely God since everyone is God. However, some people manifest God more clearly than others. Jesus falls into this category: He is one of many manifestations of God. He is not the way of salvation. He is one of many way-showers.

Buddhism, in its traditional form, is an agnostic faith; it questions God's existence. Still, in Buddhist circles, Jesus is honored as a great moral teacher who had much to offer the world. However, Jesus is not God. In fact, He is demoted to less than that of Buddha, the ultimate enlightened one.

The New Age Movement is very similar to Hinduism in its thought. Many New Agers share the Hindu beliefs that God is the universe (pantheism) and man is God. Therefore, Jesus is not uniquely God, but is one of many special manifestations of God. As a great manifestation of God, Jesus has much to teach us; but He is not the Savior and He is not uniquely God.

The Bahai Faith teaches that it is the fulfillment of Judaism, Christianity, and Islam. Devotees of this relgion believe that Baha'u'llah is the messenger from God for this age and that all religions of the world should now unite under the Bahai Faith. Jesus is considered to be one of several manifestations of God. Buddha, Muhammad, and Baha'u'llah are other manifestations of the glory of God. Since Baha'u'llah is the last, he is the greatest messenger of God. The Bahai reject Jesus as the unique manifestation of God; they deny Christ's unity deity and salvation through Him alone.

Atheism, also known as **Secular Humanism**, declares Jesus to be merely a man. Atheists deny the existence of God, the hereafter, and the possibility of miracles. To the atheist, Jesus was nothing more than a man and a religious teacher. He was not God. He will not save us.

The False Christs of Postmodernism

Postmodernism is a recent philosophical mindset that rejects absolute, universal truth and man's ability to know it. Truth claims are relegated to the realm of "stories" or "narratives." No individual stands alone; each person is a product of his community and the narrative his community chooses to embrace. Postmodern thought has given birth to many different narratives which have ironically become dogmatic ideologies—exactly what postmodernists loathe. These ideologies all reject absolute truth and any objective, real history. Therefore, they produce a Jesus who has little resemblence to the true Jesus of the Bible. Below are a few examples of postmodern perspectives of Jesus. Each perspective of Jesus is dictated by the narrative of the particular postmodern community.

Liberation Theology was created by postmodern Marxists (communists). Since they deconstruct history, as well as literature, and read it through the lenses of their narrative (i.e., Marxist philosophy), they twist the Jesus of the Bible into the greatest Marxist revolutionary who ever lived. The sole purpose of Christ's ministry was to free the impoverished masses from the evil capitalists who enslaved them. The Jesus of Liberation Theology is certainly not God, nor is He the Savior of our souls. He merely came to rescue the poor through communist revolution.

Black Christology is that brand of postmodern thought that stems from the narrative of the Black rights movement. Through this lense, Jesus is transformed into the ultimate civil rights advocate. Some Black Christologists go so far as to make Jesus a member of the Black community. Whatever the case, in postmodern Black Christology, Jesus is not the Creator God and the Savior of lost mankind.

Feminist Christology grew out of the radical women's liberation movement as it began to embrace postmodern thought. Theologians sharing this perspective read the Gospels by allowing their narrative (i.e., the struggle of women for their rights throughout history) to shape the content. The result is a Jesus who came to set women free, a Jesus whose priority was to fight for women's rights. Christ's deity is dismissed as being an ancient, outdated male chauvenistic myth (i.e., a male God rather than a female goddess) devised to help suppress women's rights.

Narrative Theology is the postmodern perspective that rejects the notion that the Bible teaches theological doctrines. Since doctrines (i.e., teachings) entail the acceptance of absolute truths—truths that are true for all people, at all times, and in all places—these postmodern theologians reject the idea that the Bible teaches doctrines. Instead, the Bible only tells stories that religiously inspire people. The stories are not true, nor do they teach doctrines that we should believe. Hence, when the Bible calls Jesus "God" or attributes divine attributes to Him, this should not be taken literally. Scripture should be viewed as a collection of stories intended to spiritually and emotionally move us; the Bible was not written to instruct us in theological doctrines.

Mythological Theology also rejects the deity of Christ. Jesus is not viewed as God and He did not come to save us from our sins. Rather, the incarnation is a myth—a story proclaiming some eternal principle—that teaches us that we can be one with God. The incarnation should not be taken literally—God did not become a man in the Person of Jesus of Nazareth. Instead, the incarnation should be viewed as a myth. We need to look behind the story to find the "truth" that lies behind it. The traditional view that God became a man is replaced by a postmodern narrative that proclaims that man can become God.

Gay Theology is the false teaching of homosexual postmodernists who present Jesus as someone who came to fight for gay rights. Some extreme gay theologians even teach that Jesus was Himself a practicing homosexual. The politically-correct gay narrative totally replaces the biblical portrait of Jesus.

With all postmodern theologies, the theologian or historian is free to rewrite history from the perspective of his or her community's narrative. After all, according to the postmodernist, there is no real, objective history. In postmodern times, what previously would be considered nonsense, is now respected as if it were the intellectual "cutting edge" thought.

The True Jesus of the Bible—Four Key Doctrines

We have briefly examined ancient and contemporary Christological heresies—false Christs who cannot save. It is now time for us to examine the biblical portrait of Jesus, the traditional Jesus. The Bible teaches that Jesus always existed as God, the second Person of the Trinity (John 1:1, 14; Titus 2:13; 2 Peter 1:1). At a point in time, He became a man by adding to His Person a human nature (John 1:14; 1 Timothy 2:5; Philippians 2:5-8). He did this without ceasing to be God. Four key doctrines proclaimed by the early church may help shed light on the biblical perspective of Jesus. It is important to note that these doctrines were not "created" by church leaders, nor did these doctrines slowly evolve into existence. The components of these doctrines were clearly and originally taught in the New Testament, but had to be systematized in a coherent fashion in order to refute false views of Jesus.

The Doctrine of the Trinity teaches that there is only one true God, but that this one true God exists throughout all eternity as three co-equal Persons (the Father, Son, and Holy Spirit). Jesus is the second Person of the Trinity. Only He became a man. The Father did not become a man, nor did the Holy Spirit become a man. The Father, Son, and Holy Spirit are three distinct Persons; yet they are only one God. They are not each one-third God; they are each fully God. Still, though they are one in nature, they are three in Personhood. Throughout all eternity, they existed as three distinct Persons, yet as only one God.

Though no single passage of Scripture exhaustively teaches the doctrine of the Trinity, the sub-points that comprise the doctrine of the Trinity are clearly taught throughout the Bible, especially in the New Testament. The Bible repeatedly and unambiguously teaches us that there is only one true God (Isaiah 43:10; 44:6; 46:9; 1 Timothy 2:5). The Father is called God (Galatians 1:1; 1 Peter 1:1-2). The Son is called God (Titus 2:13; 2 Peter 1:1; Philippians 2:6; Romans 9:5; Colossians 2:9; John 1:1; 20:28; Isaiah 7:14; 9:6; Jeremiah 23:5-6; Zechariah 14:5). And, the Holy Spirit is called God (Acts 5:3-4; 1 Cor 3:16). Yet, they are spoken of as three distinct Persons (John 14:16, 26; 15:26; Matthew 3:16-17; Isaiah 48:16). Therefore, the one true God exists throughout all eternity as three equal Persons. It would be a contradiction to say that God is one God, but three Gods. It would also be a contradiction to say that God is one Person, but three Persons. But, it is not a contradiction to say that God is one God, but three Persons. God is one in nature, yet three in Personhood. Hence, according to the Bible, God is three Persons, and Jesus is fully God, the second Person of the Trinity.

The Incarnation is the doctrine of the Bible that teaches that God the Son became a man. Several passages mention this truth (Philippians 2:5-8; John 1:1, 14; 1 Timothy 3:16; Luke 1:35; Matthew 1:22-23; Galatians 4:4). It is not a contradiction to believe that God the second Person of the Trinity, while retaining His infinite divine nature, became a man by adding a finite human nature.

The Hypostatic Union teaches that Jesus is one Person with two distinct natures forever. In other words, He is fully God and fully man. To be fully God, Jesus continues to have all the attributes or characteristics that are essential for God to have. To be fully man, Jesus has to have all the characteristics that are essential for humans to have. It is not possible for God to cease to be God. We know that Jesus retained His divine nature while becoming a man, since Scripture commands us and thc angels to worship Him even after He became a man (John 5:22-23; Hebrews 1:6), and He continued to be called "God" after He became a man (Titus 2:13; 2 Peter 1:1). As a man, He still claimed to be equal to the Father (John 5:17-18; 10:30-33). He also claimed to be omnipresent (Matthew 28:20). The Biblical portrait of Jesus clearly indicates that He is fully God.Still, Scripture also declares Jesus to be fully a man. He is called a man (1 Timothy 2:5), was born of a woman (Galatians 4:4), and experienced the limitations of human existence (Mark 13:32; Luke 2:52; John 4:6; 19:28); yet, He was without sin (Hebrews 4:15). Therefore, Jesus had two natures: one human and one divine. These two natures remained distinct; they did not blend. If His natures blended, He would not be fully man or fully God; He would be a hybrid. Jesus is not half-God and half-man, but fully God and fully man. Was Jesus limited? Yes, but only in His human nature (Mark 13:32). Was Jesus unlimited? Yes, but only in His divine nature (Matthew 28:20). Jesus is one Person with two distinct natures forever.

The Kenosis is the doctrine that teaches that Jesus veiled His glory and humbled Himself by becoming a man (Philippians 2:5-8). Though Jesus did not cease to be God when He became a man and though He retained all of His divine attributes, He voluntarily chose to refrain from using some of His divine attributes while on earth. Instead, He depended on the Father for any supernatural assistance He needed (John 5:19-21, 30). Jesus did not use His divine powers to His advantage while on earth. In His human nature He could learn things and grow in knowledge (Luke 2:52). Even though He continued to be the all-knowing God, He chose to not tap into His divine wisdom while on earth.

These four doctrines are biblically based. They help us to understand the true identity of the Jesus of the Bible. The Bible teaches that there is only one God, but this one God is three Persons (the Trinity). God the Son became a man (the incarnation) to save mankind by dying for our sins. The Son added a human nature without losing His divine nature. Therefore, Jesus is fully God and fully man (the hypostatic union). Still, He veiled His glory by choosing to not utilize some of His divine powers while on earth (the kenosis). Instead, He lived a life of total reliance on the Father and the Father's will.

In America today, two of the most popular attacks on the true Jesus of the Bible are found in Dan Brown's novel *The DaVinci Code* and the meetings of the Jesus Seminar. There are also several other attacks on the biblical Jesus that are popular (especially on the internet). Before we provide a defense that the Jesus of the Bible is indeed the true Jesus of history, we will briefly discuss the history of the search for the historical Jesus and then refute the false Christs found in *The DaVinci Code*, the findings of the Jesus Seminar, and other recent attacks on the historical Jesus. The true Jesus of the Bible has been hijacked—it is time for the church to respond.

Chapter Two
An Overview of the History and Biases of Modern Jesus Research

Before the late eighteenth century, leading thinkers of Western Civilization usually assumed the reliability of the New Testament. Hence, these thinkers considered "the Jesus of the Bible" (also known as "the Jesus of Faith") to be identical with "the Jesus of history." No distinction was drawn between the biblical portrait of Jesus and the Jesus of history. But as the nineteenth century approached, the intellectual climate in Western Culture had changed due to a major shift in Western philosophical thought. Human reason was elevated and miracles were discounted as mere superstitions of the uneducated masses of past centuries. When this thinking was applied to the Scriptures, a great divide was erected separating "the Jesus of Faith" from "the Jesus of history."

Rene Descartes and the Elevation of Human Reason

Although a professing Christian, Rene Descartes (1590-1650) is considered by many to be the thinker responsible for the elevation and exaltation of human reason above God's revelation in Scripture. This high view of human reason ultimately led to Modernism—the attempt to find all truth and solve all problems through unaided human reason (Grenz 63). Though he was a rationalist, Descartes used skepticism as a method to find truth. He decided to doubt everything until he could find something that could not be doubted. This would be a point of certainty from which he could deduce all other knowledge. The more Descartes doubted, the more he became aware of the existence of the doubter—himself. Since doubting is a form of thinking, Descartes proclaimed his famous phrase "cogito ergo sum"—"I think therefore, I am."

Thus began the modern project and the "Age of Reason" (i.e., the Enlightenment). Modernism was characterized by the attempt to find all truth with certainty through unaided human reason. But, if man through unaided human reason could find all truth, then what need is there for revelation from God? This led to deism (the belief in a God who does not perform miracles) and atheism (the belief that no God exists). The supernatural realm was eventually rejected, and the dominant perspective of Western culture became characterized by an atheistic or deistic mindset as well as a bold confidence in the power of unaided human reason to find truth and solve the problems which mankind faced (64). Hence, Descartes' attempt to defend Christianity failed, for Modernism is no friend of Christianity.

Spinoza and Hume's Rejection of Miracles

Descartes' glorification of human reason paved the way for other thinkers who followed him. Future thinkers used human reason to sit in judgment on the Bible and decide what should be accepted as historically authentic from the Bible as opposed to what the rational person should reject from the Bible. The strongest philosophical argumentation against miracles came from the pens of Benedict Spinoza (1632-1677) and David Hume (1711-1776).

Spinoza was a pantheist (Geisler, *Miracles* 18). He believed in an impersonal god that was identical to the universe. He reasoned that an impersonal god could not choose to perform miracles, for only personal beings make choices. Whatever an impersonal god does, it must do by necessity. Spinoza believed that nature necessarily operates in a uniform manner. Therefore, he argued that the laws of nature cannot be violated. Since miracles would be violations of the laws of nature, they are impossible (15).

David Hume was a deist. He believed that after God created the universe, He no longer involved Himself with His creation. Hume reasoned that miracles, if they occur, are very rare events. On the other hand, the laws of nature describe repeatable, everyday occurrences. Hume argued that the wise man will always base his beliefs on the highest degree of probability. Since the laws of nature have a high degree of probability while miracles are improbable, Hume considered the evidence against miracles always greater than the evidence for miracles. Therefore, according to Hume, the wise man will always reject the proposed miracle (Hume, *Inquiry*, 117-141).

Thus the thought of Spinoza and Hume dealt a damaging blow to the biblical account of a supernatural Jesus, for the supernatural was rejected a priori (before an examination of the evidence). All liberal New Testament studies and liberal quests for the true Jesus of history have begun with this presupposition—miracles are impossible. If one wishes to defend the biblical portrait of a miracle-working, divine Jesus, one must first refute the arguments against miracles proposed by Spinoza and Hume.

Lessing's Contribution to Jesus Studies

The application of the philosophical rejection of miracles to biblical studies can be traced back to Gotthold Ephraim Lessing (1729-1781). Lessing was a critic of the Bible who denied biblical inerrancy. He taught that religious beliefs could not be proven through reason or historical evidences (Copleston, book 2, vol. 6, 126-131). He was a fideist—he held that faith rested on subjective experience rather than on objective evidence. He believed that religions should be judged by their effect on the moral conduct of their followers. Evidence for or against religious truth claims were irrelevant.

Lessing imagined an "ugly ditch" between faith and historical facts (Erickson, *Word*, 115). This ditch could not be crossed. No one could know for sure if the Jesus of the Gospels is in fact the true Jesus of history. Religious beliefs could not be defended by appealing to objective facts. Only practical results could be used to determine the worth of a religious system. Testing religious truths is a subjective, inward task. Any appeal to objective evidence is futile.

Christian Theologian Gregory Boyd states that "from 1774-1778, Gotthold Lessing published a number of 'fragments' of a text that was clearly written from a deist perspective." Though Lessing claimed he did not know the identity of the anonymous author, Boyd relates that "these fragments were eventually confirmed to have come from the pen of Hermann Samuel Reimarus (1694-1768), a German professor of Semitic languages." Apparently, Reimarus' daughter gave the fragments to Lessing shortly after her father's death (*Cynic Sage*, 20-21). The seventh fragment was called *On the Intention of Jesus and His Disciples*. In this fragment, Reimarus argued for a sharp distinction between the true Jesus of history and the Jesus found in the Gospels. Thus began the first quest for the historical Jesus.

The First Quest for the Historical Jesus

Hermann Samuel Reimarus (1694-1768) was the first scholar to clearly differentiate between the Jesus of history and the Jesus of the New Testament (Strimple 16-19). As a deist, he could not accept the miraculous, divine Jesus of the Scriptures as a real historical person. Reimarus proclaimed a natural religion of reason, a religion devoid of miracles. He proposed his theory that Jesus conceived of his kingdom in purely political terms, but He utterly failed to usher in God's Kingdom by failing to defeat the Romans. In short, Jesus was an unsuccessful revolutionary who was executed by the Romans. Reimarus attempted to explain away the New Testament accounts of Jesus' resurrection by speculating that the apostles stole the body of Jesus and fabricated the stories of the post-death appearances of Christ (Boyd *Cynic Sage* 20-23; Evans 18). In essence, the Jesus of

Faith (i.e., the biblical Jesus) was nothing more than the lies proclaimed by the apostles. Reimarus never explained why the apostles would be willing to die for their lies; still, his influence on the future of Jesus research was enormous.

H. E. G. Paulus (1761-1851) tried to defend Christianity from the deistic attacks it had suffered at the hands of Reimarus. Unfortunately, Paulus viewed true religion as having nothing to do with miracles; instead, true Christianity is the highest level of moral teaching. He emphasized the ethical aspects of Christianity while ignoring the eschatological focus Jesus had on God's coming Kingdom. Paulus believed the Bible was written during pre-scientific, superstitious times. He did not deny the historical events recorded in the New Testament; he reinterpreted theses events in a non-miraculous way. In the case of the resurrection accounts, Paulus argued that the apostles did not lie—they were mistaken. Jesus did not actually die on the cross; He merely "swooned" or passed out on the cross and was mistaken for dead by those who placed Him in the tomb. Jesus later revived and the apostles mistook Him for having been raised from the dead (Strimple 20-24). Hence, Paulus portrayed Jesus as a non-miraculous, moral teacher. He rejected Jesus as the miraculous God-man who died for our sins and rose from the dead. Again, a wall was erected dividing the Jesus of faith from the Jesus of history.

David Friedrich Strauss (1808-1874) published his work *The Life of Jesus Critically Examined* in 1835 when he was only twenty-seven years old (Strimple 27). Strauss, like the scholars who preceded him, rejected the possibility of miracles. Still he disagreed with Reimarus' view (the miracles of Jesus were lies) and Paulus' view (the apostles were naïve and deceived into believing Jesus rose and performed miracles). Rather, Strauss concluded that the apostles were recording myths—they were teaching spiritual truth by telling stories. In this interpretation of the Gospels, the apostles were not guilty of being naïve, nor were they deceivers. They were merely using myths as a means to convey spiritual truth (Moore, *Quest* 174-175). According to the theory of Strauss, "myth is not to be viewed as a distortion of the essential gospel message but rather as the communicative medium of that message" (Strimple 30). For Strauss, religion portrays the truth in symbolic and earthly terms. He believed that when we search for historical truth, we must begin by eliminating the supernatural, for the laws that govern nature are universal—they allow no exceptions (Strimple 33).

Adolph von Harnack (1851-1930) realized that, up to his day, the search for the historical Jesus "had produced many divergent and contradictory pictures of the 'historical Jesus'" (Moore, *Quest* 175). Von Harnack decided to take a different approach by ignoring any attempt to discover the events of the life of Jesus; instead He chose to simply focus on the teachings of Jesus (175-176; Kee 24). In 1900 von Harnack wrote *What is Christianity*, a work which eliminated any reference to eschatology (i.e., issues such as the end time judgment, return of Christ, etc.) and molded the teachings of Jesus so that they were compatible with nineteenth century liberal theology (denial of miracles, inherent goodness of man, no need for salvation from sin, etc.). Von Harnack accommodated the message of Jesus to the dominant philosophies of his day by removing any "offensive" material from the teachings of Christ (Moore, *Quest* 176). Therefore, von Harnack removed any reference to miracles, the end time judgment, and eternal damnation (177).

Albert Schweitzer (1875-1965) is credited for putting an end to the First Quest for the historical Jesus (Moore, *Quest* 177). In his work, *The Quest for the Historical Jesus*, Schweitzer argued that if one rejects the overwhelming presence of Jesus' eschatological teachings, the end result will be a Jesus created in the image of the scholar doing the investigation (Moore, *Quest* 176, 178; Schweitzer 396). Schweitzer brought to the forefront Jesus' teachings about the end of days. Unfortunately, however, Schweitzer also created a Jesus in his own image. Schweitzer taught that though Jesus predicted He would usher in the Kingdom of God during His lifetime, He failed to do so (Strimple 82). Schweitzer's thesis (i.e., the historical Jesus cannot be separated from His teachings about the end times) was so unpopular in scholarly circles that when he submitted his dissertation at the university he attended, it was rejected (Moore, *Quest* 178).

The Period of "No Quest"

The period from the printing of Schweitzer's work *The Quest for the Historical Jesus* in 1906 until the end of World War II is now known as the period of "No Quest" (Moore, *Quest* 178). In the 1930's Rudolph Bultmann (1884-1976) proclaimed that almost nothing can be known about the Jesus of history (Bultmann 1-44). He believed that the Gospels were so filled with legendary material that it was no longer possible to find the historical Jesus on their pages. This expressed the general climate of this period. The quest for the historical Jesus had been dismissed as a failure. As an alternative to the Jesus Quest, Bultmann proposed that the real Jesus was to be found in the preaching of the church, not in the Jesus who lived in history. What Jesus did or said was no longer considered important. All that mattered was what was believed and proclaimed about Him in the church. During this period, following Butlmann's lead, New Testament scholars gave up searching for the true Jesus of history—they believed He could not be found. All that mattered was the Christ of Faith—the Jesus proclaimed by the church. However, these scholars, due to their bias against miracles, believed that the Christ of Faith was different from the Jesus of history. Their view concerning the historical Jesus was one of total skepticism.

The Second Quest for the Historical Jesus

The "New Quest" is also known as the "Second Quest." This search for Jesus was started just after World War II by former students of Bultmann. These scholars came to disagree with their mentor's assertion that nothing could be known about the historical Jesus. Thus began the "Second Quest" for the Jesus of history. Unfortunately, this group of scholars, like Bultmann and the scholars associated with the "First Quest" before him, continued to reject anything miraculous found in the Scriptures. Their bias against miracles dictated that they repudiate much of the New Testament portrait of Jesus (Moore, *Quest* 183-185).

Norman Perrin from the University of Chicago was a famous representative of the Second Quest for the historical Jesus. In 1974 he listed what he and his colleagues considered well-established facts about the life of Jesus. According to New Testament scholar Craig Blomberg, in his article titled *Where do We Start Studying Jesus?*, Perrin's list included: Jesus' baptism by John, His proclamation of the present and future Kingdom of God, His teaching in parable, His gathering of disciples, His Last Supper, opposition from the Jewish religious leaders of Jesus' day, His arrest and trials, His being charged with blasphemy by the Jewish religious leaders and sedition by the Romans, and His death by crucifixion (Wilkins and Moreland 25-26). Though this list admitted we could know much about the Jesus of history, a large portion of the Gospel material concerning Jesus was rejected. The growing dissatisfaction with this led numerous scholars to embark on the "third quest" for the historical Jesus.

The Third Quest for the Historical Jesus

The third quest began in the early 1980's. The defining aspect of the third quest for the historical Jesus is the emphasis on placing Jesus in His first-century, Jewish cultural context. Any description of Jesus that does not account for this is usually rejected by the scholars of this quest (Habermas, *Historical Jesus* 24). Both liberal and conservative New Testament scholars in this quest attempt to place Jesus in His Jewish culture. Blomberg states that "the most significant observation about the third quest is that none of its major contributors are evangelical Christians . . ." (Wilkins and Moreland 27). Blomberg lists some of the world's leading New Testament scholars who are at the forefront of the third quest for the historical Jesus. This list includes: Ben Meyer of McMaster University, E. P. Sanders of Duke University, James Charlesworth of Princeton University, Geza Vermes of Oxford, Richard Horsley of the University of Massachusetts, Gerd Theissen of Heidelberg, and A. E. Harvey of Oxford (26). All of these scholars, as well as many others, paint a believable portrait of Jesus by viewing Him through the lenses of first-century Judaism. And, contrary to the scholars of the former quests, many of the details of the New Testament Jesus are recovered. The skepticism of Rudolph Bultmann concerning the historical Jesus has been replaced by a confidence that, through serious historical research, we can uncover much about the true Jesus of history.

The only exception among current New Testament scholarship today is that of the Jesus Seminar. This group of scholars and their disciples (not all members of the Jesus Seminar have established their scholarship in the area of New Testament studies) are a throw-back to an earlier time when skepticism reigned concerning the historical Jesus. We will devote an entire chapter to an exposition and refutation of the conclusions drawn by the members of the Jesus Seminar. Contrary to the American media's portrayal of the Jesus Seminar as mainstream, the views and the conclusions of the Jesus Seminar are considered radical by the majority of New Testament scholars belonging to the third quest.

Identifying the Primary Liberal Presuppositions for Jesus Research

When one examines the history of Jesus research and the conclusions drawn by the researchers, several of their presuppositions become evident. It should be noted that these scholars were theologically liberal—they rejected traditional Christian beliefs such as the deity of Christ, the doctrine of the Trinity, and the divine inspiration of the Bible. Although these critics claim to have proven much, their conclusions are contradictory (they lead to several totally different and irreconcilable descriptions of Jesus' life) and are based upon assumptions that have no evidential basis in history. They go where their biases lead them, not where the evidences point. After examining a list of liberal presuppositions, we will attempt to identify the primary assumptions that form the foundation for the other presuppositions.

First, the liberal New Testament scholars believed they needed to search for the "real" Jesus of history because they assumed that miracles are impossible. Since they deny miracles, they cannot acknowledge the existence of a miracle-working, divine Jesus who bodily rose from the dead. Hence, they assume that the "real" Jesus of history must be a non-miraculous first-century Jew. The important issue is this: they never disprove the miraculous, divine Jesus of the Bible; they merely assume His non-existence and then speculate to try to produce an alternative, non-supernatural Jesus. This anti-supernaturalistic bias of liberal Jesus scholars leads them to make several other unreasonable assumptions and dictates their unorthodox conclusions.

Christian scholar Gregory Boyd, in his thoroughly researched book *Cynic Sage or Son of God*, commented on this foundational liberal bias that jump-started the search for the so-called "historical Jesus." Boyd states:

> It is this deistic Enlightenment mind-set that supplied both the historical-critical method and the quest for the historical Jesus with their original philosophical and religious presuppositions. Chief among these presuppositions was the rejection of the ideas of the supernatural and divine revelation, presuppositions that were, a priori, at odds with the biblical worldview and its claims. . . These presuppositions entail that the search for the "historical" Jesus is, almost by definition, a search for an alternative, "de-supernaturalized" Jesus (23).

Second, liberal New Testament scholars believe the New Testament books should be viewed as false until proven true. This contradicts the approach scholars take when studying non-biblical, ancient documents: they consider all other documents true until evidence can be produced calling their reliability into question. There is no reason for someone to be biased against the New Testament books before examining and researching their historical background.

Third, liberal scholars tend to assume the latest date possible for each book. Since liberal scholars reject the miracle-working, divine Jesus, they do not want to acknowledge that the New Testament books were written by eyewitnesses or people who knew eyewitnesses. The later the date for the composition of each book, the easier it is for scholars to doubt that it reports historically accurate information.

Fourth, the writers of the New Testament books, especially the four Gospels, are biased accounts (i.e., propaganda) because they were written by believers—followers of Jesus. There is no good reason to assume that the followers of Jesus were not capable of recording accurate information about their rabbi. Liberal critics assume the Gospels are biased accounts in order to prove they are biased accounts. In short, they are guilty of circular reasoning.

Fifth, liberal scholars assume that the apparent contradictions in the Gospel accounts cannot be resolved, and that these contradictions prove that the accounts, as a whole, cannot be trusted. First, even if there are contradictions in the Gospels, a point contested by conservative scholars, if these contradictions deal only with peripheral issues, then there would still be good reason to accept the reliability of the main events being recorded since the Gospels agree on these points. For instance, all four Gospels agree that Jesus was a miracle-worker who claimed to be Savior and was tried by Pontius Pilate, sentenced to death by crucifixion, but rose from the dead on the third day after His death. There is no reason to reject these accounts of Christ's miracles, teachings, death, and resurrection merely because the minor details of the accounts may be difficult to harmonize. Law enforcement investigators encounter this phenomenon on a regular basis—eyewitnesses often report the same events from different perspectives and may even seem to contradict each other until further questioning explains the differences. Second, New Testament scholar N. T. Wright states that the harmonizing of distinct accounts of the same event is a normal part of historical studies when dealing with more than one source. Wright states:

> I am, after all, suggesting no more than that Jesus be studied like any other figure of the ancient past. Nobody grumbles at a book on Alexander the Great if, in telling the story, the author "harmonizes" two or three sources; that is his or her job, to advance hypotheses which draw together the data into a coherent framework rather than leaving it scattered (*Quest* 36-37).

Sixth, liberal scholars (and now many conservative scholars who follow their lead) assume that Mark's Gospel was written first, and that Matthew and Luke borrowed much of their material from Mark.

It is also assumed that John's Gospel was written much later than the other three. According to liberal scholars, none of the four Gospels was written by an eyewitness. This contradicts the unanimous testimony of the early church. New Testament scholar Craig Blomberg states:

> . . . the uniform testimony of the early church was that Matthew, also known as Levi, the tax collector and one of the twelve disciples, was the author of the first Gospel in the New Testament; that John Mark, a companion of Peter, was the author of the Gospel we call Mark; and that Luke, known as Paul's "beloved physician," wrote both the Gospel of Luke and the Acts of the Apostles. . . There are no known competitors for these three Gospels. . . Apparently, it was just not in dispute (Strobel, *Case for Christ* 22-23).

Blomberg points out that the case for the traditional authors of Matthew, Mark, and Luke is strengthened by the fact that they were unlikely candidates. Mark and Luke were not even of the original twelve apostles, while Matthew was known as a former tax collector, a profession that aroused hatred in many first-century Jews (Strobel, *Case for Christ* 23). If the early church invented the names of the authors of the first three Gospels, they would have most certainly chosen names from among the twelve apostles, but not one who was a former tax collector, considered a traitor by many Jews.

Blomberg admits that there is some difficulty in identifying the author of the Gospel of John (23). This is due to the fact that an early church father named Papias, writing about 125 AD, speaks of John the Apostle and John the elder (Lightfoot and Harmer 528). It is unclear if Papias considered them two separate people or two different ways to refer to the Apostle John. Whatever the case, Blomberg states that apart from the ambiguous passage from Papias,

". . . the rest of the early testimony is unanimous that it was John the Apostle—the son of Zebedee—who wrote the Gospel" (Strobel, *Case for Christ* 23).

Seventh, liberal New Testament critics presuppose that Paul did not accurately represent the original beliefs of Christianity; supposedly, he was an innovator whose beliefs differed from the original Jerusalem Church. Though liberal scholars agree that Paul wrote his letters between 49 and 67 AD, they claim he invented doctrines such as Jesus' resurrection, His deity, His claim to be Messiah, and His death for the sins of the world. Liberal scholars acknowledge that Paul is the author of Galatians; yet, in this letter, Paul claims that he and Barnabas received the right hand of fellowship from the leaders of the Jerusalem church (i.e., Peter, James, and John) in the late 40's AD (Galatians 2:1-10). Most scholars, even of the most liberal sort, would admit that Paul was an honest man. Hence, it is hard to believe that the gospel Paul preached was any different in important aspects to the gospel preached by the first generation Jerusalem church.

Eighth, liberal New Testament scholars assume that there had to be an original non-supernatural collection of the original sayings of Jesus. They call this imaginary document "Q" from the Greek word "Quelle" which means source. "Q" consists of the sayings of Jesus found in both Matthew's Gospel and Luke's Gospel, but are absent in Mark's Gospel. The belief in "Q" is now so widespread that even many conservative scholars accept the existence of "Q." Liberal critics assume the existence of this ancient sayings document merely because they assume that Jesus was primarily a teacher and a speaker who did not really perform miracles. These critics believe that the gospel was originally the sayings of Jesus, and that, years later, fictional events were added to these sayings. However, this is circular reasoning. These scholars assume that the miraculous works of Christ are not in the original manuscripts in their attempt to prove that Jesus was not a miracle-worker.

Ninth, many liberal scholars believe that the early church was not concerned with recording accurate history. It is assumed that the authors of the New Testament books were superstitious and pre-scientific, and therefore unable to separate fact from fiction. Supposedly, the apostles did not have any real interest in reporting accurate history. However, we have much recorded history from this period, showing that ancient Jews were concerned with history. The writings of the Jewish historian Josephus (37-97 AD) is an example of a first century Jew who attempted to record accurate history.

Tenth, New Testament critics believe that the similarities found in the Gospels of Matthew, Mark, and Luke prove that the authors borrowed material from each other's writings. However, there are other possible ways to explain these similarities. First, the apostles may have taken notes or memorized many of Jesus' teachings. Second, the apostles may have kept copies of these notes. Third, if the gospel authors were eyewitnesses of Jesus' ministry or knew eyewitnesses of Jesus' ministry, this would explain much of the similarities found in the four Gospels, especially the first three (Matthew, Mark, and Luke).

Eleventh, these critics, at the start of their investigation, assume that the Jesus of the Gospels is not the true Jesus of history. Since they reject the possibility of miracles, they cannot accept the miracle-working Jesus portrayed in the pages of the New Testament. Hence, they are forced to try to discover a non-miraculous Jesus in history. This is a crucial point: they have not proven that the true Jesus of history is not the Jesus of the Gospels—they assume this to be the case before they began their investigation.

Twelfth, they assume that Matthew, Mark, and Luke are closer to the historical Jesus than the Jesus of the Gospel of John. Because it appears that John emphasizes Jesus' deity more than the other

Gospels, liberal critics dismiss it as a historically unreliable document. However, a strong case can be made for the apostle John as the author of the fourth Gospel, thus making Him an eyewitness of the events he records (Thiessen, *Introduction to the New Testament* 162-170). Even if one denies the traditional view that the Apostle John was the author, a robust case can still be made that the author of the fourth Gospel was an eyewitness who knew Jesus (Bauckham, *Testimony of Beloved Disciple* 12-16, 25-29, 238).

Thirteenth, these scholars presuppose that the authors of the New Testament were superstitious people with a false (supernatural) world view due to the fact they lived in the ancient, pre-scientific world. They treat the New Testament authors as somewhat gullible at times, and thus unable to adequately test miracle claims. In reality, first century Jews were not gullible; they tested the religious views of their day by their Jewish beliefs. It is actually a case of chronological snobbery when contemporary scholars assume they are much more stable-minded than first-century traditional Jews.

Fourteenth, these critics assume that they themselves are not biased and that they live in an intellectually superior age than that of the New Testament authors. These liberal New Testament critics fail to see that their own biases (i.e., anti-supernaturalism, etc.) are based upon their own questionable philosophies (i.e., deism, atheism, etc.). Conservative New Testament scholar N. T. Wright states that the motivation for critical studies of the Gospels "came from the presupposition that this or that piece of synoptic material about Jesus could not be historical" (*Contemporary Quest* 35).

Fifteenth, liberal New Testament scholars believe they have a better grasp of who Jesus really was than the New Testament authors had, despite the fact that the liberal critics are living almost two-thousand years after the events supposedly occurred and that the New Testament authors were contemporaries of Jesus. Once again, this is a case of chronological snobbery. It is an arrogance that should have no place in honest historical research. The documents should be studied based on their own merits and not based on the alleged intellectual superiority of the modern researchers.

The sixteenth liberal assumption is what is referred to as the principle of double dissimilarity. Christian scholar Gregory Boyd explains that this principle assumes that we must reject as a true saying of Jesus anything that Jesus is pictured as saying in the Gospels that either is consistent with first-century Jewish rabbinical teachings or the teachings of the first-century church (Strobel, *Case for Christ* 117). It is hard to imagine anyone considering this principle reasonable. Are we to believe that Jesus was a first-century, traditional Jew who was not influenced one bit by first-century rabbinical Judaism? Are we also to assume that Jesus is the only founder of a religion whose teachings did not resonate in the teachings of His first generation disciples? Boyd expresses this dilemma well, "the obvious problem is that Jesus was Jewish and He founded the Christian church, so it shouldn't be surprising if he sounds Jewish and Christian!" (117). The liberal critic's bias against the Jesus of the Bible forces him to believe that the first-century church put their own words and teachings in the mouth of Jesus in order to promote their own biased agenda. It seems to me that if anyone is biased here it is not the early church—it is the modern-day, liberal New Testament critics.

The seventeenth liberal presupposition is called the principle of multiple attestation. This principle would be reasonable, when used of ancient literature, if it merely meant that we can be more confident of the truth of an account if we find multiple reports of it. However, extreme liberal critics go much further with this principle. They dogmatically assert that we cannot accept as true anything found in the Gospels unless we find more than one source attesting to it. This principle is even more biased then it originally appears, for the liberal scholar assumes that Matthew, Mark, and Luke "borrowed" from each other. Therefore, the same account or saying of Jesus found in more than one Gospel is not considered reliable because it is, according to the liberal critic, derived from the same source! Boyd states, "in fact, most of ancient history is based on single sources" and that ". . . an increasing number of scholars are expressing serious reservations about the theory that Matthew and Luke used Mark" (117-118). Since most of ancient history is based on single sources and the dependency of Matthew and Luke on Mark's Gospel is assumed & not proven, the principle of multiple attestation is at best overused and at its worst should be rejected.

After examining these seventeen presuppositions of liberal scholars, it becomes apparent that four of these assumptions are foundational: they force the critics to accept the other thirteen presuppositions. Therefore, we will take a closer look at these four assumptions. If they can be shown to be unreasonable, then the entire edifice of liberal critical New Testament Jesus research can be called into question.

Refuting the Primary Liberal Presuppositions for Jesus Research

We will now take a closer look at the four primary/foundational presuppositions that dictate not only the other thirteen presuppositions, but also the conclusions of liberal New Testament studies concerning Jesus. These four presuppositions are: 1) a bias against the possibility of miracles, 2) the New Testament books should be considered false until proven true, 3) only the latest possible date of composition for each of the New Testament books should be accepted, and 4) the true Jesus of history could not possibly be the Jesus of the Bible (for this would entail the possibility of miracles).

Liberal New Testament scholars reject the possibility of miracles based upon the arguments against miracles found in the works of

Benedict Spinoza and David Hume. However, if these arguments against the possibility of miracles can be shown to be weak, then scholars should be open to the possibility of miracles rather than biased against them.

Spinoza believed miracles were impossible because he believed in the existence of a non-personal, pantheistic God. This type of God, reasoned Spinoza, does not choose to do anything and, therefore, cannot choose to do a miracle. A non-personal God can make no choices—whatever it does, it does by necessity. Hence, Spinoza concluded that the laws of nature are necessarily set in motion by God—they could not have been different. Hence, the laws of nature cannot be violated, interrupted, or superseded by miracles.

Spinoza's argument against miracles has serious problems. First, there are strong arguments against the existence of a pantheistic God—a non-personal God that is identical to the universe (Fernandes, *God Enthroned* 66-68; Geisler, *Christian Apologetics* 173-192). The existence of the physical universe (as acknowledged by common sense and experience), the beginning of the universe (proven by modern science—energy deterioration and the big bang model of the universe), the reality of moral absolutes (pointing to an absolute moral Lawgiver—i.e., a personal God), and the existence of other minds all show the pantheistic world view to be implausible (Fernandes, *God Enthroned* 66-68). Second, there is strong evidence that a theistic God (i.e., a God who is personal; a God who transcends the universe, but is also immanent in it—a God who can perform miracles) exists (Fernandes, *God Enthroned* 87-119; Geisler, *Christian Apologetics* 237-258). The beginning of the universe, the continuing existence of the universe, the intelligent design found in the universe, the existence of absolute moral laws, and the existence of absolute truths are just some of the indicators that a personal God exists and that He is capable of performing miracles (Fernandes, *No Other Gods* 71-87). Since there is strong evidence against the existence of a pantheistic

God (a God who cannot perform miracles) and a strong case for the existence of a theistic God (a God who can choose to perform miracles), then we have good reason to believe miracles are possible. Hence, miracles should not be rejected a priori—before examining the evidence concerning a particular miracle claim (134).

The second problem with Spinoza's argument against the possibility of miracles is his insistence that the laws of nature cannot be interrupted, violated, or superseded. Modern science now rejects the view Spinoza held that the laws of nature are prescriptive. Modern science now views the laws of nature as descriptive of the way things generally occur rather than prescriptive of how things must occur (135). Simply because there are general laws of nature does not make miraculous events impossible.

Third, Spinoza's definition of a miracle as a violation of the laws of nature can be questioned. It is possible that miracles do not violate the laws of nature, and that they merely supersede the laws of nature. The great Christian apologist C. S. Lewis argued along these lines (*Miracles* 59-60).

The fourth problem with Spinoza's rejection of the possibility of miracles is this: if God created the universe, then the laws of nature are subject to Him. God can choose to suspend the laws of nature anytime He chooses (Fernandes, *God Enthroned* 135). Hence, Spinoza failed to show that miracles are impossible.

Hume, unlike Spinoza did not argue for the impossibility of miracles. Instead, he argued that miracles were so unlikely that the evidence against them will always be greater than the evidence for them. Hume argued that miracles are improbable, and that the wise man will only believe that which is probable. Hence, the wise man will never accept any evidence for a miracle (135).

The traditional Christian can respond to Hume's faulty reasoning in the following manner. Just because usual events (i.e., the laws of nature) occur more often does not mean the wise man will never believe that an unusual event (i.e., a miracle) has occurred (Geisler, *Miracles* 23-31). The wise man should not a priori rule out the possibility of miracles. The wise man will examine the evidence for or against a miracle claim, and base his judgment on the evidence. Since the Apostle Paul stated that he knew of over five-hundred witnesses who claimed to have seen Jesus risen from the dead, a wise man would not reject the miracle of the resurrection merely because all other men he knew of remained dead. It seems that a wise man should examine a miracle claim if there are reliable eyewitnesses. Without good reasons for rejecting the testimony of the witnesses, it seems that a wise man would accept their testimony that a miracle has occurred (Fernandes, *God Enthroned* 135-136).

In summary, it is apparent that the arguments of Spinoza and Hume against miracles are clearly circular—they assume miracles are impossible or unbelievable in an attempt to prove miracles are impossible or unbelievable. Spinoza and Hume assumed what they were claiming to have proved. Therefore, the New Testament critic should not assume miracles are impossible before examining the data of the New Testament. Instead, the New Testament critic should examine the New Testament with an open mind and allow the historical evidence to guide his conclusions.

We must now consider the second foundational presupposition of the liberal New Testament critic: his belief that the New Testament books are false until proven true. This is a totally unfair approach to take since, except for the Bible, all other ancient literature that portrays itself as being historically accurate is considered to be true until proven false. This bias against the Bible flows directly from the liberal New Testament critic's bias against miracles. The critic's anti-supernaturalistic bias forces him to view Scripture with suspicion.

The third foundational assumption of the liberal New Testament critic is his prejudicial dating of the New Testament books—the idea that we should accept the latest possible dates for the composition of each book. Common sense dictates that the New Testament books be treated like all other literature in this regard: when one is trying to date the composition of a written work, one should attempt to establish both the earliest and the latest possible dates of composition, and then work within those parameters to narrow down the approximate date.

The fourth foundational assumption of liberal New Testament scholarship is that the true Jesus of history cannot possibly be the Jesus portrayed on the pages of the New Testament. This is a viscous example of arguing in a circle, for the liberal starting point (a non-miraculous, non-divine Jesus) dictates the liberal conclusion (a non-miraculous, non-divine Jesus).

Proposing Neutral Presuppositions for Jesus Research

We have seen that the four foundational biases of liberal New Testament scholarship are unreasonable principles to use when searching for the true Jesus of history. These biases do not promote an honest examination of the historical evidence. Rather, they encourage the creation of a false Jesus made in the image and likeness of the researcher himself. Instead of examining the evidence in an unbiased manner and trying to determine if the Jesus of the Bible is the true Jesus of history, these liberal critics assume that the Jesus of the Bible cannot possibly be the true Jesus of history, since they reject any possibility of a miracle-working, divine, risen Jesus. The faulty presuppositions of these critics lead inevitably to contradictory views of Jesus or a total skepticism about His life and work, despite so much first century data about His life.

Current research (ironically, even liberal research) on New Testament studies and Jesus studies has provided much evidence for the evangelical belief that the Jesus of the Bible is the true Jesus of history. A growing number of New Testament scholars acknowledge so much in the New Testament as historically reliable that the case for Christ's resurrection and deity is stronger today than at any other time during the last two centuries. Still, many liberal scholars (especially those affiliated with the Jesus Seminar) refuse to go where the evidence leads them and continue to create contradictory lives of Jesus, each liberal scholar creating a Jesus in his own image. The liberal presuppositions for Jesus studies are biased, unreasonable, and lead to either contradictory lives of Christ or skepticism about the Jesus of history. Hence, these liberal presuppositions should be replaced by alternative presuppositions which are more conducive to a fair treatment of the historical data in question.

Unfortunately, many conservative evangelical scholars use the same liberal presuppositions in their Jesus studies. Therefore, I propose a reformation in Jesus studies. I propose that we abandon the biased foundation of liberal New Testament scholarship and propose four alternative presuppositions for future Jesus research. These four presuppositions are much more in line with the honest examination of other ancient works, and the results they produce are not contradictory. The four alternative presuppositions are neutral presuppositions—they are neither liberal nor conservative.

If we were to use conservative/evangelical presuppositions in our Jesus research, they would be as follows: 1) the true Jesus of history is the miracle-working, divine Jesus, 2) the Jesus of the Bible is identical to the true Jesus of history, 3) the New Testament books are inspired by God and totally without errors, and 4) we should accept the traditional dates of composition and the traditional authorship of each of the New Testament books. Though conservative/evangelical scholars believe these four presuppositions, they can, for the sake of unbiased historical research, lay aside these assumptions and utilize four neutral presuppositions in their research. My thesis is that both liberal and conservative scholars, like any good historian, should lay aside their philosophical or religious beliefs and use four neutral presuppositions before embarking on their search for the historical Jesus. The historian should not allow his pre-conceived ideas to dictate his conclusions; rather, he should examine the evidence before drawing his conclusions, and his conclusions should be based on the evidence. The neutral presuppositions I propose are: 1) we should not rule out the possibility of miracles at the outset of our research—miracles may be possible; historical evidence will help us determine if they in fact occurred in history, 2) we must be open to the possibility that the Jesus of the Bible is an accurate depiction of the true Jesus of history, 3) we must consider the New Testament books (like all other ancient writings which purport to be historical) as true until proven false—the New Testament books should be given the benefit of the doubt (as is the case with the study of all literature), and 4) we should not be forced to accept the latest date of composition for each of the New Testament books; instead we should establish the parameters by identifying the earliest possible date, as well as the latest possible date, for each New Testament book. As we utilize these neutral presuppositions, the historical evidence we uncover may favor the liberal or conservative/evangelical position. The honest historian must go wherever the evidence leads.

The third quest for the historical Jesus surprisingly has shown that even research tainted with biased, liberal presuppositions can lead us extremely close to the Jesus of the Bible (assuming the liberal critic will go where the evidence leads him). Neutral presuppositions—presuppositions that are more balanced—may lead us all the way to the Jesus of the Bible. We must not allow liberal critics to dictate the presuppositions for Jesus research, for that will always corrupt the conclusion to one degree or another.

If liberal scholars refuse to use neutral presuppositions in their search for the historical Jesus, then their quest is a pseudo-historical search that is actually a philosophical bias (i.e., anti-supernaturalism) masquerading as an unbiased historical investigation. The researchers are not really conducting a historical investigation; instead, they are forcing their philosophical world view on the data in question.

In the following pages, we will show that an unbiased examination of the historical data, using neutral presuppositions, will lead us directly to the Jesus of the Bible. In short, once set free from the bondage of liberal, biased presuppositions, honest New Testament research will provide a strong case that the true Jesus of history is in fact the Jesus of the Bible.

Different Starting Points For Jesus Research

Liberal Presuppositions	Neutral Presuppositions	Conservative Presuppositions
1) miracles are impossible	1) miracles may be possible	1) Jesus is God and He actually performed miracles
2) the Jesus of the Bible is not the true Jesus of history	2) the Jesus of the Bible might be the true Jesus of history	2) the Jesus of the Bible is the true Jesus of history
3) New Testament books are false until proven true	3) New Testament books should be considered true until proven false	3) New Testament books are totally true
4) accept only the latest possible dates of New Testament books	4) find earliest possible dates as well as oldest possible dates & then research within these parameters	4) accept the traditional dates & authors of the New Testament books

Chapter Three
The DaVinci Code

Dan Brown's bestselling book *The Da Vinci Code* would be more appropriately titled *The Da Vinci Fraud.* Brown claims that "all descriptions of artwork, architecture, documents, and secret rituals in this novel are accurate" (1). He gives the reader the impression that though his work is fiction, it is based upon genuine historical data. However, this is not the case, for the novel abounds with historical inaccuracies, especially when dealing with the history of Christianity.

Brown's novel discusses the unravelling of a supposed two-thousand year old conspiracy which hides the "fact" that Jesus was married to Mary Magdalene, and that she bore his child. Mary is the Holy Grail, for the bloodline of Jesus comes from her womb. The descendents of Jesus are hidden in France; they are royalty and are the rightful rulers of Christendom.

The Da Vinci Code claims that the Christian Church has suppressed the details of Jesus' marriage to Mary because the Church promotes patriarchy (male leadership) and is opposed to matriarchy (female leadership). One of the key characters of Brown's imaginative novel is Sophie Neveu, whose name means "new wisdom." Sophie, towards the end of the novel, finds out that she is a direct descendent of Jesus. (Sorry if I ruined the novel for you.) Brown, through several of his characters in his story, claims that early Christianity believed in a merely human Jesus, but that Emperor Constantine, at the Council of Nicaea, turned Jesus into a God. Constantine then had the true gospels of Jesus burned, leaving us with a New Testament that is "anti-woman" and proclaims a divine Jesus that the early church never knew.

BROWN'S HIDDEN AGENDA

Brown's novel is not based upon true history; rather, it is built upon an agenda. This agenda is anti-Christian at its core. It seeks to replace traditional Christianity with pagan goddess worship blended with the ancient heresy called Gnosticism. Ironically, not only does Brown misrepresent the beliefs of early Christianity, but he also gives an inaccurate picture of ancient Gnostic beliefs. Brown may be a talented writer who is able to hold the attention of his readers, but he is obviously no historian. His religious agenda dictates his revision of history so that he can educate his readers in the "new wisdom," the Sophie Neveu.

HISTORICAL & THEOLOGICAL INACCURACIES OF *THE DA VINCI CODE*

There are so many distoritions of church history and Christian beliefs in Brown's work that we will be able to discuss only a few. First, Brown is mistaken to claim that the early church, before the Council of Nicaea in 325 AD, believed Jesus to be merely human (pages 233-234). The evidence clearly indicates that the Christian Church taught Jesus' deity long before the fourth century Council of Nicaea.

The pupils of the apostles who were selected by the apostles to lead the early church were called the apostolic fathers. Ignatius wrote in 107 AD, while Polycarp wrote around that same time. Ignatius was the Bishop of Antioch in Syria, while Polycarp was the Bishop of Smyrna. They both refered to Jesus as God in their writings.

Church fathers that follwed the apostolic fathers continued to call Jesus God. Justin Martyr (about 150 AD), Irenaeus (about 180 AD), and Tertullian (about 200 AD) were early church fathers; they all proclaimed Jesus as God in their writings. Today, even the far left

Jesus Seminar admits that Jesus was already considered God in the first century, and that the Apostle Paul proclaimed Jesus as God in his writings which date from 50 to 67 AD. A New Testament scholar at the University of Edinburgh named Larry Hurtado argues that Jesus was universally declared to be God by the early church as far back as the early 30's AD. That is nearly a full 300 years before the Council of Nicaea!

Second, Brown is totally mistaken about the Council of Nicaea. The debate was not concerning the question of whether Jesus was merely human or merely divine. Both sides in the debate agreed that Jesus was fully human. However, one side (the bishops who followed Athanasius) believed Jesus also to be fully divine, while their opposition (the bishops who sided with Arius) argued that Jesus was a lesser god and not fully God. The Arians believed that Jesus was the first thing God created and that Jesus then created everything else. In short, none of the participants in the debate believed Jesus to be only (or merely) human. The debate was about whether Jesus was a lesser god similar in nature to the Father (homoiousios), or fully God and thus sharing the same nature as the Father (homoousios). Emperor Constantine did not make Jesus God at the Council of Nicaea; rather, the vote of the bishops confirmed what the church always taught: that Jesus, though being fully human, is also fully God and of the same nature as the Father. Brown is also greatly mistaken when he claims that the council's vote was extremely close. A vote of 316 to 2 in favor of Christ's full deity is not my idea of a close vote. Even the 2 who voted against Christ's full deity disagreed with Brown's view of a merely human Jesus; they believed Jesus to be a lesser god and the creator of the universe.

Third, Brown is incorrect when he states that miracle stories recorded in the Bible are metaphors and were never meant to be taken literally (342). Believers of the early church were not willing to suffer persecution and death because they believed in a metaphorical resurrection. They believed that Jesus had literally risen and had literally performed miracles during His life. This gave them the courage to die for their faith knowing that Jesus had literally conquered death for them.

Fourth, Brown denies that the Bible was written by God through human authors. He claims that the Bible is merely a human product (231). Later in this book we will show that Jesus Himself believed that the Old Testament was written by God and that Jesus promised to preserve His teachings in the New Testament. We will also make a strong case for the divine inspiration of the Bible.

Fifth, Brown is incorrect when he accuses traditional Christianity of being anti-women. Brown has the audacity to accuse the church of executing over 5 million women "during three hundred years of witch hunts" because she feared the "dangers of freethinking women" (125). First, the inquisitions were acts taken by Roman Catholicism, not by Bible Christians (i.e., those who consider the Bible, not the Pope, the final authority). Second, no honest historian claims that millions were killed by the Catholic Church, male or female, during the middle ages. Conservative estimations are in the thousands, not the millions. Third, if the church was so anti-woman then why was the status of Mary the mother of Jesus elevated to such an extent in some Christian circles? Though the Bible does teach that women and men often have different roles within society due to different abilities and strengths, the Bible proclaims women to be equal to men (Galatians 3:28). This is why the women's rights movement was begun by Christians. (Eventually, however, the women's rights movement was taken over by anti-Christian radicals.)

Sixth, there is absolutely no historical evidence for Brown's wild assertion that Mary Magdalene was the wife of Jesus and the mother of His daughter, hence the "Holy Grail"—the vessel which carried the royal bloodline of Jesus. Several recent books written by Christian researchers (i.e., Ben Witheringtom III, Darrell Bock, James Garlow,

Peter Jones, Erwin Lutzer, Richard Abanes, and Amy Welborn) have documented the total lack of evidence for this thesis. We know Mary was not married since only single ladies were named after their towns—married women were called "the wife of" their husbands. There is nothing in the Gospels that imply that Mary Magdalene was either young and attractive. (Mary is often mistaken for a former prostitute or the woman caught in adultery. However, the Bible no where identifies her with these two other ladies.) In fact, it is unlikely that any young, attractive ladies would have taveled with Jesus and the apostles without causing great scandal in first-century Judaism. She, like the other ladies who accompanied Jesus and the apostles, was probably an elderly lady.

Seventh, Brown presupposes political correctness and the new morality when he states that Christian morality is outdated and "not workable in today's society" (416). I would argue that this is one of his biases that causes him to search for *The Da Vinci Code*; for, since he has rejected traditional Christianity for moral (or immoral) reasons, he needs to develop an alternative theory for the source of traditional Christianity. In essence, he uses wild speculation to formulate a theory of the earliest stage of Christianity as a religion that shares his views about Jesus, salvation, and morality. He creates a Christianity taylor-made for his politically correct views. His politically correct prejudices and biased historical research determine his conclusions.

Eighth, after slamming traditional Christianity and glorifying ancient paganism, Brown ironically claims that Christianity has pagan roots (232). Now it seems to me that if Brown wants to exalt ancient paganism while discrediting traditional Christianity, it damages his case to claim paganism as the true source of the Christian faith. Is ancient paganism a good thing or a bad thing? Brown seems confused on this point.

Ninth, Brown argues for spiritual enlightenment through sexual intercourse! The sex act is referred to as "Hieros Gamos" (125, 310).

It amazes me that people are embracing Brown's radical ideas. Is Brown's thesis really that convincing? Was original Christianity really a sex cult? Were Constantine and fourth-century Christian leaders really so anti-sex and anti-women that they had to re-invent Christianity in such a way so as to deify Christ (thus stamping out ancient goddess worship), stifle the freedoms of females, and denounce sex as carnal? It seems that Brown is going way out on a limb to Christianize his own lifestyle choices. Brown is free to make his own moral choices, but that does not give him the right to rewrite the history of Christianity to justify his distaste for biblical morality. All the available evidence indicates that the early church got much of their moral views from the Old Testament. Where in the Old Testament can anyone find the idea that spiritual enlightenment and salvation come through sexual intercourse? Only a gullible public, lacking a solid grasp of ancient history, will fall for Brown's revisionist history.

Tenth, in his attempt to portray ancient Gnosticism in a positive light, Brown misrepresents the Gnostic belief system. Brown argues that before Jesus was transformed into a God at the Council of Nicaea in 325 AD, the early church taught that Jesus was merely human. Hence, while trying to make a case for Gnosticism as the ealiest form of Christianity, Brown fails to realize that Gnosticism rejected the humanity of Christ—ancient gnostics were docetists—they believed that Jesus was divine but only appeared to be a man—He was not really human. Ancient Gnostics believed the spirit realm to be totally good while the physical realm was totally evil and unredeemable. Hence, God could not become a man and take on human form. Also, Brown's glorification of sex is not consistent with ancient Gnosticism, for Gnosticism denounced sex and other physical pleasures. Brown attempts to merge ancient goddess worship—which promoted sexual promiscuity—with ancient Gnosticism—which denounced the pleasures of the flesh. Thus, Brown displays his igorance of ancient religious belief systems, an ignorance only surpassed by his ignorance of church history. Brown portrays traditional Christianity as being anti-woman's rights, while painting a picture of ancient Gnosticism as a defender of woman's rights. But, once again, this is not the case, for, in Gnostic thinking, "females are not worthy of life" and "every female who makes herself male will enter the Kingdom of Heaven" (*The Gospel of Thomas*, 114). If Brown thinks Gnosticism is pro-women's rights, he should read this quote from the Gnostic *Gospel of Thomas* at a women's rights rally and wait for the response of the audience. If a woman wanted salvation in Gnostic circles, she had to renounce her womanhood. Hence, Brown misrepresents ancient Gnosticism in order to make it politically correct.

Eleventh, Brown is wrong to portray original Christianity as Gnostic. In fact, Simone Petrement has shown that a fully developed Gnosticism could not possibly predate Christianity since Gnosticism is based upon a perversion of some of the key themes (flesh vs. spirit, divine wisdom, etc.) found in the writings of the apostles Paul and John. Petrement's work *A Separate God: The Origins and Teachings of Gnosticism* refutes the popular, but unsubstantiated, theory of a pre-Christian Gnosticism.

And, twelfth, Brown is incorrect for attacking the New Testament canon (i.e., the list of books in the New Testament). Brown is mistaken in his assertion that the canon was not settled until the Council of Nicaea in 325 AD (231-234). Whereas the earliest Gnostic writings date to the mid second-century AD, the entire New Testament dates from the mid to late first-century AD (when eyewitnesses who knew Jesus where still alive & some of them leading the church).

Today, the vast majority of New Testament scholars, many of whom are not evangelical Christians, accept several of Paul's letters as being authentic (i.e., Romans, 1 & 2 Corinthians, Galatians,

Philippians, Philemon, and 1 Thessalonians). They date Paul's writings from 49 to 64 AD. Even a cursory reading of Paul's letters reveal that he taught the full deity and full humanity of Jesus, salvation through faith in Him alone, His substitutionary death for our sins, and His bodily resurrection from the dead. These doctrines support traditional Christian doctrines rather than the esoteric, speculative ramblings of the Gnostic heretics.

A strong case can be made for pre-61 AD dates of composition for the Gospel of Luke and the Book of Acts. Acts is the sequel of Luke since both were written to a man named Theophilus (Luke 1:1-4; Acts 1:1-3). The introduction to the Book of Acts mentions the earlier work (i.e., the Gospel of Luke); hence, Acts was written after Luke. Yet, when we examine the Book of Acts, we find several suprising omissions. Though the author of Luke writes in detail about the ministries of Peter, Paul, and James (the half-brother of Jesus), accounts of their deaths are mysteriously absent from the book. Peter and Paul were martyred in 67 AD, while James was executed in 62 AD. The temple receives much attention in Acts, yet the author does not mention its destruction which occurred in 70 AD. The best explanation for the omissions is that Acts was written before these events occurred (i.e., before 62 AD). This also explains why Acts ends abruptly and anti-climatically with Paul in Rome under house arrest in 61 AD. The best explanation is that Acts was completed in 61 AD. But, this means that, since Acts is the sequel to the Gospel of Luke, Luke's Gospel must have been written before 61 AD.

There is also strong evidence for early dates of Matthew and Mark. Papias was the Bishop of Hierapolis in Asia Minor. He was an Apostolic Father, a pupil of the apostles selected by the apostles for a position of leadership in the early church. Around 130 AD, he confirmed in his writings that Matthew and Mark wrote their Gospels. He stated that Matthew the Apostle wrote his Gospel first and that it was originally written in Hebrew, but later translated into Greek.

Papias related that Mark based his Gospel on Peter's preaching and wrote his Gospel when Peter departed from Rome in the mid 40's AD.

Papias and two other Apostolic Fathers, Polycarp and Ignatius, quote from or paraphrase portions of John's Gospel. It should be noted that Ignatius was the Bishop of Antioch and he wrote his letters in 107 AD when he was en route to be martyred. In 150 AD, an early church father named Justin Martyr also refers to John's Gospel in his writings. The evidence clearly indicates that the four Gospels (and Paul's writings) were accepted by large portions of the church as Scripture as early as the beginning of the second century AD.

It should also be noted that the early church would not have claimed that three of the Gospels were written by Matthew, Mark, and Luke if this were not the case. Mark and Luke were not numbered among the apostles—why fabricate non-apostolic authorship? Although Matthew was one of the original twelve apostles, he was a tax collector—he made his living collecting taxes from the Jews for the Romans. He would have been considered a traitor by the Jews. If the early church decided to fabricate the identity of the author of Matthew's Gospel, she would not have chosen Matthew—that would have been a public relations disaster. The early church was trying to convince the Jews to accept Jesus as their Messiah. Promoting a Gospel composed by a tax collector makes no sense unless Matthew, the tax collector, was the real author.

If someone rejects the Apostle John as the author of the fourth Gospel, then he must explain why it is the only cannonical Gospel in which John's name is never mentioned. John is referred to as "the disciple whom Jesus loved." Also, the enemy of the early church is portrayed as being the Jewish religious leaders, not the Roman governing authorities. This may argue for an early date for John's Gospel since the Jewish religious authorities were the primary threat to the early church before the temple was destroyed in 70 AD. In fact,

Princeton New Testament scholar James Charlesworth dates John's Gospel as early as the fifties AD, much earlier than many evangelical scholars date this Gospel (Thiede, *Dead Sea Scrolls* 181). Whatever the case, whether one accepts the Apostle John as the author or not, and whether one accepts an early date (50's AD) or a later date (90 AD), there is extremely good evidence that John's Gospel is based on reliable eyewitness testimony (Bauckham *Testimony of the Beloved Disciple* 12-16, 25-29, 238).

The evidence also indicates that the Book of Hebrews was written before the destruction of the temple in 70 AD. The recipients of this letter were Jews who professed faith in Jesus, but then, due to persecution, were tempted to return to Judaism. The author argues that Jesus' sacrifice of Himself on the cross alone is sufficient to atone for our sins, and that the bloodshed of animals does not take away sin. The author sees the fact that the temple priests are still standing and still offering animal sacrifices as evidence that their work is not finished—the people's sins are not forgiven. On the other hand, Jesus' work is done—He offered Himself on the cross once for all for the sins of mankind and now He is seated at the Father's right hand. His mission (to forgive sin) is accomplished. If the Book of Hebrews had been written after the destruction of the temple in 70 AD, then his argument would have been very different. He would have reasoned that his readers should not depart from the Christian Faith because God showed them that the temple sacrifices were temporary by allowing the Romans to destroy the temple. Since he did not use this argument and his argument presupposes the temple sacrifices are still being offered, the Book of Hebrews had to be composed before 70 AD.

The Muratorian Fragment of the latter half of the second century lists as Scripture all the books of the New Testament except for Hebrews, James, and the epistles of Peter. Hebrews may have been ommitted due to the fact that the author's name has been lost to history. The Book of James may be absent because of the difficulties in harmonizing James' teachings about salvation with the teachings of Paul. However, assumed contradictions are reconciled when we realize that James defined his terms (i.e., justification, faith) differently than did Paul. It is possible that Peter's epistles may not have yet been fully circulated throughout the ancient world, and that the Christians who drew up this list may not have had access to them.

Still, if one takes a closer look at early Christianity, one finds strong evidence that the New Testament books were already acknolwedged as fully authoritative Scripture in the latter half of the first-century AD. Paul quotes a passage from Luke's Gospel as "Scripture" (1 Timothy 5:18), and Peter refers to Paul's writings as "Scripture" (2 Peter 3:15-16). Even if liberal scholars reject Paul as the author of First Timothy and Peter as the author Second Peter, they still acknowledge that these letters were written in the first-century. Hence, Luke and Paul's writings were already accepted as Scripture in the first-century. Also, three bishops in the early church (i.e., Clement of Rome, Ignatius, and Polycarp), writing before 110 AD, quoted from or alluded to twenty-five out of the twenty-seven New Testament books as authoritative Scripture (Barnett, *Is the New Testament Reliable?* 39-41). Hence, the early church recognized the New Testament books as having Apostolic authority and as being reliable witnesses to the true Jesus of history.

The point is this: the evidence indicates that all New Testament books were first-century documents written by eyewitnesses of the events or people who knew the eyewitnesses. On the other hand, the Gnostic Gospels all date after 140 AD, a full generation after the eyewitnesses died and more than one hundred years after the events occurred. Philip Jenkins, Distinguished Professor of History and Religious Studies at Penn State University, notes that *The Gospel of Thomas*, though probably the ealiest of the Gnostic Gospels, "contains many sayings which unmistakenly suggest Gnosticism and other heresies which developed during the mid- and late second century . . ." (*Hidden Gospels*, 70). New Testament scholar Ben Witherington III relates that *The Gospel of Thomas* manifests a knowledge of the material found in all four Gospels, showing that it was written much later than the four cannonical Gospels at a time when all four Gospels were well-known and widely distributed throughout the church (*The Gospel Code*, 103).

It is doubtful that any first-century church had the entire set of the New Testament books. But, by the mid second century false, heretical writings were being circulated and portrayed as authentic writings from the apostles. This forced the leaders of the early church to collect and determine which books were authentic and which books were forgeries. The early church had several tests for the canonization (recognizing a book as belonging in the Bible) and authenticity of a manuscript. First, the book had to have apostolic authorship or authority. If an apostle did not write the book, the author had to be a trusted colleague of an apostle, and his writing had to have the approval of the apostle. Second, the book had to be spiritually edifying for the entire church. And, third, the book had to be consistent with what God had previously revealed in Scripture (both Old and New Testaments). Since Gnostics proclaimed a different Jesus (divine in some sense, but not really human) and a different way of salvation (salvation through secret knowledge that only the initiated could know), their writings were recognized as heretical. Since they rejected the Old Testament and declared the Old Testament God to be evil, the early church (which accepted the Old Testament as God's inspired Word and equated the Old Testament God with the New Testament God) could not accept the Gnostic writings as Scripture. Also, the Gnostic writings were written far too late and could not claim apostolic authorship or authority. In short, the early church had good reasons for rejecting the Gnostic writings as spurious, as well as good reasons for acknowledging the New

Testament writings as Scripture and as the completion of the Old Testament.

The Gnostic writings taught an entirely different religion than the Old and New Testament books. Gnosticism proclaims a different Jesus and a different way of salvation. Gnosticism worships a different god (i.e., it rejects the God of the Old Testament). Gnostics stressed subjective, secret knowledge rather than the objective truth and objective history proclaimed by Christianity.

It is interesting to note that even though the Jesus Seminar represents the extreme left in the world of New Testament scholarship, it is no where near as far left as the non-scholarly conclusions drawn by Dan Brown, author of the historically-challenged novel *The Da Vinci Code*. Robert M. Price, writing in the Jesus Seminar's magazine *The Fourth R*, accuses Brown of writing historical "fiction." Price notes that the idea that Jesus' deity was invented in the fourth century Counicl of Nicaea is inaccurate since New Testament scholars agree that Jesus was considered divine by the church in the first century. Price also picks apart other wild theories of *The Da Vinci Code* in his article entiled "The Da Vinci Fraud." Therefore, we must remind ourselves that the views of the Jesus Seminar are as far left as New Testament scholarship allows. Brown's *The Da Vinci Code* is not a scholarly work as far as New Testament scholarship is concerned. Historically speaking, it is pure fabrication.

Chapter Four
The Jesus Seminar:
The Far Left of Current New Testament Scholarship

Currently, the New Testament's portrait of Jesus is under attack. Television documentaries, magazine articles, and college professors often present a Jesus much different from the Jesus found on the pages of the four Gospels. The scholars who comprise the Jesus Seminar are often the first to be interviewed concerning the Jesus of history. In this chapter, we will examine the Jesus Seminar and critique their radical conclusions. The remainder of this book will attempt to refute their views (and other false views) about Jesus and argue that the Jesus of the Bible is the true Jesus of history.

The Jesus Seminar: An Overview

The Jesus Seminar is a group of New Testament scholars who began to meet in 1985 to vote on which sayings of Jesus, recorded in the New Testament, are authentic. They were led by recognized New Testament scholars such as Marcus Borg, John Dominic Crossan, Robert Funk, and Burton Mack.

In the book *Jesus Under* Fire (Wilkins and Moreland), evangelical New Testament scholar Craig Blomberg gives an excellent overview and critique of the Jesus Seminar in his chapter "Where do We Start Studying Jesus?" (18-25). Blomberg informs us that the Seminar originally had 200 members, but attendance was down to 74 by the mid 1990's. He observes that, due to the fact that the Jesus Seminar continues to receive much media attention, many now believe that this radical group of scholars represents mainstream New Testament scholarship (20). However, this is not the case. The Jesus Seminar is a throwback to outdated liberal scholarship. The Seminar goes against the thrust of Jesus research as embodied in the scholarly work being done in the third quest for the historical Jesus.

The Jesus Seminar dates the four Gospels found in the New Testament to have been written in the late first century AD. Supposedly, they were not authored by eyewitnesses who knew Jesus or by people who knew eyewitnesses. The Seminar also believes *The Gospel of Thomas* to be as reliable (or as unreliable) as the four traditional Gospels (i.e., Matthew, Mark, Luke, and John). The Jesus Seminar published the resuls of their research in their book *The Five Gospels* in 1993. It contains the four traditional Gospels and *The Gospel of Thomas*. *The Five Gospels* is color-coded based upon the votes taken by by the Seminar members: words in red contain statements that, according to the Jesus Seminar, Jesus definitely said. Words in pink were probably spoken by Jesus, while gray-lettered words were only possibly spoken by Jesus. Finally, words in black were statements that Jesus definitely did not say (18).

The Five Gospels contain some startling conclusions. A few examples will suffice. The Gospel of John has only one statement of Jesus in red, just one in pink, and only a few statements in gray. Over 82% of Jesus' sayings recorded in the four Gospels combined are rejected, whereas only 15 sayings of Jesus are red-lettered (18-19). According to the the Jesus Seminar, Jesus never claimed to be God, Messiah, or Savior. Hence, the Jesus Seminar rejects the Jesus found in the New Testament and presents the public with a "politically-correct" Jesus. We will now survey some of the views of two of the Jesus Seminar's leading members: Marcus Borg and John Dominic Crossan.

Marcus Borg

Marcus Borg is the Distinguished Professor of Religion at Oregon State University. He is considered one of the world's leading New

Testament scholars. Borg believes that Christianity needs to be reinterpreted in light of our culture (Borg, *Heart* 18-19). He views the older paradigm (traditional Christianity) as outdated and in need of transformation. Borg proposes what he calls the "emerging paradigm." This new paradigm rejects the Bible as being inspired by God; rather it is a human product (45). Borg denies that the Bible is "absolute truth" or "God's revealed truth." Rather, he views the Bible as "relative and culturally conditioned" (45). In other words, the Bibile is not an infallible authority from which to interpret culture; instead, culture becomes the authoritative principle through which we reinterpret the Bible.

The miraculous events of the Bible, says Borg, are to be interpreted metaphorically, not literally. In his view, the miracles of the Bible should be interpreted as stories or parables—the important thing is not whether or not it was true, but the spiritual truth being taught through figurative language (12-15). Borg views the Christian Faith as our experience with God, yet rejects the traditional idea that Christianity also entails a set of doctrinal truths (40-41).

Though Borg rejects the reality of miracles, he believes that Jesus was some how in touch with a spiritual reality in a special way. Jesus was able to, in some mysterious way, bring healing to people's lives. This transcends a mere psychological explanation, but Borg still falls short of acknowledging the reality of miracles—supernatural works of God (Borg, *A New Vision* 33-34). Borg also acknowledges that this mysterious ability is common to mystics of other world's religions as well.

Borg is pluralistic in his thought. He believes that "God is also known in other ways in other religions" (*Heart* 43). He rejects the idea that Jesus is the only way for man to be saved and he insists that we do not have to believe that Jesus literally died for our sins to be saved (44). It appears that Borg's religion is determined by his politically correct view of tolerance. He detests the idea that there is only one way to heaven. Concerning Jesus' death, Borg states, "I have trouble imagining that Jesus saw His own death as salvific" (Wright and Borg 81). Therefore, Borg denies the substitutionary atonement of Jesus; according to him, Jesus did not literally die for our sins.

Borg rejects the literal, bodily resurrection of Jesus. Instead, he views Christ's resurrection metaphorically; the message is that Jesus is alive to us—His message of love still lives (*Heart* 54). Still, in his written dialogue with conservative scholar N. T. Wright, Borg had a difficult time explaining away the post-resurrection appearances of Christ. Knowing that the past alternative/naturalistic explanations of the resurrection have failed, Borg does not claim that the apostles hallucinated. Rather, he acknowledges that the apostles had "visions" or "apparitions" of Jesus after His death (Borg and Wright 132-133). Borg does not explain what he means by this; however, it is clear that, while he rejects the resurrection, he offers no plausible alternative explanation of the New Testament data.

Borg draws a clear distinction between what he calls the "pre-Easter Jesus" and the "post-Easter Jesus" (*Heart* 82). The pre-Easter Jesus is the true Jesus of history—the first century Jew who was crucified and died and is no more. The post-Easter Jesus is the Jesus of faith—the Jesus of Christian experience and tradition (82). The post-Easter Jesus is the experience within the hearts of Christians of the divine reality; but, there is no real continuity between the pre-Easter Jesus (the historical Jesus) and the post-Easter Jesus (the Christian's experience of God). Like Bultmann before him, Borg draws a clear distinction between the Christ of Faith and the true Jesus of history.

Borg denies what he calls "supernatural theism" (the traditional view of God), and expouses the world view called panentheism (65-70). In this view, the "universe is not separate from God, but in God" (66). In short, Borg's view of God is much closer to the pantheistic view of God held by New Agers—the view that God is the universe—

than the traditional view of the miracle-working personal Creator God of the Bible. Evangelical scholar Ben Witherington III describes Borg's non-traditional view of God as follows: "he wishes to deny the sense of God as 'Holy Other' and affirm a God who is around and within us all, apparently without regard to our belief or behavior" (*Quest* 106).

Borg does not accept the true deity of Christ. In his view, Jesus showed us what God is like. It is only in this sense that deity can be figuratively asserted of Jesus (Wright and Borg 150). While denying Jesus' literal deity, Borg is honest enough to admit that, before the Gospels were written, "prayers were addressed to Jesus as if to God" (153).

John Dominic Crossan

Jesus Seminar member John Dominic Crossan is a New Testament scholar with a very unique perspective: he does not believe Jesus was buried in a tomb. Instead, he believes that Jesus' body was either left on the cross or buried in a mass, shallow grave with deceased criminals. In either case, Crossan speculates that Jesus'body was probably consumed by wild beasts (*Jesus: A Revolutionary Biography* 152-158). Though Crossan's view is not widely accepted by New Testament critics, a brief response will be given.

Christian apologist Gary Habermas identifies several problems with Crossan's theory that Jesus was not buried and His body was eaten by wild beasts (Habermas, *Historical Jesus* 127-134). First, all four Gospels agree on the burial account. Second, no early documents deny the burial accounts. Hence, there is absolutely no historical evidence for Crossan's theory. Third, the Jewish religious leaders did not contest the burial accounts. Fourth, the Jewish religious leaders, while arguing against the resurrection, admit both the burial and the empty tomb (Matt 28:11-15). Fifth, the pre-Markan passion accounts acknolwedge both the burial and the empty tomb. Sixth, at a time when a woman's testimony was not held in high regard, the Gospels record women as the first witnesses of the empty tomb, thus accepting that Jesus was buried in that tomb. There is no reason for the apostles to fabricate accounts with women witnesses. Seventh, Jesus' burial is supported by ancient creeds (i.e., 1 Corinthians 15:3-7; Acts 13:29) that go back to the early 30's AD, the earliest days of the church. And finally, the earliest preaching of the Gospel (i.e., the sermons in the first twelve chapters of Acts) in Jerusalem included the burial.

Due to these factors, virtually no other leading New Testament scholars agree with Crossan's denial of Jesus' burial. As far as most New Testament critics (even most members of the Jesus Seminar) are concerned, Jesus' death by crucifixion and His burial in a tomb are not in dispute—they are accepted as historical facts.

The Jesus Seminar: A Critique of Their Views

Contrary to the public's perception of the Jesus Seminar, they do not represent the common findings of current New Testament scholarship. Its members make up a very small, radical subset of New Testament scholarship. Almost half of their 74 members earned their graduate degrees from one of three of the most liberal schools in the world when it comes to New Testament studies: Harvard, Claremont, and Vanderbilt. European scholars, often considered to be on the cutting edge of New Testament scholarship, are not represented in the Jesus Seminar. And, obviously, Evangelical scholars—New Testament scholars who believe the Bible is the inspired Word of God—are not to be found among the members of the Jesus Seminar.

In short, the general conclusions of the Seminar's voting should not have surprised anyone: only like-minded, radical New Testament scholars were invited to attend their meetings. If the Evangelical Theological Society decided to take votes on which sayings of Jesus found in the New Testament are authentic, no one would consider it news worthy. Because evangelical scholars believe the Bible is God's Word, they would accept all of Jesus' sayings as authentic—their conclusions would be predetermined by their conservative theological and biblical views. Yet, the opposite is the case with members of the Jesus Seminar. Their radical, liberal views of the Bible predetermine their conclusions. Hence, the conclusions of the Jesus Seminar are not really news worthy. Apparently, all the media coverage the Jesus Seminar receives is merely the result of its agreement with the media's bias against the traditional Jesus. It has nothing to do with suprising results . . . because the results are not suprising. No one should be schocked when liberal scholars reach liberal conclusions. If a fair number of European and Evangelical scholars were invited to the meetings and allowed to vote, the results would be vastly different.

It should also be noted that more than half of the 74 members of the Seminar are relative unknowns in the field of New Testament studies. They have yet to be published in circles of New Testament scholarship; hence, their scholarship in New Testament studies has not been established.

The members of the Jesus Seminar share a bias against the traditional Jesus. This effects the way they vote and, hence, the conclusions of their "research." Many of the members are biased against the supernatural—they either deny the existence of God (atheism) or they deny that God can perform miracles (deism). Some members of the Jesus Seminar, like Marcus Borg, are willing to acknowledge Jesus as a religious leader with great charisma and spiritual power, and that He could heal people and cast out demons. However, Borg's panentheism (his belief that the universe is God's body) will not allow him to accept a Jesus who claimed to be uniquely God (Borg believes that we are all "divine" in some sense) or a Jesus who claimed to be the only way for a person to be saved (Borg believes that all religions lead to God). In other words, the biases of the members of the Jesus Seminar determine the way they vote. Their conclusions are not determined by historical evidence.

The Jesus Seminar, like much of liberal New Testament scholarship, rejects what the Gospels teach, unless they are proven true by outside sources. In response, several points need to be made. First, this violates Aristotle's dictum, which says that a historical document should be considered true unless strong evidence is found to diprove the account. Second, the members of the Jesus Seminar argue in a circle. They say they will accept a saying of Jesus if it is related by more than one source. This is called "double attestation." However, they rarely accept sayings of Jesus even if they are found in more than one Gospel. To justify this, the Jesus Seminar usually treats the Gospels as one source, believing that Matthew and Luke copied much of their material from Mark's Gospel (despite the fact that all the early church fathers who wrote on the subject stated that the Gospels were written independently of one another). Third, if we treated all of ancient literature the way the Jesus Seminar treats the Gospels, then all of ancient literature would be rejected as historically inaccurate. There is simply no good reason to assume the unreliability of the Gospels or the New Testament until their reliability can be proven by outside sources. In other words, the Jesus Seminar is correct in that we can know very little of what Jesus said and was like only if we assume the Gospel accounts of Jesus are unreliable. The Jesus Seminar has not proven that the Gospels are unreliable; they have merely assumed them to be unreliable.

Another problem with the Jesus Seminar is that they assume the existence of a nonsupernatural original manuscript, which no one has ever seen, called "Q." Many New Testament scholars outside the Jesus Seminar also believe in the existence of "Q." Still, it is very suspect to believe in the existence of a document which has never been mentioned in the history of Christian literature and of which no copy has ever been found. This curious document called "Q" is the invention of the imaginations of liberal scholars who assume that the real Jesus of history did not say or do the things we find in the Gospels today. Today, we have over 24,000 copies of the New Testament. No one has ever found a copy of the imaginary document called "Q."

The Jesus Seminar is wrong to consider *The Gospel of Thomas* as being as reliable as the four Gospels (Matthew, Mark, Luke, and John). The wealth of ancient manuscript evidence for the antiquity and reliablity of the New Testament is totally absent for *The Gospel of Thomas*. Also, the early church fathers refered to the four Gospels as authoritative in their writings, but any mention they gave of *The Gospel of Thomas* was to show that it was not really written by the apostle Thomas, that it was a heretical writing, and that it held no authority in the early church. Most New Testament scholars agree that *The Gospel of Thomas* was a heretical document written around 140AD, more than 100 years after the death of Christ. On the other hand, as we will show in this work, the evidence is overwhelming that the Gospels and most (if not all) of the New Testament were written before 70AD, within a generation of the death of Christ and while eyewitnesses were still alive and leading the early church.

Members of the Jesus Seminar accept Paul as the author of most of the New Testament books credited to him today.They acknowledge that Paul taught that Jesus is God and that He rose from the dead. Hence, there are several questions that the Jesus Seminar cannot satisfactorily answer. Does the Jesus Seminar really expect us to believe that within 20 to 25 years of Jesus' death, the apostles allowed Paul to totally transform the person, work, and life of Christ? Do they believe Paul was lying when he said that he and Barnabas received the right hand of fellowship from Peter, James, and John (Galatians 2:7-9)? Would these leaders of the early church accept Paul's message if he distorted the truth about Jesus? Are we to believe that the first generation of Christian leaders allowed the greatest perversion to the Gospel narratives, whereas all following generations devoted themselves to faithfully preserving the New Testament texts handed down to them? Does the Jesus Seminar sound convincing when they imply that the apostles, who were first century orthodox Jews, were not concerned about accurately reporting the history and teachings of their rabbi (Jesus)? Why should we accept the Jesus Seminar's view of Jesus as being more accurate than Paul's portrait of Christ? Since even the Jesus Seminar agrees that Paul wrote between 50 and 64 AD, why should anyone accept the views of these late comers as more trustworthy than Paul's depiction of Christ?

Why doesn't the Jesus Seminar admit the obvious—that Paul's writings and the four Gospels all share the same basic outline of the events of Christ's life, death, and resurrection, and that they teach the same things about Christ's person and works? The reasoning of the Jesus Seminar begs the question. They believe that Paul's theology of the person and works of Christ is far more developed than that of the original form or early stages of the synoptic Gospels (Matthew, Mark, and Luke). Hence, the Jesus Seminar concludes that Paul wrote before the final stage of the composition of the synoptic Gospels. This, claims the Jesus Seminar, explains the high Christology (i.e., Jesus is God, He rose from the dead and died for our sins, etc.) of the present form of the synoptic Gospels. However, isn't it simpler to acknowledge that Paul and the Gospel authors had the same core understanding of Jesus' person and works so that Paul's writings and the synoptic Gospels could have been written independently and around the same period of time? Of course, Paul's rabbinical training would have enabled him to present a more developed theology, but the similarities in the portraits of Christ found in the synoptic Gospels and Paul's writings are best explained by acknowledging that there was universal agreement throughout the early church about the person and works of Jesus. This conclusion has been confirmed by the New

Testament scholar from the University of Edinburgh, Larry Hurtado, in his recent work entitled *Lord Jesus Christ: Devotion to Jesus in Earliest Christianity*. Hurtado argues persuasively that the doctrines of the deity and resurrection of Christ date back to the early 30's AD (101, 128-129, 131-137, 650). It is interesting to note that once we acknowledge that Paul and the Synoptic Gospels both proclaim a fully-divine, resurrected Jesus who died for our sins, then the main objection for questioning the reliability of the Gospel of John has been removed.

Most New Testament scholars date the ancient creeds and sermons found in the New Testament to within ten years of the crucifixion. Can the Jesus Seminar give us another ancient example of legends overwhelming core historical data in less than ten years? The work of historian A. N. Sherwin-White, who specialized in the history of ancient Rome, has conclusively shown that it takes at least two generations for this to occur (*Roman Society and Roman Law in the New Testament* 188-191).

The rest of this book will be devoted to a thorough refutation of the radical conclusions drawn by the Jesus Seminar. We will examine the manuscript evidence for the reliability of the New Testament, as well as the views of the early church fathers concerning the New Testament documents. We will look at what ancient secular (non-Christian) authors wrote concerning the beliefs of the early (i.e., first generation) church. We will discuss archaeological confirmation of the New Testament and survey ancient creeds, found in the New Testament, which predate the New Testament, often originating during the decade of the crucifixion (the 30's AD). We will demonstrate, beyond reasonable doubt, that the Jesus of the Gospels is in fact the true Jesus of history.

Chapter Five
The Synoptic Problem

Matthew, Mark, and Luke are commonly referred to as the "Synoptic Gospels" because the material they contain has much more in common with each other than with the fourth Gospel—the Gospel of John. The Christian church throughout the ages held that Matthew, Mark, and Luke, though very similar in content, were written independently of each other. However, with the advent of the Enlightenment, biblical scholars began to attempt to explain the similarities found in the Synoptic Gospels as due to a dependence between them (i.e., the authors borrowed material from one another—their Gospels were not written independently of each other).

The different dependence theories of the origin of the Synoptic Gospels were formulated by scholars who did not believe the Bible was inspired by God and inerrant. These scholars viewed the Bible as merely a human book and they attempted to explain the similarities found in Matthew, Mark, and Luke. It is rather sad that today many evangelical (i.e., Bible-believing) New Testament scholars accept one of the dependence theories for the origin of the Synoptic Gospels.

The Three Main Views of the Origin of the Synoptic Gospels

There are three main views concerning the origin of the Synoptic Gospels: the Markan Priority Hypothesis, the Two-Gospel Hypothesis (which views Matthew as the first Gospel written but accepts a literary dependence between the Synoptic Gospels), and the Literary Independence Theory. The Literary Independence theory is by far the oldest theory of the origin of the Gospels of Matthew, Mark, and Luke. I will argue that this theory (the Literary Dependence Theory) should not have been abandoned by many contemporary evangelical

New Testament scholars. But, first I will comment briefly on the two newer theories.

Adherents of the Markan Priority Hypothesis believe that Mark was the first to write his Gospel based upon Peter's preaching. Mark himself was not one of the original apostles. There are two subcategories within the Markan Priority Hypothesis: the Two-Source View and the Four-Source View. The Two-Source View declares that Mark's Gospel and a no longer extant document called "Q" formed the foundation for the Gospels of Matthew and Luke. The Two-Source adherents believe that Matthew and Luke received much of their material from Mark, but the material common to Matthew and Luke but not found in Mark came from a hypothetical document called "Q." No one has ever found a copy of the supposed ancient document called "Q." In fact, many New Testament scholars doubt it ever existed.

The Four-Source View within the Markan Priority Hypothesis posists the existence of two additional hypothetical documents called "M" and "L." According to this speculative theory, "M" was an ancient source used by Matthew in addition to Mark and "Q." And "L" was supposedly an ancient source used by Luke in addition to Mark and "Q." Like "Q," no copy of "M" or "L" has ever been found. Again, many New Testament scholars doubt that these hypothetical documents ever existed.

The Two-Gospel View of Synoptic Dependence claims that Matthw was written first, followed by Luke and Mark. Supposedly, Luke utilized Matthew as a source, whereas Mark "borrowed" from both Matthew and Luke. What the two Markan Priority views and the Two-Gospel View have in common is that Matthew, Mark, and Luke were not written independently of each other. The Gospels of Matthew, Mark, and Luke were dependent upon each other.

The Literary Independence Theory disagrees. This view accepts the unnimous testimony of the early church fathers that the Synoptic

Gospels were written independently of each other. The main reason for the origin of the various dependence theories of the Synoptic Gospels is to discredit the historical reliability of the Gospel accounts. It is therefore suprising that so many evangelical New Testament scholars would embrace these dependence theories. I agree with Robert L. Thomas and F. David Farnell (two New testament scholars from the Master's Seminary in Sun Valley, California) in their assessment that evangelical scholars should never have forsaken the Literary Dependence Theory. Their ideas are spelled out in *The Jesus Crisis* and *Three Views on the Origins of the Synoptic Gospels*.

A Defense of the Literary Independence Theory

Farnell makes a strong case for the Literary Independence Theory in Robert L. Thomas' book *Three Views on the Origins of the Synoptic Gospels*. Farnell begins his defense by exposing the presuppositions that led to the dependence theories of the Synoptic Gospels (226-233). Farnell states, "Historical-critical ideologies were not initiated to affirm but to negate the historical integrity of the Gospels" (231). He credits the pantheist philosopher Spinoza with being the founder of historical criticism of the Bible. Spinoza rejected the divine authorship of the Scriptures and sought to call into question its historical reliability (232-233). He questioned the widespread acceptance of the traditional authors and traditional dates of composition of the Biblical books. In all this, Spinoza presupposed that the personal God of traditional Christianity and Judaism did not exist and, therefore, could not write a book. Spinoza's views led to the Enlightenment view of God called Deism—the idea that God created the world but does not intervene by performing miracles. Deism became very popular among European intellectuals in the eighteenth century. Due to this popularity, the traditional doctrines of inspiration (that God guided human authors to record His Word in written form) and inerrancy (that the Bible is totally without errors in its original form) fell into disfavor. Rather than continuing to acknowledge a supernatural origin of the Scriptures, Enlightenment thinkers began to propose non-supernatural explanations for the origin of the biblical books. Hence, the traditional view concerning the authorship of the Gospels was rejected. Early dates of the composition of the Gospels were also discarded. An evolutionary view of the origin of the Gospels became popular—the idea that the Gospels were not written by eyewitnesses or people who knew eyewitnesses; rather, the Gospels were written in layers over different stages of time, with one Gospel writer borrowing his material from other sources. In short, Farnell traces the rise of dependency theories of the origin of the Gospels to the bias against miracles that grew out of the Enlightenment (233-234).

Farnell points out that throughout the history of the church until the rise of Enlightenment Deism, the independence theory of the Synoptic Gospels reigned supreme as the dominant view of scholars. Only with the rise of antisupernaturalism (the philsophical assumption that miracles are impossible) did the independence theory fall out of favor among scholars (235). The demise of the independence theory was not due to evidence found within the pages of the Gospels; rather, it was caused by a philosophical bias against the possibility of miracles. Hence, it is rather strange that evangelical (Bible-believing) New Testament scholars of the twentieth century would so quickly abandon the independence theory, for evangelical scholars believe in miracles and accept the traditional doctrines of inspiration and inerrancy.

Farnell notes that some twentieth-century evangelical New Testament scholars refused to compromise—they continued to hold to the independence theory of the Synoptic Gospels. Some of these scholars noted by Farnell are: Louis Berkhof, Henry C. Thiessen, Eta Linnemann (a former historical-critical scholar), Robert Gromacki,

Merrill C. Tenney, Jacob Van Bruggen, and John M. Rist. Farnell aslo informs us that John Wenham and Bo Reicke hold to modified independence theories of the origin of the Synoptic Gospels (242-249). There is no reason why contemporary evangelical New Testament scholars should continue to promote dependence theories.

Farnell gives an overview of the early church's view of the origin of the Synoptic Gospels. Speaking about the view of the early church fathers, Farnell states that "the Fathers' writings verify a unanimous consensus that Matthew, not Mark, was the first Gospel written and that the Gospel writers wrote independently of each other." Farnell adds that "The Fathers' writings also reveal that Luke probably wrote second and Mark third, although at times Mark is placed second" (237).

Farnell shows that the Apostolic Father named Papias, writing about 110 AD, wrote that Mark based his Gospel on Peter's preaching, not on Matthew's Gospel (237). Farnell notes that Eusebius, the great historian of the early church, quotes Clement of Alexandria (150-215 AD) as giving the chronological order of the composition of the Gospels as: Matthew, Luke, Mark, and John (238). Farnell adds that Clement of Alexandria is in general agreement on these issues with other early church fathers such as Papias, Ireneaeus, and Tertullian, and that there is no hint of any literary dependence between the Gospel authors whatsoever (239-241).

It should also be mentioned that the early church had no reason to lie and claim that Matthew, Mark, and Luke authored the Synoptic Gospels. We must remember that Matthew, though one of the original apostles, would have been considered by many Jews a traitor. He was formerly a tax collector who was paid by the Romans to collect taxes from the Jews for the Romans. To pretend that he was an author of one of the Gospels would not have been a major public relations success. The only reason for the early church to claim that Matthew wrote a Gospel would be that Matthew actually wrote a Gospel. Also, why would the early church claim that Luke wrote Luke and Mark wrote Mark if this was not actaully the case? Neither Luke nor Mark were members of the original twelve apostles—they would be unlikely candidates for authorship of the Gospels—unless, of course, they actually were the authors. Hence the only reason why the early church claimed that Matthew, Mark, and Luke wrote the Synoptic Gospels is that they actually did author these works.

Farnell offers his own defense of the independence theory of the Synoptic Gospels. While acknowledging that the differences in the Gospels are due to the fact that the authors did not borrow from one another (the Gospel writers were not dependent upon one another for their information), Farnell lists five factors that explain the common aspects found in the Synoptic Gospels (273-294). First, the authors had direct, eyewitness knowledge of the events they recorded. Farnell points out that the early church fathers unanimously considered the Gospels written by the apostles or their close associates. Therefore, they had access to eyewitness information.

Second, the authors had access to oral tradition based upon the teachings of the apostles. The early church inherited their respect for oral tradition and their memorization skills from the first-century AD Jewish culture. Rabbis expected their disciples to memorize and pass on their key teachings to others. There is no reason to believe that oral tradition had any less of an important role in the early church (279-281).

Third, Farnell states that, besides the first-century AD Jewish emphasis on oral tradition, the authors of the Synoptic Gospels probably had access to short written accounts. Several New Testament scholars (even some dependence theory advocates) suspect that Matthew may have been the "note-taker" for the apostles (283). In fact, Jesus refers to His disciples as "scribes" in Matthew 13:51-52 (see also Matthew 23:34), implying that they took notes of His sermons.

Fourth, Farnell notes that the authors of the Synoptic Gospels (Matthew, Mark, and Luke) probably had personal contacts with each other (291). A careful study of the Book of Acts and Paul's letters reveal that the apostles met in John Mark's home (Acts 12:12; the full name of the author of the Gospel of Mark was John Mark) and that John Mark and Luke were close associates of each other and of the Apostle Paul (Colossians 4:10, 14; Philemon 24). Luke accompanied Paul on several of his journies, which would have given him numerous occassions to meet with some of the original apostles.

And fifth, Farnell reminds evangelical New Testament scholars that, as evangelicals, they are supposed to believe in the inspiration of the Holy Spirit. That is, the Holy Spirit guided the Gospel authors to record His Word without error (292). Since they were protected from introducing errors into the biblical texts, it is no surprise that we would find so many similarities in the three Synoptic Gospels.

Farnell's Case for the Indepence Theory of the Origin of the Synoptic Gospels can be summarized as follows. 1) The early church fathers taught that the authors of the Synoptic Gospels worked independently of each other. 2) This view was held by the Christian Church throughout the centuries until the advent of the Enlightenment. 3) The dependence theory of the origin of the Synoptic Gospels was produced by Enlightenment thinkers who rejected the possibility of miracles. 4) Evangelical New Testament scholars believe that God performed miracles such as the inspiration of Scripture. Therefore, they should not have abandoned the traditional view of the Christian church because of the anti-supernaturalistic bias of Enlightenment thinkers. 5) Numerous evangelical scholars, though in the minority, were able to prove their scholarship without abandoning their adherence to the independency theory. And, 6) evangelical scholars can explain the similarities found in the Synoptic Gospels without accomodating to the dependency theories.

It is my opinion that Farnell's defense of the Independent Theory of the origin of the Synoptic Gospels is sound. Therefore, I join with scholars like Farnell and Thomas as they call evangelical scholars to reject dependency theories and return to the position that the Christian Church had held for the first seventeen centuries of her history. Now is not the time to compromise. The same presupposition (i.e., bias against miracles) that led to the dependency theories of the origin of the Synoptic Gospels has also led to the denial of the Christian doctrines of inspiration and inerrancy. Evangelicals should not cave in to pressure from the world to compromise. There is no reason to reject the Church's view on the Synoptic Gospels—there is no reason to reject the independence theory of the Gospels.

Chapter Six
New Testament Reliability

Christianity is a religion with deep historical roots. For example, if Jesus did not rise from the dead (a historical event), then the Christian Faith cannot save (1 Corinthians 15:14, 17). If He did not die on the cross for the sins of mankind (a historical event), then Christianity offers no hope (1 Peter 2:24; 3:18). Proving the New Testament can be trusted will go a long way to establishing Christianity as the one true faith.

This chapter will attempt to show that if we use honest, neutral presuppositions in our study of the New Testament, we will see that it is historically reliable. It can be shown that the New Testament accounts were written by eyewitnesses who knew Christ, or persons who knew the eyewitnesses. This chapter will not deal with defending the Bible as the inspired and inerrant Word of God; the purpose of this chapter is to merely show that the New Testament documents can be shown to be historically reliable when the researcher does not use biased, liberal presuppositions.

Manuscript Evidence for the New Testament

Many historical scholars believe that one cannot know the true Jesus of history since no one no has the original writings of those who knew Him. Only copies of the originals are in existence today. Ironically, these historical scholars will often quote from Plato, as well as other ancient writers, as if they can know with certainty what Plato originally wrote. This clearly unveils a double standard: ancient secular writings can be trusted based on late copies, but the New Testament cannot be trusted since the original manuscripts are missing!

Any honest examination of the manuscript evidence will reveal that the New Testament is by far the most reliable ancient writing in existence today. There exist today nearly 25,000 hand-written copies (5,686 of them in the original Greek language) of the New Testament, either in whole or in part (McDowell, *New Evidence* 34; Geisler and Turek 225). This should be compared with the fact that only 7 copies presently exist of Plato's Tetralogies (McDowell, *Evidence* 42-43). Homer's Iliad is in second place behind the New Testament among ancient writings with just 643 copies (43).

The earliest copy of Plato's Tetralogies is dated about 1,200 years after Plato supposedly wrote the original (43). Compare this with the earliest extant copy of the New Testament: the John Ryland's Papyri. It contains a portion of John 18. This fragment is dated at about 125 AD, only 25 years after the original is thought to have been written (43).

In fact, based on the research of a distinguished German papyrologist named Carsten P. Thiede, there are possibly even earlier New Testament fragments that were found among the Dead Sea Scrolls. One fragment is called 7Q5; it is dated earlier than 70AD. Though there is heated debate about this manuscript, it has been argued that it is a part of Mark 6:52-53 (Thiede, *Rekindling*, 50, 114). Another possible New Testament fragment found in cave 7 of the Dead Sea Scrolls is 7Q4, identified by Thiede as 1 Timothy 3:16-4:3 (174). Thiede builds upon the work of the late papyrologist Jose O'Callaghan and makes a solid case that these fragments can only be identified as from Mark 6 and 1 Timothy 3 and 4. Thiede states that the only reason why New Testament scholars reject these fragments as being from the New Testament is due to their critical theories, which we have shown to be based upon biased presuppositions (169-204). Carsten B. Thiede has also argued that three tiny fragments of the twenty-sixth chapter of Matthew's Gospel which belong to

Magdalen College, Oxford, date to the mid first century AD (Thiede and D'Ancona 1-2).

Still, even if one rejects the conclusions drawn by Thiede, we must remember there is no debate about the early dating of the John chapter eighteen fragment. So a gap of only twenty-five years is established. Again, Homer's Iliad takes second place among ancient writings, second only to the New Testament. The earliest copy of any portion of Homer's Iliad is dated about 500 years after the original writing (McDowell, *Evidence* 43).

When the contents of the extant manuscripts of the New Testament are compared, there appears to be 99.5% agreement. There is total agreement in the doctrines taught; the corruptions are mainly grammatical (43). Homer's Iliad once again takes second place behind the New Testament among ancient documents. Homer's Iliad has a 95% accuracy when its copies are compared (43). Since there are so few remaining copies of Plato's writings, agreement between these copies is not considered a factor (they are probably all copies of the same copy). When one compares the accuracy of the New Testament copies with that of Homer's Iliad, one can appreciate the extreme care that went into the copying of the New Testament. For the 99.5% accuracy of the New Testament copies means that only 5 letters out of every one-thousand are in question. On the other hand, the second place 95% accuracy of the Homer's Iliad manuscripts means that 50 letters out of every one-thousand are in question. This makes the New Testament manuscripts ten times more accurate than any other ancient writng! It should also be noted that, with the high number of New Testament manuscripts and the high degree of agreement between them, textual experts are extremely confident that, by examining the thousands of New Testament copies, we can arrive at an exact replica of the original New Testament.

The manuscript evidence for the New Testament can be clearly seen when we examine the following data adapted from a chart found in Josh McDowell's *New Evidence that Demands a Verdict* (38):

Comparison of Ancient Writings

Author	Book	Date Written	Earliest Copies	Time Gap	No. of Copies
Homer	*Iliad*	800 B.C.	400 B.C.	400 yrs.	643
Herodotus	*History*	480-425 B.C.	A.D. 900	1,350 yrs.	8
Thucydides	*History*	460-400 B.C.	A.D. 900	1,300 yrs.	8
Plato		400 B.C.	A.D. 900	1,300 yrs.	7
Demosthenes		300 B.C.	A.D. 1100	1,400 yrs	200
Caesar	*Gallic Wars*	100-44 B.C.	A.D. 900	1,000 yrs.	10
Livy	*History of Rome*	59 B.C.- A.D. 17	4th century (partial) 10th century (most)	400 yrs. 1,000 yrs.	1 partial 19 copies
Tacitus	*Annals*	A.D. 100	A.D. 1100	1,000 yrs.	20
Pliny Secundus	*Natural History*	A.D. 61-113	A.D. 850	750 yrs.	7

New Testament		A.D. 50-100	114 A.D. (fragment) 200 A.D. (books) 250 A.D. Most of N.T. 325 A.D. (complete N.T.)	14 yrs. 100 yrs. 150 yrs. 225 yrs.	Nearly 5,700 Greek copies Nearly 25,000 copies total

In short, historical scholars can consider the extant New Testament manuscripts to be reliable and accurate representations of what the authors originally wrote. Since the New Testament is by far the most accurately copied ancient writing, to question its authenticity is to call into question all of ancient literature.

The following manuscripts are some of the better known copies of the New Testament. The John Rylands Papyri is the oldest undisputed fragment of the New Testament still in existence. It is dated between 125 and 130 AD. It contains a portion of John 18 (McDowell, *Evidence* 46). The Bodmer Papyrus II contains most of John's Gospel and dates between 150 and 200 AD (46-47). The Chester Beatty Papyri includes major portions of the New Testament; it is dated around 200 AD (47). Codex Vaticanus contains nearly the entire Bible and is dated between 325 and 350 AD (47). Codex Sinaiticus contains nearly all of the New Testament and approximately half of the Old Testament. It is dated at about 350 AD (47-48). Codex Alexandrinus encompasses almost the entire Bible and was copied around 400 AD. Codex Ephraemi represents every New Testament book except for 2 John and 2 Thessalonians. Ephraemi is dated in the 400's AD (48).

ANCIENT GREEK NEW TESTAMENT COPIES

Manuscript	**Contents**	**Date**
John Rylands Papyir	Portion of John 18	125 A.D.
Bodmer Papyrus II	Most of John's Gospel	150-200 A.D.
Chester Beatty Papyri	Major portions of the N.T.	200 A.D.
Codex Vaticanus	Almost entire Bible	325-350 A.D.
Codex Sinaiticus	All of N.T. & half of O.T.	350 A.D.
Codex Alexandrinus	Almost entire Bible	400 A.D.
Codex Ephraemi	Most of N.T.	400's A.D.

The very early dates of these manuscripts provide strong evidence that the content of the current New Testament is one and the same with the original writings of the apostles. There is no logical reason to doubt the reliability of these manuscripts.

It should also be noted that, besides ancient Greek manuscript copies of the New Testament, there there also exist today ancient New Testament copies in other languages. The *Old Syriac Version* and the *Syriac Peshitta* date back to the fourth and fifth centuries, yet experts believe they were copies of second century New Testament manuscripts. The *Old Latin Version* of the New Testament and the *African Old Latin Version* also show signs of having been copied from second century manuscripts (McDowell, *New Evidence* 41).

After assessing the manuscript evidence for the reliability of the New Testament, the world renown manuscript expert Sir Frederick Kenyon stated:

> The interval then between the dates of original composition and the earliest extant evidence becomes so small as to be negligible, and the last foundation for any doubt that the Scriptures have come down to us substantially as they were written has now been removed. Both the authenticity and the general integrity of the books of the New Testament may be regarded as finally established (*Bible and Archeology* 288).

The Testimony of the Apostolic Fathers

The New Testament manuscript copies are not the only evidence for the reliability of the New Testament. Another source of evidence is found in the writings of the apostolic fathers. The apostolic fathers were leaders in the early church who knew the apostles and their doctrine (Cairns 73). Most of their writings were produced between 60 and 130 AD.

As we have shown, liberal scholars have attempted to find the so-called true Jesus of history. It was their goal to find a non-supernatural Jesus who never claimed to be God. These scholars believe that Christ's claim to be God and Savior, and His miraculous life (especially His bodily resurrection from the dead) are merely legends. The true Jesus of history was a great teacher; still, He was merely a man (Habermas, *Ancient Evidence* 42). Therefore, if it can be shown that early church leaders, who personally knew the apostles, taught that the miraculous aspects of Christ's life actually occurred and that Jesus did in fact make the bold claims recorded in the New Testament, then the legend hypothesis fails. Historians recognize that legends take generations to develop (McDowell and Wilson 130). A legend is a ficticious story that, through the passage of time, many people come to accept as historically accurate. A legend can begin to develop only if the eyewitnesses and those who knew the eyewitnesses are already dead. Otherwise, the eyewitnesses or those who knew them would refute the legend. Therefore, a legend begins to compete with the historical facts a generation or two after the event or person in question has passed. However, before a legend receives wide acceptance, several generations (sometimes centuries) are needed, for there is still a remembrance of the person or event due to information passed on orally from generation to generation. After several centuries, new generations arise without the sufficient knowledge of the person or event necessary to refute the legend. If a written record compiled by eyewitnesses is passed on to future generations (as is the case with the New Testament), legends can be easily refuted.

A. N. Sherwin-White, a historian who specialized in ancient Greek and Roman history, has studied the development of ancient legends. He concluded that more than two generations are needed for legendary speculation to wipe out core historical facts (*Roman Society and Roman Law in the New Testament* 188-191). When we read the apostolic fathers—those trained by the apostles themselves—we find the same teachings about the person and work of Jesus found in the New Testament. Hence, there was insufficient time for legends to develop.

One apostolic father, Clement, was the Bishop of Rome. Before he became bishop, he wrote his letter to the Corinthians in 70 AD. The following is a brief quote from this letter:

> Let us fear the Lord Jesus (Christ), whose blood was given for us. . . The Apostles received the Gospel for us from the Lord Jesus Christ; Jesus Christ was sent from God. . . He made the Lord Jesus Christ the firstfruit, when He raised Him from the dead (Lightfoot and Harmer 67, 75, 68).

It is important to note that Clement of Rome referred to Jesus as "the Lord." This is an obvious reference to Christ's deity, for he uses the Greek word "Kurios" with the definite article—Christ was the Lord, not a Lord (Lightfoot and Harmer 17). Clement also spoke of Christ's blood as being shed for us, indicating a belief in Christ's saving work. He declared that the apostles received the Gospel directly from Jesus. Clement also spoke of God raising Jesus from the dead. If any of these statements were opposed to the doctrines of the apostles, the Apostle John, who was still alive at the time, would have openly confronted this first century bishop. However, he did not. Therefore, the writing of Clement of Rome provides strong confirmation of the original message of the Apostles. We know that Clement of Rome wrote his letter before the temple was destroyed in 70 AD since he spoke of the temple sacrifices still be offered (41.2). Hence, contrary to the wishful thinking of skeptics, the teachings of the first century church are exactly what one finds in today's New Testament.

The apostolic father, Ignatius, bishop of Antioch, wrote his letters around 107 AD. During that time, he was travelling from Antioch to Rome to be martyred (97). Ignatius openly wrote about the deity of Christ. He referred to Jesus as "Jesus Christ our God," "God in man," and "Jesus Christ the God" (137, 139, 149-150, 156). Ignatius stated that "there is one God who manifested Himself through Jesus Christ His Son" (144). Besides ascribing deity to Christ, Ignatius also wrote of salvation in Christ and expressed belief in Christ's virgin birth, crucifixion, and resurrection. He referred to Jesus as "Christ Jesus our

Savior" and wrote "Jesus Christ, who dies for us, that believing on His death ye might escape death" (137, 141). Ignatius also wrote concerning Jesus:

> He is truly of the race of David according to the flesh, but Son of God by the Divine will and power, truly born of a virgin (156).
> Be ye deaf therefore, when any man speaketh to you apart from Jesus Christ, who was born of the race of David, who was the Son of Mary, who was truly born and ate and drank, was truly persecuted under Pontius Pilate, was truly crucified and died in the sight of those in heaven and those on earth and those under the earth; who moreover was truly raised from the dead, His Father having raised Him . . . (148).

The writings of Ignatius show that only ten to fifteen years after the death of the Apostle John the central doctrines of the New Testament were already being taught. It is highly unlikely that the New Testament manuscripts, referenced by Ignatius, could have been corrupted in such a short amount of time. It is also important to remember that Clement of Rome taught the same doctrines while the Apostle John was still alive.

Another apostolic father named Polycarp (70-156 AD) was the Bishop of Smyrna. He was a personal pupil of the Apostle John (Cairns 74). Had any of the other apostolic fathers perverted the teachings of the apostles, Polycarp would have set the record straight. However, Polycarp's teachings are essentially the same as that of Clement of Rome and Ignatius. Of all the apostolic fathers, Polycarp knew better than any the content of the original apostles' message. Liberal scholars display tremendous arrogance when they assume that they have more insight into the original apostolic message than Polycarp. Polycarp studied under the Apostle John (85-95 AD?);

contemporary scholars live nearly 2,000 years later. In his letter to the Philippians, Polycarp wrote the following about 107 AD:

> . . . Jesus Christ who took our sins in His own body upon the tree, who did no sin, neither was guile found in His mouth, but for our sakes He endured all things, that we might live in Him (Lightfoot and Harmer 180).
> For they loved not the present world, but Him that died for our sakes and was raised by God for us (180).
> . . . who shall believe on our Lord and God Jesus Christ and on His Father that raised Him from the dead (181).

Here we see that Polycarp called Jesus "our Lord and God," and proclaimed Jesus' sacrificial death for us and His resurrection from the dead. If the apostles did not teach such things, then why would their successors?

While discussing the writings of Clement of Rome, Ignatius, and Polycarp, Christian scholar Paul Barnett points out that, by 110 AD, these three early church leaders quoted from or referred to twenty-five of the twenty-seven New Testament books, proving that the entire New Testament was in circulation and accepted as authoritative by the early church by the close of the first century AD (*Is the New Testament Reliable?* 40-41). Barnett adds that "The silence of Clement, Ignatius, and Polycarp with respect to 2 John and Jude need not imply that these books were not written, only that those authors failed to quote from them or refer to them" (41).

Another student of the Apostle John was Papias, the Bishop of Hierapolis. Papias was born between 60 and 70 AD and died between 130 and 140 AD (Lightfoot and Harmer 514). Papias wrote that he did not accept the words of any self-proclaimed teacher. Instead, he would talk to others who, like himself, had known at least one of the original apostles. In this way, Papias could discover the teachings of

Christ from the sources closest to Christ Himself, rather than rely on hearsay testimony (527-528).

Papias wrote of his discussions with persons who spoke with with apostles such as Andrew, Peter, Philip, Thomas, James, John, or Matthew (528). Papias stated that Mark received the information for his Gospel from the Apostle Peter himself. Papias also related that Matthew originally recorded his gospel in Hebrew, but that it was later translated into Greek to reach a wider audience (529).

The testimony of the first-century and early second-century church should be considered extremely reliable. Many of these early Christians were martyred for their beliefs. Since people will only die for what they truly believe, it is reasonable to conclude that the early church sincerely believed thay were protecting the true apostolic faith from possible perversions. If they had tampered with the teachings of the apostles, they certainly would not have died for their counterfeit views.

The following conclusions can now be drawn: first, the apostolic fathers form an unbroken chain from the apostles to their day. Second, people who personally knew the apostles accepted the leadership of the apostolic fathers. Third, the apostolic fathers taught essentially the same thing as the New Testament. Fourth, the apostolic fathers and their followers were willing to die for the teachings passed down to them from the apostles themselves. Therefore, our New Testament accurately represents the teachings of the apostles. This includes such key doctrines as the deity of Christ, His substitutionary death, virgin birth, bodily resurrection, and salvation through Him alone.

The Testimony of Ancient Secular Writers

Besides references to Christ in Christian literature which date back to the first and second centuries AD, there are also ancient secular writings which refer to Christ from that same time period. The significance of these non-Christian writings is that, though the secular authors themselves did not believe the early church's message, they stated the content of what the early church actually taught.

In 52 AD, Thallus recorded a history of the Eastern Mediterranean world. In this work, he covered the time period from the Trojan War (mid 1200's BC) to his day (52 AD). Though no manuscripts of Thallus' work are known to currently exist, Julius Africanus (writing in 221 AD) referred to Thallus' work. Africanus stated that Thallus attempted to explain away the darkness that covered the land when Christ was crucified. Thallus attributed this darkness to an eclipse of the sun (Habermas, *Ancient Evidence*, 93). This reveals that about twenty years after the death of Christ, non-believers were still trying to give explanations for the miraculous events of Christ's life.

In 115 AD, a Roman historian named Cornelius Tacitus wrote about the great fire of Rome which occurred during Nero's reign. Tacitus reported that Nero blamed the fire on a group of people called Christians, and he tortured them for it. Tacitus stated that the Christians had been named after their founder "Christus." Tacitus said that Christus had been executed by Pontius Pilate during the reign of Tiberius (14-37 AD). Tacitus related that the "superstition" of the Christians had been stopped for a short time, but then once again broke out, spreading from Judaea all the way to Rome. He said that multitudes of Christians (based on their own confessions to be followers of Christ) were thrown to wild dogs, crucified, or burned to death. Tacitus added that their persecutions were not really for the good of the public; their deaths merely satisfied the cruelty of Nero himself (87-88).

These statements by Tacitus are consistent with the New Testament records. Even Tacitus' report of the stopping of the "superstition" and then its breaking out again appears to be his attempt to explain how the death of Christ stifled the spreading of the gospel, but then the Christian message was once again preached, this time spreading more rapidly. This is perfectly consistent with the New Testament record. The New Testament reports that Christ's disciples went into hiding during His arrest and death. After Jesus rose from the dead (three days after the crucifixion), He filled His disciples with the Holy Spirit (about fifty days after the crucifixion), and they fearlessly proclaimed the gospel throughout the Roman Empire (Acts 1 and 2).

Both the Bible (Acts 5:33-39) and the Jewish historian Josephus tell their readers that many men claimed to be the Jewish Messiah in ancient times. Eventually, these would-be-messiahs were crushed by the Roman military. Once the self-proclaimed Messiah died, his movement died with him. Tacitus tells us that Jesus died and that His movement was stifled temporarily, but then His movement was somehow "jump-started" and spread throughout the Roman Empire. Since dead Messiah equals dead Messiah movement, historians have had a hard time explaining what Tacitus reported: Jesus' Messiah movement died when He died, but then shortly thereafter His movement came back to life. Since the Messiah was supposed to rescue Israel from her enemies (what Jesus will do when He returns), when a supposed Messiah dies without delivering Israel, His movement dies as well. When Jesus died, His Messiah movement died with Him. But, then His Messiah movement came back to life and continues to spread nearly two-thousand years later. Since dead Messiah equals dead Messiah movement, if Jesus' movement was resurrected, the only explanation is that Jesus the Messiah came back to life as well. Dead Messiah equals dead Messiah movement; resurrected Messiah movement equals resurrected Messiah. Apart from the resurrection, there is no way that Jesus' Messiah movement would have been revived after Jesus' death as reported by Tacitus.

Suetonius was the chief secretary of Emperor Hadrian who reigned over Rome from 117 to 138 AD. Suetonius refers to the riots that occurred in the Jewish community in Rome in 49 AD due to the instigation of "Chrestus." Chrestus is apparently a variant spelling of

Christ. Suetonius refers to these Jews being expelled from the city (90). Seutonius also reports that following the great fire of Rome, Christians were punished. He refers to their religious beliefs as “new and mischievous” (90).

Pliny the Younger, another ancient secular writer, provides evidence for early Christianity. He was a Roman govenor in Asia Minor. His work dates back to 112 AD. He states that Christians assembled on a set day, sangs hymns to Christ as to “a god,” vowed not to partake in wicked deeds, and shared “ordinary” food (94). This shows that by 112 AD, it was already common knowledge that Christians worshiped Christ, sang hymns to Him, lived moral lives, assembled regularly, and partook of common food (probably a reference to the celebration of the Lord’s Supper).

The Roman Emperor Trajan also wrote in 112 AD. He gave guidelines for the persecution of Christians. He stated that if a person denies he is a Christian and proves it by worshiping the Roman gods, he must be pardoned for his repentance (96).

The Roman Emperor Hadrian reigned from 117 to 138 AD. He wrote that Christians should only be punished if there was clear evidence against them. Mere accusations were not enough to condemn a supposed Christian (97). The significance of these passages found in the writings of Trajan and Hadrian is that it confirms the fact that early Christians were sincere enough about their beliefs to die for them.

The Talmud is the written form of the oral traditions of the ancient Jewish Rabbis. A Talmud passage dating back to between 70 and 200 AD refers to Jesus as one who “practiced sorcery” and led Israel astray. This passage states that Jesus (spelled Yeshu) was hanged (the common Jewish term for crucifixion) on the night before the Passover feast (98). This is a very significant passage, for it reveals that even the enemies of Christ admitted there were supernatural aspects of Christ’s life by desribing Him as one who “practiced sorcery.” This source also confirms that Jesus was crucified around the time of the Passover feast.

Another anti-Christian document was the Toledoth Jesu, which dates back to the fifth century AD, but reflects a much earlier Jewish tradition. In this document, the Jewish leaders are said to have paraded the rotting corpse of Christ through the streets of Jerusalem (99-100). This obviously did not occur. The earliest preaching of the gospel took place in Jerusalem. Therefore, parading the rotting corpse of Christ through the streets of Jerusalem would have crushed the Christian faith in its embryonic stage. However, some of the other non-Christian authors mentioned above stated that Christianity spread rapidly during the first few decades after Christ's death. The preaching of Christ's resurrection would not have been persuasive if His rotting corpse had been publicly displayed.

It is also interesting to note that the Jewish religious leaders waited quite a long before putting a refutation of the resurrection into print. Certainly, it would have served their best interests to disprove Christ's resurrection. But as far as written documents are concerned, the first century Jewish authorities were silent regarding the resurrection of Jesus.

Lucian was a Greek satirist of the second century. He wrote that Christians worshiped a wise man who had been crucified, lived by His laws, and believed themselves to be immortal (100). Thus, this ancient secular source confirms the New Testament message by reporting the fact that Jesus was worshiped by His earliest followers.

Probably the most interesting of all ancient non-Christian references to the life of Christ is found in the writings of the Jewish historian named Josephus. Josephus was born in 37 or 38 AD and died in 97 AD. At nineteen, he became a Pharisee—a Jewish religious leader and teacher of the Old Testament (90). The following passage is found in his writings:

> Now there was about this time Jesus, a wise man, if it be lawful to call him a man; for he was a doer of wonderful works, a teacher of such men as receive the truth with pleasure. He drew over to him both many of the Jews and many of the Gentiles. He was (the) Christ. And when Pilate, at the suggestion of the principal men amongst us, had condemned him to the cross, those that loved him at the first did not forsake him; for he appeared to them alive again the third day; as the divine prophets had foretold these and ten thousand other wonderful things concerning him. And the tribe of Christians, so named after him, are not extinct at this day (Josephus 480).

Since Josephus was a Jew and not a Christian, many scholars deny that this passage was originally written by him. These scholars believe this text was corrupted by Christians. Gary Habermas, chairman of the the philosophy department at Liberty University, dealt with this problem in the following manner:

> There are good indications that the majority of the text is genuine. There is no textual evidence against it, and, conversely, there is very good manuscript evidence for this statement about Jesus, thus making it difficult to ignore. Additionally, leading scholars on the works of Josephus have testified that this portion is written in the style of this Jewish historian. Thus we conclude that there are good reasons for accepting this version of Josephus' statement about Jesus, with modifications of questionable words. In fact, it is possible that these modifications can even be accurately ascertained. In 1972 Professor Schlomo Pines of the Hebrew University in Jerusalem released the results of a study on an Arabic manuscript containing Josephus' statement about Jesus. It

> includes a different and briefer rendering of the entire passage, including changes in the key words listed above. . . (*Ancient Evidence* 91).

Habermas goes on to relate the Arabic version of this debated passage. In this version, Jesus is described as being a wise and virtuous man who had many followers from different nations. He was crucified under Pontius Pilate, but his disciples reported that, three days later, He appeared to them alive. Josephus added that Jesus may have been the Messiah whom the prophets had predicted would come (91-92).

It is highly unlikely that both readings of this controversial passage are corrupt. One of these two readings probably represents the original text. The other reading would then be a copy that was tampered with by either a Christian or a non-Christian. Whatever the case may be, even the skeptic should have no problem accepting the Arabic reading. Still, even if only this reading is accepted, it is enough. For it is a first-century testimony from a non-Christian historian that declares that those who knew Jesus personally claimed that He had appeared to them alive three days after His death by crucifixion under Pilate.

Several things can be learned from this brief survey of ancient non-Christian writings concerning the life of Christ. First, His earliest followers worshiped Him as God. The doctrine of Christ's deity is therefore not a legend or myth developed many years after Christ's death (as was the case with Buddha). Second, they claimed to have seen Him alive three days after His death. Third, Christ's earliest followers faced persecution and martyrdom for their refusal to deny His deity and resurrection. Therefore, the deity and resurrection of Christ were not legends added to the text centuries after its original composition. Instead, these teachings were the focus of the teaching of Christ's earliest followers. They claimed to be eyewitnesses of

Christ's miraculous life and were willing to die horrible deaths for their testimonies. Therefore, they were reliable witnesses of who the true Jesus of history was and what He taught.

The Evidence From Ancient Sermons

Christian philosopher J. P. Moreland, in his book *Scaling the Secular City*, discusses another important evidence that indicates the New Testament we have today is an accurate representation of the teachings of the early church leaders—the apostles (155-156). Moreland points to the "evangelistic speeches" found in Acts chapters one through twelve as strong evidence that the apostles did proclaim Jesus to be the Jewish Messiah who had died on the cross and rose from the dead, and that these speeches date back to the earliest years of Christianity—the early 30's AD.

Moreland gives five aspects of these speeches indicating they are extremely early. First, these speeches "translate well into Aramaic." This cannot be said of the sermons found in Acts chapter thirteen and beyond. This probably indicates that these speeches were originally spoken in Aramaic to Jewish audiences (155). Aramaic was the common language of first-century Judean Jews. Before the gospel was proclaimed to the Gentiles, it was almost exclusively preached to the Jews.

Second, the speeches of Acts chapters one through twelve have a "unique vocabulary, tone, style, and theology" in contrast to the rest of Acts (155). This shows that in Acts chapters one through twelve we find material that predates the writing of the book of Acts, and that the author of Acts referred to this earlier material to compile Acts one through twelve.

Third, Moreland states that "the theology of these speeches is primitive; that is, it does not reflect a great deal of developed thinking." In other words, these speeches were given before the early church had sufficient time to contemplate the person and works of Jesus to formulate systematic doctrines. Moreland shows that the Messiahship of Jesus is emphasized, rather than His deity (which is what we would expect to be the case when the gospel was first preached to Jewish audiences). Primitive phrases are used to refer to Jesus such as "Jesus the Nazarene" and "thy holy Child Jesus." These phrases were not commonly used by the early church after the first decade of its existence. Moreland adds that a primitive concept of redemption is used in these speeches—Jesus is viewed as the one who redeems the nation of Israel, rather than as the Savior of the world (155).

Fourth, the vocabulary, style, and emphasis of the speeches given by Peter in the first twelve chapters of Acts are very similar to the material found in 1 Peter and the Gospel of Mark (the early church fathers told us that Mark received his Gospel from the Apostle Peter). This gives one the impression that the speeches were in fact given by the same person—the Apostle Peter (156).

And, fifth, according to the first two chapters of Acts, these speeches represent the earliest preaching of the gospel and were preached in Jerusalem just seven weeks after Jesus was crucified. Moreland reasons that this information (the preaching in Jerusalem and the seven week gap) is probably reliable since it would have been counter-productive for the early church to invent the seven week interval before the gospel was publicly proclaimed (156). Why have the apostles wait seven weeks before proclaiming Christ's resurrection unless that is what actually happened? But that means that the early church actually preached that Jesus had risen from the dead just seven weeks after He was crucified. The resurrection was not a legend that evolved into existence over a prolonged period of time; it was publicly preached in Jerusalem (the easiest place on earth to refute a resurrection hoax) only weeks after Christ's death.

Moreland concludes that the evidence indicates these sermons are extremely early, taking us back to within weeks of Christ's death. Yet, when we examine the content of these speeches, we see that Jesus is proclaimed as the Jewish Messiah and the Savior, and that the apostles declare themselves to be eyewitnesses of His resurrection (156; Acts 2:22-24, 32, 38; 3:15; 4:10-12; 5:30-32; 10:38-43). Therefore, the supernatural aspects of Jesus' life were proclaimed by the early church from the beginning; the miraculous aspects of Christ's life are not legends, but the testimony of the people who knew Him.

The Evidence From Ancient Creeds

The writings of both the apostolic fathers and ancient non-Christian authors declare that the earliest Christians did in fact teach that Jesus is God and that He rose from the dead. We have seen that the manuscript evidence for the New Testament is stronger than that of any other ancient writing. Ancient sermons found in the first twelve chapters of Acts also show the New Testament portrait of Jesus to be accurate. Another piece of evidence for the authenticity and reliability of the New Testament manuscripts is the ancient creeds found in the New Testament itself.

Most scholars, whether liberal or conservative, date Paul's epistles before the Gospels were put into written form (McDowell and Wilson 168-170). Just as the teachings of the Jewish Rabbis had originally been passed on orally, it appears that the Gospel was first spread in the form of oral creeds and hymns (170). J. P. Moreland states that Paul's epistles contain many of these pre-Pauline creeds and hymns, that they were originally spoken in the Aramaic tongue (the Hebrew language of Christ's day), and that most scholars date these creeds and hymns between 33 AD and 48 AD (*Scaling the Secular City* 148-149). Since Paul's writings are dated in the 50's or 60's AD by most scholars, the creeds he recorded in his letters point to an oral tradition which predates his writings. Most scholars will at least admit that these ancient creeds originated before 50 AD (148-149).

Excerpts from some of these ancient creeds found in the letters of Paul are as follows:

> . . . that if you confess with your mouth Jesus as Lord, and believe in your heart that God raised Him from the dead, you shall be saved (Romans 10:9).
>
> Have this attitude in yourselves which was also in Christ Jesus, who, although He existed in the form of God, did not regard equality with God a thing to be grasped, but emptied Himself, taking the form of a bondservant, and being made in the likeness of men. And being found in appearance as a man, He humbled Himself by becoming obedient to the point of death, even death on a cross. Therefore also God highly exalted Him, and bestowed on Him the name which is above every name, that at the name of Jesus every knee should bow, of those who are in heaven, and on earth, and under the earth, and that every tongue should confess that Jesus Christ is Lord, to the glory of God the Father (Philippians 2:5-11).
>
> And He [Christ] is the image of the invisible God, the first-born of all creation. For by Him all things were created, both in the heavens and on earth, visible and invisible, whether thrones or dominions or rulers or authorities—all things have been created by Him and for Him. And He is before all things, and in Him all things hold together (Colossians 1:15-17).

The creed found in 1 Corinthians 15:3-8 provides extremely strong and early evidence for Christ's resurrection. It is often assumed by anti-Christian skeptics that the resurrection of Jesus Christ from the dead is nothing more than an ancient myth or legend, having no basis in historical fact. However, this is not the case. In the Apostle Paul's First Letter to the Corinthians, we find excellent eyewitness testimony concerning the resurrection that nearly dates back to the event itself. The Apostle Paul wrote:

> For I delivered to you as of first importance what I also received, that Christ died for our sins according to the Scriptures, and that He was buried, and that He was raised on the third day according to the Scriptures, and that He appeared to Cephas, then to the twelve. After that He appeared to more than five hundred brethren at one time, most of whom remain until now, but some have fallen asleep; then He appeared to James, then to all the apostles; and last of all, as it were to one untimely born, He appeared to me also (1 Corinthians 15:3-8).

Most New Testament scholars, liberal and conservative alike, agree that this passage is an ancient creed or hymn formulated by the early church. In our task of ascertaining when the creed of 1 Corinthians 15 was created, it is first necessary to determine when Paul wrote 1 Corinthians. In this way, we will establish the latest possible date for the creed. We can then work our way back in time from that date, following any clues based upon the internal evidence found in the creed itself. Christian philosopher J. P. Moreland has correctly stated that for the past one hundred years almost all New Testament critics have accepted the Pauline authorship of 1 Corinthians (*Scaling the Secular City* 148). A comparison of 1 Corinthians 16 with Acts 18, 19, and 20 provides strong evidence that 1 Corinthians was written by Paul in 55 AD while in Ephesus (Morris, *1 Corinthians* 1995). Scholars such as John A. T. Robinson, Henry C.

Thiessen, A. T. Robertson, Douglas Moo, Leon Morris, and D. A. Carson all concur that 1 Corinthians was written in the mid 50's AD.

We have established 55 AD as the date for the composition of 1 Corinthians. This means that the ancient creed quoted by Paul in 1 Corinthians 15:3-8 had to originate before this date. However, there is strong evidence found in the creed itself that points to its development at a much earlier time.

Christian apologist Gary Habermas discusses at least eight pieces of evidence from within the creed that indicate a very early date. First, the terms "delivered" and "received" have been shown to be technical rabbinic terms used for the passing on of sacred tradition (*Ancient Evidence* 124). Second, Paul admitted that this statement was not his own creation and that he had received it from others. Third, scholars agree that some of the words in the creed are non-Pauline terms and are clearly Jewish. These phrases include "for our sins," "according to the Scriptures," "He has been raised," "the third day," "He was seen," and "the twelve." Fourth, the creed is organized into a stylized and parallel form; it appears to have been an oral creed or hymn in the early church (125). Fifth, the creed shows evidence of being of a Semitic origin and, thus, points to a source that predates Paul's translation of it into Greek. This can be seen in the use of "Cephas" for Peter, for "Cephas" is Aramaic for Peter (which is Petros in the Greek). J. P. Moreland notes additional evidence for the Semitic origin of this creed by relating that the poetic style of the early creed is Hebraic (*Scaling the Secular City* 150). Sixth, Habermas reasons that Paul probably received this creed around 36-38 AD, just three years after his conversion, when he met with Peter and James in Jerusalem, as recorded by Paul in Galatians 1:18-19 (*Ancient Evidence* 125). Jesus' death occurred around 30 to 33 AD, and Paul was converted between 31 and 35 AD. Seventh, Habermas states that, due to the above information, "numerous critical theologians" date the creed "from three to eight years after Jesus' crucifixion." Eighth, since it would have taken a period of time for the beliefs to become formalized into a creed or hymn, the beliefs behind the creed must date back to the event itself (125).

Hence, there is strong evidence that the creed of 1 Corinthians 15:3-8 originated between three to eight years after Christ's crucifixion, and that the beliefs which underlie this creed must therefore go back to the event itself. Now we must briefly examine the content of this ancient creed.

First, the creed mentions the death and burial of Christ. Second, it states that Christ was raised on the third day. Third, it lists several post-resurrection appearances of Christ. These include appearances to Peter, to the twelve apostles, to over 500 persons at one time, to James (the Lord's brother), to all the apostles, and, finally an appearance to Paul himself.

It should be noted that scholars differ as to the exact contents of this ancient creed in its most primitive form. It seems that Paul added verse eight (detailing his own eyewitness account) to the original creed, as well as a portion of verse six (a reminder that most of the 500 witnesses were still alive). This in no way lessons the force of this ancient creed. In fact, it strengthens it as evidence for the resurrection, for Paul adds his own testimony and encourages his readers to question the many eyewitnesses still living in his day. Whatever the case, most New Testament scholars accept a large enough portion of the creed for it to be considered a valuable piece of eyewitness evidence for the resurrection of Christ from the dead.

Having argued for a very early date for its origin, we must now ascertain the evidential value of this creed. Simply stated, the early date of the 1 Corinthians 15 creed proves that the resurrection accounts found in the New Testament are not legends. Christian philosopher William Lane Craig, while commenting on the work of the great Roman historian A. N. Sherwin-White, stated that "even two generations is too short a time span to allow legendary tendencies to wipe out the hard core of historical facts" (*Reasonable Faith* 285). If two generations is not enough time for legends to develop, then there is no way that a resurrection legend could emerge in only three to eight years.

It should also be noted that, in this creed, Paul is placing his apostolic credentials on the line by encouraging his Corinthian critics to check out his account with the eyewitnesses who were still alive. These eyewitnesses not only included over 500 people, but also Peter, James, and the other apostles—the recognized leaders of the early church (Galatians 2:9). It is highly improbable that Paul would fabricate the creed and jeopardize his own position in the early church.

Finally, it should be obvious to any open-minded person who examines the evidence that Paul was a man of integrity. He was not lying. Not only did he put his reputation and position in the early church on the line, but he was also willing to suffer and die for Christ. Men do not die for what they know to be a hoax. Paul was a reliable and sincere witness to the resurrection of Christ.

The creed of 1 Corinthians 15:3-8 provides us with reliable eyewitness testimony for the bodily resurrection of Jesus Christ. Not only did Paul testify that he had seen the risen Christ, but he also identified many other witnesses to the resurrection that could have been interrogated. Contrary to the futile speculations of liberal scholars, Paul was not devising myths behind closed doors. No, from the beginning he was preaching a risen Savior who had conquered death and the grave, a risen Savior who had met him on the road to Damascus and changed his life forever.

When taken together, these ancient creeds (Romans 10:9; Philippians 2:5-11; Colossians 1:15-17; 1 Corinthians 15:3-8; etc.) clearly prove that the first generation Christians believed that Jesus had bodily risen from the dead, that He is God, and that salvation comes through Him (Moreland, *Scaling the Secular City* 149). The followers of Buddha attributed deity to the founder of their religion centuires after his death (McDowell ans Stewart, *Today's Religions* 307-308). However, the earliest followers of Christ, those who knew Jesus personally, considered Him to be God during their lifetimes (Moreland, *Scaling the Secular City* 150). It is almost universally recognised by New Testament scholars today that these creeds were formulated before 50 AD, some of these creeds going back to the early 30's AD. Therefore, these creeds represent the gospel in its original form, the gospel preached by the early church—the apostles themselves.

Hence, the belief in Christ's deity and resurrection is not based on later corruptions of the New Testament text as liberal scholars believe. The doctrines of Christ's deity and resurrection are not legends that took centuries to develop. These doctrines were held by the first generation church, those who knew Jesus personally. The gospel message found in the New Testament is the same message proclaimed by the apostles themselves.

Less than twenty years after Christ's death, hymns were already being sung in Christian churches attributing deity to Christ. The apostles were still alive and had the authority to supress the doctrine of Christ's deity if it was a heresy; but, they did not. All the available evidence indicates that they not only condoned it, but that it was their own teaching. Therefore, liberal scholars such as John Hick have no justification for their claims that the deity of Christ was a legend that developed near the end of the first century AD (*Center* 27-29). The historical evidence indicates that the Christian church always believed in Christ's deity. Therefore, to deny that Christ claimed to be God is to call the apostles liars.

Nearly 2,000 years after the death of Christ a forum of liberal scholars called the "Jesus Seminar" began meeting in 1985. These scholars voted to decide which biblical passages they believed Jesus actually said (Moreland and Wilkins 2-3). This is ironic since the evidence shows that Christianity proclaimed Christ's deity and resurrection from its inception. The early church accepted the deity of Christ and His bodily resurrection. The first believers were willing to suffer horrible persecution for these beliefs. Sincere eyewitness testimony should not be ignored by contemporary scholars.

The Letters of Paul and the Historical Jesus

Liberal scholars, as well as many evangelical scholars who accept liberal presuppositions, believe that Paul's letters comprise the earliest New Testament writings. Several of Paul's letters (i.e., Romans, 1 Corinthians, 2 Corinthians, Galatians, Philippians, 1 Thessalonians, and Philemon) are accepted as authentic by the vast majority of New Testament critics today. The reasons given by liberal scholars for rejecting the other six Pauline letters (i.e., Ephesians, Colossians, 2 Thessalonians, 1 Timothy, 2 Timothy, and Titus) are not convincing. The early church fathers accepted all thirteen of Paul's letters as being authentically written by him. The burden of proof is on the liberal scholars if they wish to deny Pauline authorship of these other letters. These letters were collected very early by the church, and there is no reason to assume that the early church was mistaken. The apostolic fathers (i.e., leaders in the early church who were trained by the apostles themselves) quoted from or alluded to all thirteen of Paul's letters as authoritative by 110 AD (Barnett, *Is the New Testament Reliable?* 39-42). Are we really to believe that the early church leaders were mistaken? Again, the burden of proof is on those who choose to deny the Pauline authorship of these letters.

In Paul's letters (both the accepted letters and the debated letters), one can find an outline of the life, ministry, and teachings of Jesus. Paul Barnett lists aspects of Jesus' life known and proclaimed by Paul (*Is the New Testament Reliable?* 140-141). Paul related that Jesus was a descendent of both Abraham and David (Galatians 3:16; Romans

1:3), that He was born of a woman under the Jewish Law (Galatians 4:4), and that He lived a life of humble service despite the fact that He was rejected and insulted during His life (Philippians 2:5-8; Romans 15:3). Paul knew that James was Jesus' brother and that Jesus had other brothers (Galatians 1:19; 1 Corinthians 9:5). Paul knew the Apostle Peter enough to know that Peter was married (1 Corinthians 9:5). Paul knew of the Last Supper, the betrayal of Christ, and His trial before Pilate (1 Corinthians 11:23-26; 1 Timothy 6:13). Paul also taught that Jesus is God (Philippians 2:6; Romans 10:9; Titus 2:13; Colossians 2:9), He is Messiah (Galatians 1:1; Romans 1:1), He is Savior (Titus 2:13), and He died on the cross for our sins (1 Corinthians 15:3). Paul relates that Judean Jews played a role in Jesus' death (1 Thessalonians 2:14-15), and that Jesus was buried, but rose from the dead and appeared to numerous people on several occassions (1 Corinthians 15:4-8).

It must be remembered that Paul recorded these events of Christ's life just twenty to thirty years after Christ's death. Still, Larry Hurtado of the University of Edinburgh points out that the evidence for the historical Jesus found in Paul's writings is stronger than that. Hurtado relates that Paul constantly argued for his views when others in the church disagreed with him. Yet, states Hurtado, Paul never argues that Jesus is God or Messiah, or that Jesus rose from the dead. He merely states these doctrines as if they were universally accepted by the Christian church at the time of his writings. Hence, Hurtado argues that the worship of Jesus as God, the acknowledgment of Him as Messiah, and the belief in His resurrection all date back to the early 30's AD—the approximate time Paul met with the leaders of the Jerusalem church (Hurtado, *Lord Jesus Christ* 101, 128-129, 131-137, 650). Paul was not an innovator; he did not create a new religion; he taught the same Gospel as Peter and John—the original followers of Jesus.

Jesus was crucified around 30 to 33 AD (Witherington III, *The Paul Quest* 307). Paul became a Christian just a year or two later (31-35 AD?). Just three years after he was converted, about 34 to 37 AD, Paul traveled to Jerusalem to meet with the leaders of the Jerusalem church (309). At that time, Paul met with Peter and James, the half-brother of Jesus (Galatians 1:18-19). Fourteen years after his conversion (45-48 AD?), Paul again went to Jerusalem, and he and Barnabas met with Peter, James, and John (317). These leaders of the Jerusalem church acknowledged that Paul and Barnabas were preaching the same Gospel as they were; they extended the right hand of fellowship to Paul and Barnabas (Galatians 2:1-10). This would not have occurred if Paul was preaching a different Gospel. In short, Paul's Gospel of Jesus as the Messiah, God, and risen Savior was the same Gospel as the original followers of Jesus proclaimed.

Liberal New Testament critics are guilty of trying to invent a "Jesus of the gaps." These critics believe that Paul wrote the earliest portions of the New Testament, yet they reject the Jesus whom Paul proclaims. Therefore, they contend that the true Jesus of history was transformed into imaginary Jesus of Paul's writings. However, this cannot be the case. Even these critics do not question Paul's honesty; yet, Paul claimed that the leaders of the Jerusalem church confirmed that his Gospel was one and the same as their's. In other words, there is no gap. Paul's writings, the ancient sermons of Acts chapters one through twelve, and the ancient creeds found in the New Testament all take us back to Christianity's earliest years, and, at this early date, we find the same Jesus found in Paul's letters and the rest of the New Testament as well. In short, there can be no "Jesus of the gaps" because there are no gaps (see 1 Corinthians 15:1-11). We can trace the Gospel to the early 30's AD, and, when we do, we find that the true Jesus of history is identical to the Jesus found in the New Testament.

The First-Century AD Dates of the New Testament Books

Liberal critics acknowledge most of Paul's writings as having been authored by the Apostle Paul between 50 AD and 64-65 AD. But, arguments for early dates of other New Testament books are also very convincing. We will look at three New Testament books to illustrate this point.

Both the Gospel of Luke and the Book of Acts were written to the same recipient—a man named Theophilus (Luke 1:1-4; Acts 1:1-3). The prologues of these books show us that Acts is the sequel of Luke; therefore, Luke was written before Acts. Acts focuses on the key characters Peter, Paul, and James (the half-brother of Jesus), yet it does not record their deaths. Peter and Paul died between 64 and 67 AD, while James died in 62 AD. Since Acts records the deaths of people less significant to the purposes of the book (i.e., Ananias, Sapphira, Stephen, James son of Zebedee, and Herod Agrippa), it appears that Acts must have been written before Peter, Paul, and James were executed (before 62 AD). Also, though Jerusalem is one of the major cities of the Book of Acts and the temple plays a key role in Acts, no mention is made of the war with the Romans (started 66 AD) and the destruction of the temple (70 AD). This is further confirmation that Acts was written early. Acts is a book filled with adventure, yet it ends anti-climatically with Paul in Rome in chains in 61 AD. This makes no sense unless Acts was completed in 61 AD and then sent to Theophilus. And, since Acts is the sequel to Luke's Gospel, the Gospel of Luke had to be written at an even earlier date. This is also confirmed by the fact that Paul quotes from Luke's Gospel as Scripture (1 Timothy 5:18). Therefore, both Luke and Acts were written before 62 AD.

The Book of Hebrews was written for the purpose of trying to prevent Jews who had accepted Jesus from abandoning the Christian faith due to persecution. The author of the Book of Hebrews argues that the temple priests are still standing and still offering sacrifices. Therefore, their animal sacrifices have failed to take away our sins. The author of Hebrews then reasons that since Jesus is seated at the Father's right hand, His work is done and His sacrifice of Himself on the cross has accomplished its purpose—our sins are forgiven. This argument makes no sense if the Book of Hebrews was written after 70 AD (the year the temple was destroyed by the Romans). If Hebrews was written after 70 AD, the author would have argued that it is impossible for his readers to return to the animal sacrifices since God allowed the temple to be destroyed. Instead, his argument only works if the temple is still standing and the temple sacrifices are still being offered. Hence, Hebrews was written before 70 AD.

Paul's accepted writings, Luke, Acts, and Hebrews all portray Jesus as God, Messiah, and risen Savior. Yet, these books were all written at least between 50 and 70 AD. The ancient creeds and sermons, dating to the early 30's AD, found in the New Testament, also paint the same picture of Jesus. Hence, the Jesus of the New Testament can be traced all the way back to the start of the church. The biblical Jesus is not a legend; Paul was not an innovator. The Jesus of the Bible is the true Jesus of history.

As the chart below indicates, there exists an unbroken chain of evidence for Jesus' claims to be God, Messiah, and the risen Savior who died for our sins. There is no gap—there is absolutely no room for legends or perversions of the Gospel message to take place.

Dates	**Evidences**
30's & 40's AD	ancient creeds found in New Testament ancient sermons (Acts 1-12) hypothetical "Q" document the Book of James Matthew, Mark, Luke ?

	(Could they be this early?) Paul's teachings before he wrote his letters
50's & 60's AD	Paul's writings Gospels (if we accept conservative dates) Gospel of John (could it be written this early?) Acts & Luke (written before 61 AD) Hebrews (written before 70 AD) Possible NT fragments (Dead Sea Scrolls) The Didache (teaching of the 12 Apostles)
70's-90's AD	Gospels (if we accept liberal dates) Non-Pauline New Testament letters? Clement of Rome's letter Epistle of Barnabas Shepherd of Hermas
90's-150's AD	Writings of other apostolic fathers Writings of ancient secular authors Fragment of John 18
150's -325 AD	Extant New Testament manuscripts Early church fathers before Nicea
325 AD-today	Early church after Nicea to the reformers to the conservative evangelical church today

The Opinions of the Experts

The testimonies of some of the world's leading experts can be called upon to further verify the authenticity and reliability of the New Testament manuscripts. Dr. John A. T. Robinson, one of England's leading New Testament critics, came to the conclusion that the entire New Testament was written before the fall of Jerusalem in 70 AD (McDowell, *Evidence* 63).

Sir William Ramsey was one of the world's greatest archaeologists. His thorough investigation into Luke's Book of Acts led him to the conclusion that Acts was a mid-first century document that was historically reliable (Varghese 267-268). William F. Albright is one of the world's foremost biblical archaeologists. He stated that there is no evidential basis for dating any New Testament book after 80 AD (267). Sir Frederic Kenyon was one of the world's leading experts on ancient manuscripts. His research led him to conclude that the New Testament is essentially the same as when it was originally written (274).

Millar Burrows, the great archaeologist from Yale, stated that there is no doubt that archaeological research has strengthened confidence in the historical reliability of the Bible. Burrows also stated that the skepticism of liberal scholars is based on their prejudice against the supernatural, rather than on the evidence itself (McDowell, *Evidence* 66).

F. F. Bruce, New Testament scholar from Manchester University in England, stated that if the New Testament writings had been secular works, no scholar would question their authenticity. Bruce believes that the evidence for the New Testament outweighs the evidence for many classical works which have never been doubted (Varghese 274).

Bruce Metzger was a famous textual critic from Princeton. He has stated that the New Testament has more evidence in its favor than any other writings from ancient Greek or Latin literature (205).

It is clear that the evidence favors the authenticity and reliability of the New Testament. Scholars who do not allow their bias against the supernatural to influence their conclusions have recognized this fact. Scholars who reject the reliability of the New Testament manuscripts do so because they chose to go against the overwhelming evidence. However, such a rejection is not true scholarship; it is an a priori assumption. If one uses neutral presuppositions rather than liberal, anti-supernatural presuppositions, then the outcome is clear: the New Testament portrait of Jesus is historically accurate.

Jesus' Inner Circle

It is interesting to note that a strong case can be made from the writngs of the early church fathers that all the books found in the New Testament can be traced back to the authority of Jesus' inner circle—those who knew Jesus more intimately than anyone else. The early church (i.e., Papias, Ireneaus, Clement of Alexandria, Tertullian, etc.) told us that Matthew wrote the Gospel bearing his name. Since Matthew was one of the original apostles, he was in Jesus' inner circle. The early church also told us that John the apostle wrote his Gospel, his three epistles, and the Book of Revelation. Peter, another apostle, wrote two epistles and his preaching formed the basis for Mark's Gospel. The apostle Paul wrote thirteen epistles. Luke was Paul's colleague and he wrote his Gospel and the Book of Acts. The author of Hebrews knew Timothy (a colleague of Paul) and apparently knew Paul's theology; hence, he was probably also an associate of the apsotle Paul. And, finally, James and Jude were Jesus' half brothers, and they each authored a New Testament epistle. Hence, all twenty-seven New Testament books can be traced back to

Matthew, John, Peter, Paul, or Jesus' brothers (i.e., Jesus' inner circle). This explains why these twenty-seven books were canonized (i.e., accepted as the list of books that belong in the Bible), whereas many other books were rejected.

Conclusion

Evidence from the existing New Testament manuscripts, from the writings of the apostolic fathers, from the works of ancient secular authors, from the ancient sermons, creeds, and hymns found in the New Testament, and from the opinions of the world's leading experts has been examined. Evidence from Paul's writings, Luke, Acts, and Hebrews has been presented. All this evidence leads to the conclusion that the existing New Testament manuscripts are reliable and authentic testimony of what the apostles wrote. The Jesus of the New Testament is the Jesus of history. A person is free to deny this conclusion, but to do so is to go against all the available evidence. The key point is that the original apostles taught that Jesus rose from the dead, and that He claimed to be God incarnate and the Savior of the world.

In the next chapter, we will briefly argue for a re-examination of the dates of composition for some of the New Testament books. Is it possible that several New Testament books should be dated much earlier than they are now dated?

Chapter Seven
Redating the New Testament Books

Evangelical pastors often accept the earliest dates for New Testament books allowed by liberal New Testament critics. But, this should not be the case. Though there are solid arguments for the traditional dates of the New Testament books, a stronger case can be made for even earlier dates for some of the New Testament books. Liberal scholars, due to their biases against miracles and traditional Christianity, assume that Paul's letters were written before any of the Gospels were written. Liberal critics assume that decades passed before any Gospel was recorded in writing. They also assume that no eyewitnesses wrote any of the Gospels. Evangelicals should question these liberal assumptions. Evangelicals should take a second look at the dating of the New Testament books.

In Paul's letters, Paul would first teach Bible doctrines (i.e., theology) and then he would move on to practical application. This was due to the fact that Paul believed that our behavior should be based on true beliefs. But, Paul was a Jew, and the Jewish faith was based on history (i.e., the Old Testament Jewish history). In Paul's writings he alludes to historical events from the life of Jesus. Hence, early Christianity more likely progressed in this order: history, doctrine, and practice. Therefore, it makes more sense that the early church would have been motivated to record in writing the historical data of the life of Christ before dealing with doctrinal issues in print. The historical data (i.e., the Gospels) would establish the basis for Christian doctrines (i.e., Jesus' deity and Messiahship, salvation through His death and resurrection, etc.). The liberal assumption that the early church would initially be interested in recording doctrine and practice, and only later be concerned about recording historical events, seems unlikely. The early church would have been greatly concerned with the historical aspects of Jesus' ministry—His life and teachings. Then after these matters are recorded and proclaimed, theological and practical implications would be drawn from this historical data. Therefore, it is possible that at least some of the Gospels were in print before the Apostle Paul began to write his doctrinal and practical letters.

There have been scholars in the past and present who have speculated that the Gospels (as well as other New Testament books) may have been written much earlier than liberal critics will allow. A few examples will suffice. New Testament scholar John A. T. Robinson, in his book *Redating the New Testament*, dated the composition of the entire New Testament to before the destruction of the Jewish temple in 70 AD (352). This was because no New Testament book mentions the destruction of the temple, though the temple plays a very significant role in the New Testament (10).

William F. Albright, one of the world's leading archaeologists, stated that there is absolutely no good reason to date any New Testament book after about 80 AD. He even went so far to say, "In my opinion, every book of the New Testament was written by a baptized Jew between the forties and the eighties of the first century AD" (McDowell, *Evidence that Demands a Verdict* 62-63).

New Testament scholar John Wenham rejects the later dates for the synpotic Gospels (i.e., Matthew, Mark, and Luke) given by liberal New Testament critics. In Wenham's work entitled *Redating Matthew, Mark, and Luke*, he dates Matthew's Gospel at around 40 AD, Mark's Gospel at about 45 AD, and Luke's Gospel at around the early 50's AD (243). New Testament scholar Henry Thiessen also gives early dates for the four Gospels and the other New Testament books (*Introduction to the New Testament*).

Roman Catholis scholars such as Claude Tresmontant and Jean Carmignac date the synoptic Gospels (i.e., Matthew, Mark, and Luke) as early as the forties or fifties AD (Keating, *What Catholics Really*

Believe 40-44). There is no reason for evangelicals to accept, without question, the late dates of the New Testament books promoted by liberal New Testament critics. If we are not biased against the possibility of miracles, we should be open to early dates of the New Testament books. This is especially true when we consider what the early church fathers wrote about the composition of the New Testament books.

If scholars are to be unbiased in their studies of the New Testament, then they must be open to the earliest possible dates of the composition of each New Testament book, rather than merely accept the latest possible date. In this chapter, we will look at evidence for the earliest possible dates of the New Testament books. Though we must be tentative in dating ancient works, since the early church fathers generally accepted the earlier dates, honest scholarship should at least be open to the possibility of these early dates.

John Wenham, in his work *Redating Matthew, Mark, and Luke*, gives an interesting quote from the Yale scholar and expert on Semitic languages C. C. Torrey:

> I challenged my New Testament colleagues [in 1934] to designate even *one* passage from any of the four Gospels giving clear evidence of a date later than 50 A.D. . . . The challenge was not met, nor will it be, for there is no such passage (Wenham, 299).

The truth of the matter is this: only liberal, anti-Christian assumptions prevent evangelicals from dating the New Testament books earlier than we normally date them. We must not be content with accepting only the earliest dates that far left, critical New Testament scholars will allow. We must be willing to think "outside the box." Conservative evangelical scholars must be willing to ask the question: "How early could the New Testament books have been written?"

Before we discuss the New Testament books themselves, we must look at the writings of the Apostolic Fathers, as well as possible ancient fragments of the New Testament. This will help us to more accurately date the New Testament books.

The Apostolic Fathers

The Apostolic Fathers were selected by the Apostles and their colleagues for positions of leadership in the church as the Apostles grew older. In short, the Apostles passed the baton of leadership to the Apostolic Fathers. Since the Apostolic Fathers quoted from or alluded to many of the New Testament books, we must date the New Testament books they quote before the writings of the Apostolic Fathers. For this reason, liberal critics, who do not want to date the New Testament books early, will often date some of the works of the Apostolic Fathers later than they should be dated. We will now examine some of these writings and attempt to determine the approximate dates of their composition. This will help us to more accurately date the New Testament books which, in most cases, preceded them.

The Didache is also called *The Teaching of the Twelve Apostles*. This document has many hints of an extremely early date of composition. First, it speaks of "the two ways," one way leading to life and the other leading to death. This was a similar theme among pre-Christian Jewish writings such as the *Qumran Manuel of Discipline* found in the Dead Sea Scrolls. It is also similar to one of the themes found in Jesus' Sermon on the Mount (Matthew 7:13-14). Second, *The Didache* is a very practical writing; it is concerned with practice, not doctrine. Yet, the church organization found in this document is very primitive—it is not the advanced stage of church organization found in second-century documents. In *The Didache*, the bishops are merely the elders, the leaders of the local congregations.

The bishop is not part of a hierarchy; he is not the head of a collection of churches in a city or region. The church organization is rather like that of Paul's epistles (the 60's AD) and the Book of Acts (i.e., elders and deacons). It is clearly primitive, first-century church organization (which implies a first-century document).

Third, the offices of "apostles and prophets" are still functioning—this indicates a very early stage in church history. Fourth, set days for fasting are prescribed and dietary instructions are given. This implies that the church is functioning as if it is still a branch of Judaism. In fact, Friday is still called the day of preparation—the day set aside to prepare for the Sabbath Day—this also implies close ties to Judaism. Still, Sunday corporate worship (i.e., the Lord's Day) is practiced as well as baptism in the name of the Triune God. In fact, instructions on how to baptize in water are given. All these factors imply a very early time in the history of the church—Christianity is still in its infancy.

For reasons such as these, John A. T. Robinson dates *The Didache* from 40 to 60 AD (*Redating the New Testament* 327, 352). At the least, it appears that *The Didache* paints a picture of Christian corporate worship that pre-dates 70 AD. Yet, this work references numerous New Testament passages from Matthew and Luke. It is possible that *The Didache* also alludes to Hebrews, Acts, and Mark, and there is even a possible parallel passage with 1 John. At a minimum, *The Didache* indicates the antiquity of Matthew and Luke.

Many scholars date the *The Epistle of Barnabas* to around 135 AD. However, Robinson argues persuasively for a 75 AD date for this writing. The unknown author—he is probably not Paul's colleague Barnabas—speaks of the temple having been recently torn down by the enemies of the Jews (16.4). Lightfoot and Harmer also date this epistle to the 70's AD, shortly after the temple was destroyed (*The Apostolic Fathers* 241). This epistle references several passages from Matthew's Gospel. It may also refer to Hebrews, 2 Peter, the Gospel of John, Acts, Romans, and Revelation. If the earlier date of *The Epistle of Barnabas* is accepted, then several of the New Testament books must be dated earlier as well.

Clement of Rome wrote a letter to the church of Corinth. Since Clement was the Bishop of Rome towards the close of the first-century, many scholars date this letter to 95-96 AD. However, in this epistle, the position of elder seems closer to what Paul described in his letters thirty years earlier (1 Timothy 3 and Titus 1). Hence, the church government resembles the pre-70 AD model, not the early second-century model which elevated the role of the bishop. It should also be noted that, in his letter, Clement never appeals to his authority as the Bishop of Rome. Due to this, Robinson believes that Clement wrote this letter while a representative of the Roman Church, but long before he was bishop. This is confirmed by Clement's statement that the Jerusalem temple was still standing at the time of this writing (41.2). Since Clement does mention the martyrdoms of Peter and Paul (5:1-7), which occurred around 67 AD, but says the temple had yet to be destroyed, Robinson concludes that Clement wrote his letter to the Corinthians in early 70 AD, before the temple was destroyed by the Romans (*Redating the New Testament* 327-335). In Clement's letter, he alludes to or quotes from Matthew, Mark, Luke, Acts, 1 Corinthians, Titus, Hebrews, James, 1 Peter, and possibly Revelation.

Scholars often date *The Shepherd of Hermas* to the mid second century due to the fact that the Muratorian Fragment identifies Hermas with the brother of Pius who was the Bishop of Rome from 141 to 155 AD (Robinson, 319). But, Robinson believes the Muratorian Fragment is incorrect on this point, for church fathers like Ireneaus, Tertullian, and Origen all treated *The Shepherd of Hermas* as if it were an ancient document, not a second-century document which had been recently authored. This would not have been the case if it was a recent composition. Though *The Shepherd of Hermas* mentions Clement of Rome as a comtemporary, Robinson believes this letter was written before Clement was the Bishop of Rome. This work speaks of the apostles, bishops, teachers, and deacons—this reflects the earliest stages of Christianity. Hence, Robinson dates *The Sheherd of Hermas* to around 85 AD (Robinson, 319-322, 352). This work mentions passages from several New Testament books: Matthew, Mark, John, 1 Corinthians, Hebrews, James, 1 Peter, 1 John, and Revelation.

The seven letters of *Ignatius* were written in 107 AD as Ignatius was enroute to be martyred for the faith. Ignatius was martyred about 107 AD; hence, Lightfoot and Harmer, as well as most scholars, date Ignatius' seven letters about 107 AD (Lightfoot and Harmer, *The Apostolic Fathers* 97). Ignatius was the Bishop of Antioch of Syria. In his seven letters he referenced Matthew, John, Acts, Romans, 1 Corinthians, Galatians, Ephesians, Colossians,1 Peter, and James.

Polycarp was a disciple of the Apostle John. He eventually became the Bishop of Smyrna. At age 86, he experienced martyrdom when he was burned at the stake in 156 AD (Cairns, *Christianity through the Centuries* 76-77). Around the time of Ignatius' martyrdom (107 AD), Polycarp wrote his *Epistle to the Philippians*. In this letter, Polycarp quotes or paraphrases from the following New Testament books: Matthew, Mark, Luke, Acts, Romans, Galatians, 1 Corinthians, 2 Corinthians, Ephesians, Philippians, 2 Thessalonians, 1 Timothy, 2 Timothy, 1 Peter, and 1 John.

The writings of *Papias* are mostly lost to mankind. Only a few fragments of his works remain, and these are found quoted by other ancient writers like Eusebius. Papias was born between 60 and 70 AD, and he died between 130 and 140 AD. He was a disicple of the Apostle John. Papias wrote his *Exposition of Oracles of the Lord*; however, as mentioned above, only fragments remain. In those fragments, Papias tells us that Matthew wrote his Gospel first, Mark's Gospel is based on Peter's preaching, and the Apostle John wrote the

Gospel of John (Lightfoot and Harmer, *The Apostolic Fathers* 527-535).

Many liberal critics date Clement's letter, the *Shepherd of Hermas*, the *Epistle of Barnabas*, and the *Didache* much later than the dates given above. But, the primitive church polity seems much closer to the church polity of Paul's epistles (50's and 60's AD) than the later church polity of the second-century AD. By the second-century AD, the the authority of the bishop was greatly elevated—this is not the case in the writings of the Apostolic Fathers mentioned above. Apparantly, the desire of the liberal critics to date the New Testament books late forces them to date some of the writings of the Apostolic Fathers late as well. However, we shall see that a strong case can be made for dating many of the New Testament books much earlier than the earliest dates allowed by liberal critics (due to their anti-supernaturalistic bias).

Possible Early Fragments of the New Testament?

Few Christians are aware of the fact that possible fragments of the New Testament exist that might date all the way back to the first-century AD. Liberal critics are not open to identifying these fragments with portions of the New Testament. This is because some of these fragments were written before the critics believe the original New Testament manuscripts were written. Some of these fragments are acknolwedged as New Testament copies by liberal critics, but they are dated late so as to not conflict with critical theories of the late dates for the Gospels and other New Testament books.

The famous John Ryland's fragment of John 18:31-33 is dated by the majority of scholars to about 125 to 130 AD. However, the late papyrologist (i.e., an expert on identifying ancient fragments) Carsten P. Thiede reminds his readers that when Colin Roberts originally dated this fragment, though he settled on a 125 AD date, he did acknowledge numerous parallels with several first-century documents. Hence, it is possible that the John Ryland's fragment of John 18 could date back to the 90's AD (Thiede, *Rekindling the Word* 10-11, 26-27). Since this copy was found in Egypt the original Gospel of John had to have been written much earlier (122).

The Chester Beatty papyri contains portions of Paul's writings. Thiede points out that though these papyri are usually dated to about 200 AD, papyrologist Young Kyu-Kim argued in 1988 that the Chester Beatty papyri should be dated to the late first-century AD (178). The idea of first-century copies of any New Testament book is too radical for most New Testament critics to accept. However, New Testament scholars should pay more attention to the results of recent research conducted by papyrologists, rather than merely dismiss any empirical evidence that contradicts liberal speculation.

The late Carsten B. Thiede, towards the end of his life, built upon the work and research of the great Spanish papyrologist Jose O'Callaghan. O'Callaghan identified several ancient fragments in cave seven of Qumran with portions of New Testament books. Though most scholars resist the notion of New Testament copies in the Dead Sea Scrolls, it is possible that the Jewish community in Qumran collected as much Jewish literature as they could, including Greek copies of New Testament writings. It must be remembered that the early church was originally considered to be a branch of Judaism, though a unique branch at that. Cave seven is the only known collection of Greek fragments in the Dead Sea Scrolls. It is possible that the research of O'Callaghan and Thiede is on target, and that fragments of copies of the New Testament existed between 50 and 70 AD—the latest possible date for any of the Dead Sea Scrolls. In cave seven of Qumran, the following fragments were found: 7Q6 (Mark 4:28), 7Q15 (Mark 6:48), 7Q5 (Mark 6:52-53), 7Q7 (Mark 12:17), 7Q6 (Acts 27:38), 7Q9 (Romans 5:11-12), 7Q4 (1 Timothy 3:16 & 4:1-3), 7Q10 (2 Peter 1:15), and 7Q8 (James 1:23-24). Though these fragments are tiny and identification can be disputed, the acknowledgement that they are copies from the New Testament should not be dismissed merely for a priori reasons (Geisler, *Baker Encyclopedia of Christian Apologetics* 530, 547-548).

Thiede also argued that the oldest existing fragments of Matthew's Gospel should be dated to the first-century AD, possibly even to pre-70 AD (*Rekindling the Word* 26-27). The oldest copies of Matthew's Gospel consist of five small scraps, three which are kept at Magdalene College, Oxford, with the other two fragments in Barcelona, Spain (20). Obviously, if these fragments are actually this old, then Matthew's Gospel must have been authored very early in the history of the Church. Since most New Testament critics reject such an early date for Matthew's Gospel, Thiede's conclusions are considered very controversial. However, if one places more confidence in the views of the early church fathers and less confidence in the speculation of contemporary liberal critics, then Thiede's work deserves consideration. Also, it should be noted that Thiede's work is not based on speculative theories like that of New Testament critics. Rather, Thiede's research was based on empirical research—comparing the ancient fragments with other ancient fragments of known date (33).

Due to a re-examination of the dates of the writings of the Apostolic Fathers, and the possible identification of ancient first-century fragments as copies of the New Testament, the dating of the New Testament books deserves a second look. We will now discuss possible dates for the composition for the twenty-seven New Testament books.

Gospel of Matthew

Most New Testament scholars assume that the Gospels were not written until after Paul's letters. This would mean that the Gospels were written, at the earliest, thirty to seventy years after Jesus' death and resurrection. But, this is not necessarily the case. Jesus referred to the apostles as "scribes" (Matthew 13:51-52; 23:34). This implies that the apostles took notes when Jesus taught them. Matthew had been a tax collector before Jesus selected him to be one of His disciples. His profession necessitated good writing skills. It is very possible that Matthew was the stenographer for the twelve apostles—he may have been the lead scribe. Since the Old Testament is in written form, it makes sense that the New Testament would be in written form as well. The apostles would have had the incentive to record in writing Jesus' sayings (and maybe His miracles as well) almost immediately. He was their rabbi (their teacher), and His miracles would have convinced them that He might be the Messiah. It is very likely that the apostles would record in writing the most important teachings and acts of Jesus' ministry.

It is possible that the original edition of Matthew's Gospel consisted of Matthew's notes on Jesus' sermons. These notes would date back to between 27 and 30 AD or between 30 and 33 AD (depending on the date of Jesus's public ministry). This may explain why the apostolic father Papias refers to the original edition of Matthew's Gospel as "the words" ("ta logia" in Greek) of the Lord (Wenham, 124).

Papias, probably writing about 110 AD, also says that Matthew was the first to write his Gospel (contrary to the popular theory among New Testament scholars that Mark wrote first), and that he originally wrote his Gospel in Hebrew (121-135). It makes sense that Matthew would be the first to write a Gospel since the original preaching of the Gospel would emphasize proving that Jesus is the Jewish Messiah. It is no coincidence that Matthew's Gospel contains many more Old Testament prophecies fuflilled by Jesus than any of the other three Gospels (Thiessen, 132, 138).

In fact, it might not be incorrect to consider Matthew's Gospel the "Jerusalem Gospel" since he includes in his Gospel several events that would have greater relevance for the Jerusalem Church than for churches located elsewhere. These events would include: the rising of recently departed saints who entered Jerusalem after Jesus' resurrection to show others they were alive (Matthew 27:52-53), the earthquake that occurred in Jerusalem as Jesus died (Matthew 27:51), the name of the field (i.e., Potter's Field) purchased with the money Judas received to betray Jesus (Matthew 27:7), and the stolen body rumor started by the chief priests (Matthew 28:11-15). The first preaching of the Gospel took place in Jerusalem. It emphasized the teaching that Jesus is the Jewish Messiah. It only makes sense that Matthew's Gospel, with its many Old Testament prophecies fulfilled by Christ and its unique Jerusalem details, would be the first Gospel written.

Thiessen correctly states that "The early church unanimously ascribed this Gospel to the Apostle Matthew" (131). First-century works (such as *The Didache*, *The Epistle of Barnabas*, and *The Shepherd of Hermas*), Ignatius' early second-century writings, and the work of mid second-century AD apologist Justin Martyr all quote from or allude to passages from Mathew's Gospel. Papias (110 AD), Irenaeus (180 AD), and Origen (230 AD) all name Matthew as the author of the first Gospel (Thiessen, 130-139; Wenham, 116-121).

It should also be noted that it is unlikely that the leaders of the early church would lie by claiming that Matthew was the author of the first Gospel (or any Gospel for that matter). Since Matthew had been a tax-collector, most Jews would not have held him in high esteem. Some would have considered him a traitor to the Jewish cause. Certainly, if the early church decided to pretend an Apostle wrote the first Gospel, Matthew would not have been their first choice. Therefore, it is unlikely that the early church lied about Matthew as the author of the first Gospel. Hence, there is excellent evidence to support Matthew as the author of the first Gospel (despite current speculation of New Testament scholars that Mark wrote first).

For the above reasons, John Wenham dates Matthew's Gospel to about 40 AD, while Henry Thiessen dates it to between 45 and 50 AD (Wenham, 243; Thiessen, 137). Robinson dates Matthew's Gospel to 40 to 60 AD (Robinson, 352). If we do not ignore the unanimous consent of the early church fathers, these early dates for the composition of Matthew's Gospel seem far more probable than the later dates given by the liberal New Testament critics of the twenty-first-century.

Archaeological corroboration for the early date of Matthew's Gospel may also exist. The late Carsten P. Thiede was an expert on fragments of ancient writings. He argued that the oldest existing fragments of copies from Matthew's Gospel should be dated to the first-century AD and not the second-century as previously assumed. He concluded that these fragments may even date to before 70 AD. Three of these fragments are kept at Magdalene College, Oxford, while the other two fragments reside in Barcelona, Spain. These fragments contain portions of Matthew 26 (Thiede, *Rekindling the Word* 3, 15, 20, 26-27). Obviously, if the earliest known copies of Matthew's Gospel are first-century copies (and not second-century copies), then the probability of an earlier date for Matthew's Gospel increases. Thiede argued that the writing style of middle first-century fragments found in the Dead Sea Scrolls match the Magdalene fragments of Matthew's Gospel (11). If Thiede is correct, we may have fragments from Matthew's Gospel that go back to the mid first-century; Matthew's Gospel would have to have been written very early (possibly as early as the mid 30's to the early 40's AD).

John Wenham reports that a sixth-century Alexandrian author named Cosmas dated Matthew's Gospel as early as 33 AD, while the late third-century church historian Eusebius dated Matthew's Gospel to the third year of Caligula's reign—approximately 41 AD (*Redating*

Matthew, Mark, and Luke 239). It is possible that Matthew may have written the first edition of his Gospel in Hebrew (this is consistent with what the Apostolic Father Papias wrote) for the Jerusalem Church in the mid 30's AD, and then translated his Gospel into Greek before leaving Jerusalem in the early 40's AD due to the persecution of the Apostles during the reign of Herod Agrippa I (Acts 12:1-19). Whatever the case, Wenham notes that conservative scholars continued to date Matthew's Gospel to the 30's and 40's AD into the nineteenth century (239).

A strong case can be made that James' epistle was written around 45 AD, and that it was one of the earliest New Testament books written. James was the undisputed leader of the Jerusalem church, at least since the mid-40's AD when the original apostles had to flee during persecution from Herod Agrippa I (see Acts 12). Yet, James' epistle shows a knowledge of Matthew's Gospel, especially Jesus' Sermon on the Mount (Matthew 5, 6, and 7). Most modern translations of the Bible list over thirty-five parallel passages in James with Matthew's Gospel. Hence, if James was written around 45 AD, then Matthew's Gospel had to be written earlier. Enough time had to pass for Matthew's Gospel to be recognized as an authoritative account of Jesus' life, ministry, death, and resurrection. This link between Matthew's Gospel and the letter of James is further confirmed by the fact that Matthew is the most Jewish of all the Gospels (i.e., it contains far more Old Testament Messianic prophecies fulfilled by Jesus than the other three Gospels), and James was the leader of the Jerusalem Church. Therefore, a 35 to 42 AD date for Matthew's Gospel is not unrealistic—it could have been written that early!

The common objection to such an early date for Matthew's Gospel is Matthew's use of the phrase "to this day." Matthew wrote that the field purchased with the betrayal money "has been called the Field of Blood to this day" (Matthew 27:8). He also wrote that the chief priests' rumor that the disciples stole the body while the soldiers slept was "widely spread among the Jews, and is to this day" (Matthew 28:15). In response, it should be noted that the phrase "to this day" does not necessitate that decades have passed since Christ's death and resurrection; one or two years would be sufficient (Wenham, 242). There is no reason why Matthew's Gospel should not be dated as early as 35 to 42 AD.

In fact, a close study of the first two chapters of Matthew may indicate that Matthew was able to interview Joseph, the step-father of Jesus, before Joseph's death. The events recorded in these chapters seem to be from Joseph's perspective. It is possible that Joseph was still alive early in Jesus' ministry. In John 6:42, Joseph is spoken of as if he is still alive. Hence, it is possible that Matthew was already taking notes of Jesus' life and teachings during Jesus' public ministry. However, it is obvious that Matthew's Gospel, in the form we have it today, was not completed until after Jesus' ascension. We do not know exactly how long it took Matthew to complete his Gospel. But, it may have been only a few years after Jesus ascended to heaven, rather than several decades.

Gospel of Mark

Since there is no mention of the destruction of the temple in the Gospel of Mark, this book was probably written before 70 AD (the year the temple was destroyed). The early church fathers Papias (110 AD), Justin Martyr (150 AD), and Irenaeus (180 AD) tell us that Mark received the material for his Gospel from the Apostle Peter's sermons (Thiessen, 140-146). Clement of Alexandria, Tertullian, Origen, and Eusebius also acknowledge that Mark was the author of this Gospel (141). Since Mark (also known in the Bible as John Mark) was not one of the original apostles (although he was a co-laborer of the Apostle Peter), it is highly unlikely that the early church lied about him being the author—there would be no reason to fabricate a lie making a non-apostle the author of a Gospel.

The unanimous consent of the early church was that Mark wrote this Gospel and got his information from the Apostle Peter. In fact, most New Testament critics acknolwedge John Mark as the author and agree he received the content of his Gospel from Peter's preaching. Still, most contemporary critics date the composition of Mark's Gospel to 67 to 69 AD. However, the real date of the writing of this Gospel may be earlier than this. Eusebius records a report that Papias claimed he received from the Apostle John:

> And the Elder said this also: Mark, having become the interpreter of Peter, wrote down accurately everything that he remembered, without however recording in order what was either said or done by Christ. For neither did he hear the Lord, nor did he follow Him; but afterwards, as I said, (attended) Peter, who adapted his instructions to the needs (of his hearers) but had no design of giving a connected account of the Lord's oracles. So then Mark made no mistake, while he thus wrote down some things as he remembered them; for he made it his one care not to omit anything that he heard, or to set down any false statements therein (Lightfoot and Harmer, 529).

In 180 AD, Irenaeus wrote, in his work *Against Heresies* (3.1.2.), that Mark was the disciple and interpreter (possibly the stenographer?) of Peter. After the death of Peter, Peter's gospel message was not lost, for Mark had already recorded, in writing, the Gospel based on Peter's sermons about Jesus' life and ministry. Many scholars believe that Irenaeus meant that Mark wrote his Gospel after Peter's death in 67 AD. However, this is not necessarily the case. Wenham and Thiede understand Irenaeus, and Papias before him, to be saying that after Peter departed Rome, Mark wrote his Gospel based on what he learned from Peter's preaching. Since Peter may have been in Rome from 42 to 44 AD (i.e., after Peter fled Jerusalem duirng Herod's persecution of the Apostles in Acts 12), Mark may have written his Gospel as early as 45 AD (Wenham, 169-172, 243).

The hypothesis that Mark wrote his Gospel while Peter was still alive is consistent with what the church fathers Papias and Clement of Alexandria reported on the matter. For, Eusebius, commenting on the writings of these church fathers from the second-century AD, relates a tradition that after Peter preached the Gospel in Rome, he departed the region. The Christians in Rome then pleaded with Mark to put into writing Peter's Gospel. Mark did so; he authored the Gospel that bears his name. When Peter learned of Mark's Gospel, he gave it his approval and allowed it to be read in the churches (Eusebius, *History of the Church* 2.15). This means that it is possible that Mark's Gospel was written as early as 45 AD. This early date is corroborated by the apostolic fathers: Clement of Rome quotes from or alludes to Mark's gospel in 70 AD, the *Didache* alludes to it in the 60's AD, while the *Shepherd of Hermas* does so about 85 AD (Lightfoot and Harmer, 12, 30, 223, 316).

Carsten B. Thiede ageed with papyrologist Jose O'Callahan that there exists archaeological evidence supporting the earlier dating of Mark's Gospel in the Dead Sea Scrolls. A growing number of papyrologists have identified a small fragment called 7Q5 as Mark 6:52-53. The latest the fragment can be dated is 68 AD (when the Qumran community was dispersed). But, some papyrologists believe the fragment should be dated as early as 50 AD. This would be a very early copy of Mark's Gospel and confirmation that the Gospel was originally written in the mid-40's AD (Thiede, *Rekindling the Word* 48-51).

Gospel of Luke & the Book of Acts

Both the Gospel of Luke and the Book of Acts were written to the same recipient—a man named Theophilus (Luke 1:1-4; Acts 1:1-3). The prologues of these books show us that Acts is the sequel of Luke; therefore, Luke was written before Acts. Acts focuses on the key characters Peter, Paul, and James (the half-brother of Jesus), yet it does not record their deaths. Peter and Paul died between 64 and 67 AD, while James died in 62 AD. Since Acts records the deaths of people less significant to the purposes of the book (i.e., Ananias, Sapphira, Stephen, James son of Zebedee, and Herod Agrippa I), it appears that Acts must have been written before Peter, Paul, and James were executed—Peter and Paul were executed about 67 AD, while James was martyred in 62 AD. Also, though Jerusalem is one of the major cities of the Book of Acts and the temple plays a key role in Acts, no mention is made of the war with the Romans (which started 66 AD) and the destruction of the temple (70 AD). This is further confirmation that Acts was written early. Acts is a book filled with adventure, yet it ends anti-climatically with Paul in Rome in chains in 61 AD. This makes no sense unless Acts was completed in 61 AD and then sent to Theophilus. This early date for Acts is confirmed by the fact that the *Didache*, which was probably written in the 60's AD, alludes to Acts 4:32.

Since Acts is the sequel to Luke's Gospel, the Gospel of Luke had to be written at an even earlier date. This is also confirmed by the fact that Paul quotes from Luke's Gospel as Scripture in the mid 60's AD (1 Timothy 5:18). Therefore, both Luke and Acts were written before 62 AD.

It is also unlikely that the early church would have made up the idea that Luke was the person who wrote this Gospel and the Book of Acts. Luke was not one of the original apostles. In fact, he probably never even met Jesus during Jesus' earthly ministry. If the apostles merely fabricated the identity of the author of Luke and Acts, they would have definitely chosen one of the original apostles to be the author.

Is it possible that the reason why Paul did not discuss, in detail, the life and ministry of Jesus in his letters was because his readers already had access to a written account of Jesus' life and ministry? Is it possible that Luke's Gospel was written even before Paul wrote his first letter (in my opinion, Paul's Letter to the Galatians)? Is it possible, as John Wenham argues, that Luke is the brother famous for his "Gospel" spoken of by Paul in 2 Corinthians 8:18? John Wenham believes that Luke's Gospel was well-known by the mid-fifties AD (*Redating Matthew, Mark, and Luke*, 243). In fact, Paul quotes Luke's Gospel as Scripture in the early 60's AD (1 Timothy 5:18). It is possible that Luke's Gospel could have been written as early as the mid-forties AD. Luke's Gospel was also referenced very early (the 60's AD) in the *Didache* (Lightfoot and Harmer, 217, 221, 223, 224).

Much of the first two chapters of Luke's Gospel seems to represent the perpective of Mary, the mother of Jesus (see Luke 1:26-56; 2:19, 51). Luke may have interviewed her for this information. This would also indicate that Luke's Gospel was written early—during the life of Mary.

In 55 AD, when Paul discusses the Lord's Supper with his Corinthian readers, he seems to be giving Luke's account of the Lord's Supper (1 Corinthians 11:23-26; Luke 22:19-20). This is another clue that Luke was written before 55 AD.

In 2 Corinthians 8:16-18, Paul tells the Corinthians that he is sending to them Titus and two other Christian brothers who have been entrusted to carry the donations for the Judean Christians. Paul refers to one of Titus' colleagues as "the brother whose fame in the gospel has spread through all the churches." John Wenham points out that many of the church fathers (i.e., Origen, Eusebius, Ephraem, Chrysostom, and Jerome) identified the brother famous in all the churches for the gospel as Luke. They believed the gospel ("euangelion" in the Greek) referred to the Gospel written by Luke (Wenham, *Redating Matthew, Mark, and Luke* 230=237).

Modern critics disagree for two reasons. First, they do not believe the Gospels were called "Gospels" in the first century AD. Second, these critics also do not believe that Luke's Gospel was written early enough to be referred to in 2 Corinthians, which was written in 56 AD.

In response to the first argument, Mark starts his Gospel with these words: "The beginning of the gospel of Jesus Christ, the Son of God" (Mark 1:1). Though it is doubtful that Mark was actually calling his book "the gospel," he was saying that his book contained the "good news" of Jesus Christ. For, gospel literally means "good news." But, it was probably not long before the early church began to call the four Gospels by the name "Gospel" due to Mark 1:1. The four recognized books that proclaim the good news of Jesus were eventually called "Gospels." But, how early did this occur? The Apostolic Father Ignatius referred to the Gospels as "the Gospel" in 107 AD, while the *Didache* in the 60's AD refers to allusions to the Gospels as "the Gospel" (Wenham, *Redating Matthew, Mark, and Luke* 234-235). Hence, it is not unrealistic to acknowledge that the mid first century church already referred to Matthew, Mark, Luke, and John as "Gospels."

In response to the second argument, it should be noted that the critics assume what they are supposed to prove—they are guilty of arguing in a circle. They assume that Luke's Gospel could not possibly have been written before 2 Corinthians (56 AD) in order to "prove' that 2 Corinthians could not possibly refer to Luke's Gospel. But, if we are correct in arguing for an early date of Luke's Gospel, then there is no reason to rule out the possibility that Paul was speaking of Luke, who was famous in all the churches of that region for his Gospel. The early church fathers had no problem interpreting this 2 Corinthians 8:18 in this light.

If Mark could refer to his written work about Jesus as "the good news" (i.e., the gospel), then there is no reason why Paul could not refer to Luke's written work about Jesus as "the good news" (i.e., the gospel). It should be noted that if Paul merely means "the brother who is famous for his *preaching* of the gospel," then it is unlikely that his readers would know about whom he was writing. There were many disciples famous for preaching the gospel to the churches. But, throughout the Corinthian region of the world—Macedonia and Achaia (i.e., the area of ancient Greece), there was probably only one written Gospel known to all the churches at that time—the Gospel of Luke.

If this reasoning is correct, then Luke's Gospel was already famous throughout ancient Greece in 56 AD (when 2 Corinthians was written). How long would it take (in the first century AD) to write a book, have copies of it made, distributed throughout Greece, and read in the churches throughout the region? And, how long would it take before the author of the book would become famous throughout all the churches of that region? It seems that if Luke was famous for his Gospel throughout the churches of the region by 56 AD, he had to write his Gospel at a significantly earlier time. Hence, a date for Luke's Gospel of between 45 and 50 AD seems appropriate.

Gospel of John

The Gospel of John had, in the past, been dismissed as a second-century document because the Christology (i.e., doctrine of Christ) appeared to be far too developed for the first-century AD. But, this is not the case, for the Christology found in Philippians (or other Pauline letters) is no more primitive. In fact, Paul already taught that Jesus is fully divine in his earliest letters (i.e., Galatians and 1 Thessalonians);

in these letters, Paul referred to Jesus as "the Lord Jesus Christ." In Philippians, Paul stated that Jesus continues to exist in nature as God and that every knee will someday bow to Jesus (Philippians 2:6-11). In other words, the fact that the Gospel of John teaches the full deity of Christ and His pre-existence is not a sufficient reason for rejecting a first-century date for its composition.

There is ample evidence for John's Gospel being a first-century document (Thiessen, 162-164). It is quoted or paraphrased frequently by the apostolic fathers (i.e., *Epistle of Barnabas*, Ignatius, and Polycarp) in the first two centuries, and by other second-century church leaders (i.e., Tatian, Theophilus of Antioch, Irenaeus, and Clement of Alexandria). The apostolic father Papias knew of this Gospel and wrote about its author. Tatian wrote his own harmony of the Gospels—he clearly taught that Matthew, Mark, Luke, and John were the only four Gospels accepted by the second-century church.

Archaeological evidence exists for the antiquity of John's Gospel—a very early fragment of John's Gospel. The John Ryland's fragment of John chapter 18 has been dated by some scholars to about 130 AD. However, papyrologist Carsten B. Thiede has persuasively argued that this fragment of a copy of John's Gospel should probably be dated earlier—as early as 100 AD. In fact, Thiede adds that there is no reason why it could not have originated in the late first-century (Thiede, *Rekindling the Word* 10-11, 26-27). Since this fragment was found in Egypt, the original of John's Gospel would have had to be written considerably earlier; for, the Gospel did not immediately spread to Egypt from Israel (122).

The author of John's Gospel refers to himself as "the disciple whom Jesus loved" (John 21:20, 24). The internal evidence of the Gospel of John shows the author to be a Palestinian Jew who had knowledge of Jewish feasts and customs, as well as an eyewitness perspective of the events he records (Thiessen, 167-169). He was the disciple who leaned on Jesus' chest during the Last Supper (John

13:23-25). Hence, he was one of Jesus' inner circle. The other Gospels reveal this inner circle to be Peter, and the two sons of Zebedee—James and John (see, for instance, Matthew 17:1). But, Peter was not the author; for, the author of John's Gospel speaks about Peter talking to "the disciple whom Jesus loved" (John 13:23-25). James son of Zebedee could not be the author for he was martyred before this Gospel was written, in the early to mid-40's AD (Acts 12:1-2). Hence, by process of elimination, the Apostle John was the author of the fourth Gospel.

Many scholars reject the Apostle John as the author of the fourth Gospel. They point to Papias' statement which seems to indicate a different John was the author, not the Apostle John. Papias wrote:

> I would inquire about the discourses of the elders—what was said by Andrew, or by Peter, or by Philip, or by Thomas or James, or by John or Matthew or any other of the Lord's disciples, and what Aristion and the elder John, the disciples of the Lord say. For I did not think that I could get so much profit from the contents of books as from the utterances of a living and abiding voice (Lightfoot and Harmer, 528).

I agree with those scholars who argue that Papias is not talking about two distinct Johns; instead, he is speaking about two different ages—the age of the original Apostles and the age of the elders. The Apostle John was an original Apostle; but, he also outlived the rest of the other original Apostles. John lived into the age of "the elders." The "elders" were leaders in the early church who personally knew Jesus, but were not necessarily of the original twelve Apostles. The Apostle John was the one person who was both a leader in the age of the Apostles and a leader in the age of the elders.

During the age of the Apostles (i.e., when most of the Apostles were still alive), their colleagues were called "elders." This can be seen in the Jerusalem church at the time of the Jerusalem Council (Acts 15:2, 22, 23). The phrase "the apostles and the elders" is repeated numerous times. Hence, the early church was led by the apostles and the elders. When all the apostles had died, except for John (and possibly a few others), then John and the elders led the church. At this time, the "age of the elders" began.

Some of the elders may have been members of Jesus' seventy disciples (Luke 10:1). They followed Jesus and were appointed positions of leadership by Him while the Apostles were alive. However, many of them outlived the Apostles—they were probably less likely to be martyred. Hence, John lived through the age of the Apostles (in fact, he was one of the Apostles) on into the age of the elders. This is why he identifies himself, later in life, as "the elder" (2 John 1 and 3 John 1).

The age of the Apostles roughly ran from 30 AD to about 70 AD. Most of the orignal Apostles had been martyred by about 70 AD. Then, the age of the elders would have extended from 70 AD to about 95 AD. With the death of the last elder, the age of the eyewitnesses would have ended. Next, came the age of the apostolic fathers. The apostolic fathers led the church from 95 AD to about 156 AD, ending with the death of Polycarp (the last living pupil of the Apostles). (Some of the writings of the "Apostolic Fathers" were actually written well before 95 AD and should therefore be classified as writings of the elders.)

If the above speculation is sound, then it makes sense that Papias would include the Apostle John in two separate lists: first with the original Apostles, later with the elders. Hence, he does not mention two Johns. Instead, he mentions two ages: the age of the Apostles and the age of the elders. John was an abiding voice in both ages.

If the Apostle John did not write this Gospel, then it is inexplicable as to why the author never mentions the Apostle John by name. This is especially true in that the Apostle John plays such a prominent role in the other three Gospels. The most reasonable conclusion is that the Apostle John wrote the fourth Gospel. This is the most prevelant view throughout the history of the church. Irenaeus and Clement of Alexandria both accepted John the Apostle as the author of this Gospel, as have most Christian thinkers before the advent of higher criticism.

However, even if someone rejects the Apostle John as the author, and instead believes John the Elder is a different person from the Apostle, it is still clear that the author ("the disciple whom Jesus loved") is an eyewitness who knew Jesus. This is the view of leading New Testament scholars such as Martin Hengel and Richard Bauckham (Bauckham, *The Testimony of the Beloved Disciple* 73-91). They deny the author was one of the original Apostles; still, they acknowledge the author was an eyewitness of Jesus and one of His most beloved disciples.

We must now attempt to answer the question as to when this Gospel was written. Due to early fragments of copies of this Gospel and many quotations found in the writings of the leaders of the second-century church, it is no longer acceptable to date the composition of this work to the second-century. It is unambiguously a first-century document. Most conservative scholars (and even some liberal scholars) date John's Gospel to around 85 to 95 AD.

Still, a minority of scholars entertain the possibility that the Gospel of John may have been written even earlier. John A. T. Robinson dates John's Gospel from 40 to 65 AD (Robinson, 352). James Charlesworth of Princeton, due to his research on the Dead Sea Scrolls, is open to the possibility that John's Gospel may have been authored as early as 50 AD (Thiede, *The Dead Sea Scrolls* 181). The hypothesis that John's Gospel has a pre-70 AD date is strengthened by the fact that John speaks of the temple grounds in the present tense in John 5:2. This strongly implies that the temple was still standing when John wrote this Gospel. Since the temple was destroyed in 70 AD, the Gospel of John had to be written at an earlier date.

Those who argue for the later date of 85 to 95 AD for John's Gospel usually assume that a considerable amount of time is needed for the development of the theology found in John's Gospel. But, this is not necessarily the case. For Paul's theology is highly developed even in his earliest letters—Galatians and 1 Thessalonians. If Paul's theology was this developed by the late 40's or early 50's AD, then there is no reason why John's theology could not be this developed at that point in time as well. And, if the other three Gospels (i.e., Matthew, Mark, and Luke) were already written in the 30's and 40's AD, then the theology of John's Gospel would not be too advanced for the mid-50's AD. Though most scholars prefer the later date, I now lean towards the earlier date—the early to mid-50's AD.

There are other good reasons for entertaining the possibility that John wrote his Gospel before the temple was destroyed in 70 AD. In John's Gospel, the enemy of the church is not the Roman Empire, but the Jewish religious leaders (John 7:1; 8:48, 52;10:31; 12:9-11). There is no hint in the Gospel of John of any opposition to the church coming from the Roman Empire. This implies that the Gospel was written before Nero's persecution of Christians in the 60's AD.

The theological thought forms in John's Gospel, rather than being too developed for first-century literature, are actually very consistent with that found in the Dead Sea Scrolls (Thiede, *The Dead Sea Scrolls* 181). Also, John emphasizes salvation through faith in Jesus more than the other three Gospels (John 1:12-13; 3:16-18; 5:24; 6:35, 47; 10:26; 20:30-31; etc.). Could it be that John's Gospel is the only Gospel written after the Jerusalem Council of 49 AD? If this is the case, John had the motive to emphasize salvation through faith in Jesus while clearly showing that salvation is not earned through the works of the Old Testament Law. John stated his reason for writing his Gospel:

> Therefore many other signs Jesus also performed in the presence of the disciples, which are not written in this book; but these have been written so that you may believe that Jesus is the Christ, the Son of God; and that believing you might have life in His name (John 20:30-31).

Hence, John wrote this Gospel to encourage people to believe in Jesus for salvation. His specific reasons for writing his Gospel may have been: 1) to more explicitly declare the deity of Christ, 2) to more clearly proclaim salvation through faith in Jesus, and 3) to show that Jesus, and not John the Baptist, is the Jewish Messiah (or, to at least show John the Baptist's disciples where the Baptist fit in the Messianic scheme of things—he was the forerunner of Messiah).

Both Irenaeus and Clement of Alexandria say that John wrote his Gospel after the other three Gospels had already been written (Thiessen, 172-173). John may have wanted to suppliment the material found in the other three Gospels (assuming he was aware of these writings). If this is the case, he may have chosen to include Jesus' most unambiguous claims to be God (John 5:17-18, 22-23; 8:23-24, 58-59; 10:30-33; 14:9; 17:5). And, since John writes after the Jerusalem Council, he may have decided to clearly annunciate Jesus' teachings about salvation through faith in Him. Christ deity and salvation through faith in Jesus were already taught in Matthew, Mark, and Luke. Still, John may have wanted to emphasize these teachings more explicitly than the other three Gospels.

Irenaeus tells us that John wrote his Gospel while in the city of Ephesus (Thiessen, 173). Even in the mid-50's AD the teachings of John the Baptist were still popular in that city (Acts 18:24-19:7). Could it be that John wrote his Gospel in the mid-50's AD while in Ephesus, and that one of his reasons for writing was to remind the Jews in Ephesus that John the Baptist was not the Messiah and that the Baptist's ministry pointed to Jesus, the true Jewish Messiah (John 1:6-8)?

John's Gospel goes to great lengths to argue for Jesus' full deity (John 1:1, 14; 20:31; etc.). This may be because he wanted to refute the Ebionite heresy. This heresy argued that, though Jesus was the Jewish Messiah, He was not God. Ebionism was one of the earliest Christological heresies that confronted the church (Erickson, *The Word Became Flesh* 42-44).

Many scholars argue that John's Gospel could not have been written in the mid-50's AD since the final chapter of John's Gospel implies that the Apostle Peter has already died (John 21:18-23). Since Peter died around 67 AD, John's Gospel had to be written after that date. But, it is also possible that the first edition of the Gospel of John was completed in the mid-50's AD, and that it contained only the first twenty chapters. Verses 30 and 31 of chapter twenty do seem like a plausible ending for this Gospel. Then, after Peter's death, John may have added chapter twenty-one to dispel the rumor that Jesus had promised that He would return before John the Apostle died. John may have felt the need to include this final chapter to set the matter straight (see John 21:18-23). Still, it is also possible that the final chapter of John's Gospel was not a later interpolation, and that it was written while Peter was aging, though still alive. This is also consistent with a mid-50's AD date. A rumor that John would still be alive when Jesus returns could have started while Peter was still alive. Whatever the case, John felt the need to set the record straight by clarifying what Jesus said, as well as what Jesus did not say, concerning the matter.

John's Gospel may explain why one of Jesus' greatest miracles (i.e., Jesus raising Lazarus from the dead) is not mentioned in the first three Gospels. For John tells his readers that the Jewish religious leaders desired to kill Lazarus after Jesus raised him from the dead (John 12:9-11). Why would Matthew, Mark, and Luke fail to mention this powerful miracle? Could it be that Lazarus was still alive when they wrote their Gospels, and that mentioning him in their Gospels would place his life in danger? Maybe Lazarus had finally died a second time before John wrote his Gospel?

Whatever the case, John does seem to indicate that the temple is still standing when he writes his Gospel (John 5:2). This indicates a pre-70 AD date for his Gospel. During the writing of this Gospel, many of the disciples of John the Baptist are probably still ministering throughout the Roman Empire (John 1:6-8, 15, 19-37; Acts 18:24-19:7). John has to clearly identify the Baptist's role in the Messianic movement—does anyone really think John would have to clarify this as late as the close of the first-century? John refutes the Ebionite heresy which denies Jesus' deity—he does not emphasize disproving the Docetist heresy which denies Jesus' humanity. The Docetist heresy did not become popular until later in the first-century; while Christ's deity was opposed from the inception of the church. Also, in John's Gospel the main opposition of the church comes form the Jewish religious leaders, not the Roman authorities. This also indicates a pre-70 AD date for John's Gospel. Hence, I favor a mid-50's AD date for the composition of John's Gospel.

Paul's Undisputed Letters: Romans, 1 & 2 Corinthians, Galatians, Philippians, 1 Thessalonians, Philemon

The vast majority of New Testament scholars have accepted the Pauline authorship of Romans, 1 Corinthians, 2 Corinthians, Galatians, Philippians, 1 Thessalonians, and Philemon. Scholars have identified the parallels between the timeline of the Book of Acts and the settings of these books, causing them to embrace the authenticity of these letters. Hence, there is no real debate concerning the dates of these books between liberal scholars and conservative scholars, with the possible exception of Galatians.

The accepted dates for these books are as follows: Romans 56-58 AD, 1 Corinthians 55 AD, 2 Corinthians 56 AD, Galatians 48 or 55 AD, Philippians 61 AD, 1 Thessalonians 51 AD, and Philemon 61 AD. A strong case can be made for the earlier date of Galatians.

In Paul's Letter to the Galatians, Paul argued that the true Gospel teaches salvation by grace through faith in Jesus (Galatians 2:21; 3:1-9; 23-26). Paul rejects the idea that salvation can be achieved by both faith and works. He disdains the false teaching that Gentiles must get circumcized and obey the Old Testament Law to be saved.

Paul builds his case for justification by faith in this letter. First, Paul establishes the fact that his apostleship came directly from Jesus and God the Father (1:1). He shares the same authority as the original Apostles; he is not a second-class Apostle. He did not receive the Gospel from the Apostles—Jesus taught Paul the Gospel. Second, Paul places the authority of the true Gospel above the authority of the Apostles (1:8-9). If the Apostles preach a false Gospel, let them be accursed. Third, Paul refers to Peter, John, and James as "reputed to be pillars" of the church in Jerusalem (2:9). Paul acts as if their authority can be rejected if they have begun to preach a different Gospel. Fourth, Paul even goes to the extreme of discussing an event where he publicly corrected the Apostle Peter for hypocrisy (2:11-14). In short, Paul's authority in Christ is as high as the authority of the original Apostles.

The only reasonable explanation for this sort of argument is that Galatians was written before the Jerusalem Council of 49 AD (Acts 15). It represents Paul's pre-emptive strike before attending the Council. Paul had heard rumors that the Jerusalem church had fallen away from the true Gospel of salvation through faith alone, and she now proclaims a false Gospel of salvation through faith plus obedience to the Jewish Law. The Jerusalem Council was called to settle the issue. Just in case the Jerusalem church (headed by James, Paul, and John) had indeed apostatized, Paul wrote this letter.

Fortunately, the Jerusalem Council agreed with Paul and produced a written decree recognizing the true Gospel (Acts 15). If Paul wrote Galatians after the Jerusalem Council, he would have merely sent a copy of the Jerusalem decree (Acts 16:4). Since this is not the case, Paul wrote Galatians in 48 or 49 AD, before he left for the Jerusalem Council.

This early date for Galatians is confirmed by the fact that Paul discusses his two visits to Jerusalem after being saved. His first visit (34 or 37 AD?) was three years after he was saved on the Road to Damascus (Galatians 1:18-19; see Acts 9:26-30). On this visit he only met with Peter and James. His second Jerusalem visit occurred fourteen years after his conversion (45 or 48 AD?). During this visit, he and Barnabas met with Peter, James, and John (Galatians 2:1-10; see also Acts 11:27-12:25). Paul only mentions these two visits to Jerusalem because he was yet to travel to Jerusalem the third time after being saved—this third visit was to attend the Jerusalem Council (Acts 15:1-30). Hence, Paul wrote his letter to the Galatians before the Jerusalem Council of 48 or 49 AD.

Ephesians, Colossians, and 2 Thessalonians

It should be noted that, in the first-century AD, a collection of letters written by Paul was already considered to be Scripture by the author of 2 Peter (2 Peter 3:15-16). If the author is actually the Apostle Peter (as we will argue below), then the recognition of Paul's letters as Scripture dates back to the time when Peter and Paul were still alive!

Whatever the case, as early as 110 AD, the leaders of the early church apparently accepted all of Paul's letters as authoritative Scripture. This can be confirmed by examining the writings of the Apostolic Fathers (the pupils of the Apostles who were selected by the Apostles to lead the early church). In the writings of just three of the Apostolic Fathers (i.e., Polycarp, Ignatius, and Clement of Rome), every one of Paul's letters was quoted or alluded to by 110 AD. The three church leaders were Polycarp (the Bishop of Smyrna and former disciple of the Apostle John), Ignatius (the Bishop of Antioch of Syria), and Clement (who later became the Bishop of Rome). It is unlikely that they were fooled by the Pauline introduction of these thirteen letters. If any of these books were written by a forger, they would have known. Yet, it seems that they accepted all thirteen of Paul's letters.

There exists no good reason to reject the Pauline authorship of Ephesians, Colossians, or 2 Thessalonians. Ephesians and Colossians were written by Paul while he was in prison (Ephesians 3:1; Colossians 4:10), probably during his first Roman imprisonment. This means that these letters were written at approximately the same time as Paul's other prison epistles—Philippians and Philemon (see Philippians 1:7 and Philemon 9). Paul probably wrote all four of these letters in about 61 AD.

Ephesians is quoted very early by the church fathers, and is even called the Epistle to the Ephesians by Clement of Alexandria and Tertullian (Thiessen, 239). Ephesians follows Paul's typical pattern: greeting and thanksgiving, doctrinal teaching, and practical teaching. The only reason why the end of Ephesians lacks any personal greetings is that it was believed to be an encyclical letter (i.e., a general letter written to numerous churches, not just one church).

Colossians is quoted very early by the church fathers—Ignatius, the Epistle of Barnabas, Justin Martyr, Irenaeus, Clement of Alexandria, and Tertullian (Thiessen, 229-230). The fact that the details of Colossians fit so perfectly with the details of Philemon argues for its authenticity. Five of the persons mentioned in Colossians 4 are also mentioned in Philemon. The advanced doctrine of the person of Christ found in Colossians is no more developed than the doctrine of Christ found in Philippians, a letter already accepted by most scholars as an authentic letter of the Apostle Paul (Thiessen, 229-231).

Also, it is simply wrong to assert that Colossians refutes full-blown second-century Gnosticism. (If that was the case, Colossians would have to be a mid second-century document.) Instead, the author of Colossians is merely addressing and refuting an earlier, first-century Jewish form of Gnosticism (not the anti-Jewish Gnosticism of the second-century). Whatever the gnostic tendencies of the Colossian heretics were, the Colossian heretics were proponents of circumcision, the Old Testament Law, and the Jewish feast days. On the other hand, second-century Gnosticism considered the Old Testament God to be an evil God and different from the New Testament God. It is clear that Paul's letter to the Colossians does not address the second-century anti-Jewish Gnosticism at all. Therefore, there is no good reason to deny the early church's view of the Pauline authorship of Colossians or a 61 AD date for this work.

2 Thessalonians is quoted very early. It is quoted in the first-century in the *Didache*, and in the second-century by Ignatius, Polycarp, Justin Martyr, Irenaeus, and Clement of Alexandria (Thiessen, 195). As in all of Paul's letters, the author of 2 Thessalonians identifies himself as the Apostle Paul (2 Thessalonians 1:1; 3:17). The evidence seems to indicate that Paul wrote 2 Thessalonians just a few months after he wrote 1 Thessalonians. Paul wrote 2 Thessalonians to clarify some of his teachings about the end times found in his first letter to the Thessalonians. Apparently, some of the Thessalonians were confused and thought that the Day of the Lord (i.e., Christ's return to gather believers to Himself) had already occurred. Hence, Paul most likely wrote 2 Thessalonians about 51 AD.

1 & 2 Timothy & Titus (The Pastoral Epistles)

The Pastoral Epistles (1 Timothy, 2 Timothy, and Titus) have been rejected as genuine Pauline epistles by most New Testament critics for four reasons. First, these letters do not fit into the timeline given concerning Paul's travels in the Book of Acts. Second, the style of writing and the vocabulary of the Pastoral Epistles does not seem to be the same as that of Paul's other writings. Third, "it is said that the Pastorals imply too advanced a stage of church organization for Paul's day." Fourth, some scholars believe these letters refute Gnosticism, a second-century ad heresy (Thiessen, 256-259).

However, each of these objections can be answered. First, Acts ends in 61 AD at the close of Paul's first Roman imprisonment. It is possible that Paul was released, continued his missionary work, was re-arrested, and matyred during his second Roman imprisonment. If this is the case, then 1 Timothy, 2 Timothy, and Titus were written after the first Roman imprisonment. These letters include details of Paul's further missionary work—ministry he did after 61 AD (256-257). This missionary work was done by Paul after the Book of Acts was written; hence, there is no mention of these details in Acts.

Second, the differences in style and vocabulary can easily be explained by the fact that Paul was dealing with a different subject (258-259). In these letters, he discussed issues of church organization. It only makes sense that a unique subject would evoke a different vocabulary from an author.

Third, the level of church organization is no more complex than that found in Acts 14:23, Ephesians 4:11, and Philippians 1:1 (259). Paul uses the terms "elders" and "bishops" interchangeably (Titus 1:5, 7). In these epistles, there is no hint of a second-century elevation of the office of bishops (259).

Fourth, fully developed second-century Gnosticism was an anti-Jewish Gnosticism that rejected the Old Testament God and

Scriptures. But, the Gnosticism Paul refutes in the Pastoral Epistles is apparently a first-century pro-Jewish Gnosticism (i.e., it promotes circumcision, adherence to Jewish feast days and practices, etc.), not the more developed and anti-Jewish Gnosticism of the second century.

In short, all four objections to Pauline authorship can be answered. There is no good reason to deny the Pauline authorship of these letters. All three letters have the common Pauline greeting, and the church fathers accepted these letters as authentic Pauline letters. These letters were already being quoted by church leaders as early as 110 AD (Barnett, *Is the New Testament Reliable?* 39-41). It is doubtful that Ignatius, Clement of Rome, and Polycarp would have been fooled by a forger. Also, the theological brilliance of the author must be taken into account. It seems that a great mind like this would more likely be a leader in the early church than a forger. It is therefore resonable to agree with the early church and accept the Pauline authorship of the Pastoral Epistles.

For the above reasons, conservative scholars accept the Pauline authorship of 1 Timothy, 2 Timothy, and Titus. Thiessen dates 1 Timothy to 64-65 AD, Titus to 65 AD, and 2 Timothy to 67 AD—just before Paul's martyrdom (Thiessen, 262-270).

Hebrews

The Book of Hebrews was written for the purpose of trying to prevent Jews who had accepted Jesus from abandoning the Jewish faith due to persecution. The author of the Book of Hebrews argues that the temple priests are still standing and still offering sacrifices. Therefore, their animal sacrifices have failed to take away our sins. The author of Hebrews then reasons that since Jesus is seated at the Father's right hand, His work is done and His sacrifice of Himself on the cross has accomplished its purpose—our sins are forgiven. This argument makes no sense if the Book of Hebrews was written after 70 AD (the year the temple was destroyed by the Romans). If Hebrews was written after 70 AD, the author would have argued that it is impossible for his readers to return to the animal sacrifices since God allowed the temple to be destroyed. Instead, his argument only works if the temple is still standing and the temple sacrifices are still being offered. Hence, Hebrews was written before 70 AD.

Even though Hebrews was written before 70 AD, it was not authored by the Apostle Paul. First, it does not have the distinct Pauline greeting. Second, Greek scholars note that the Greek of Hebrews is more advanced than Paul's Greek. And third, the author, unlike Paul, admits he never met Jesus in the flesh (Hebrews 2:3-4). Still, the theology of the book of Hebrews is definitely Pauline. Hence, the author of Hebrews probably had been a colleague of the Apostle Paul at some point and learned from his teaching. This is confirmed by the fact that the author knew Timothy, Paul's famous disciple (Hebrews 13:23). Some have suggested that Luke, Barnabas, Silas, or Apollos may have authored this work. Whatever the case, it was probably written by a former student of Paul; hence, it was considered by the early church to have Paul's apostolic authority.

James

This may be the earliest New Testament letter. It seems to represent the pre-Pauline Christianity of the early Jerusalem church. Paul's doctrine of "justification by faith" was not an official Christian doctrine at this point in the history of the church. (Though the official doctrine was yet to be fully spelled-out, the early church was already trusting in Jesus alone for salvation—the reconciliation of this with the Christian's duty to the Old Testament Law had not yet fully been resolved.) Though James preached the same Gospel Paul preached (see Galatians 1 and 2), James does not use Paul's terminology. For

Paul, "justification" means the moment a person first believes and is declared righteous by God—the moment of salvation. For James, "justification" is defined as when a person is proven to be righteous before others (i.e., when a person is vindicated). By "faith" Paul meant genuine saving faith which produces good works. But, James used the word "faith' for mere intellectual assent, not the robust saving faith of Paul's epistles. The fact that James was using his terms with different meanings than the meanings ascribed by Paul seems to indicate that James' letter was written before the Jerusalem Council of 49 AD. At this council, the apostles were able to resolve the apparent, but not actual, differences in their Gospel presentations.

James appears to have knowledge of Matthew's Gospel, especially the Sermon on the Mount (Matthew 6 and 7). This would support the early date given above for Matthew's Gospel. It would also support the notion that Matthew was the Gospel utilized by the early Jerusalem church.

James' word for church is "synagogue." This implies that this letter was written during the infancy of the church—when it was still primarily Jewish. As the church became more and more Gentile, the Greek word "ekklesia" was used for the local assemblies.

For these and other reasons, Henry Thiessen dated James from 45 to 48 AD (278), while John A. T. Robinson believed James was written about 47 to 48 AD (352). Douglas Moo also dates James early—45-48 AD (*James* 33-34). A date of 45 AD for Jame's epistle is not extreme.

1 & 2 Peter

The author of First and Second Peter claims to be the Apostle Peter (1 Peter 1:1). There is no good reason to reject the Apostle Peter as the true author of either epistle. In fact, there are many similarities and parallels noted by scholars between 1 Peter and Peter's sermons recorded in the first twelve chapters of Acts (Thiessen, 280). The early church quoted 1 Peter frequently and recognized the Apostle Peter as the author (Thiessen, 279-280).

The readers of the first epistle are called "aliens." They reside in the provinces of Asia Minor, yet their real home is in heaven with the Lord since they are believers (1 Peter 1:1). Many Jews from these provinces had accepted Christ when they were in Jerusalem for the Feast of Pentecost when Peter preached his first sermon in about 33 AD (Acts 2:8-9). Also, many Gentiles from these regions were led to Christ by Paul on his second missionary journey (Acts 16:6-7; 50-52 AD).

1 Peter was apparently written while Peter was in Rome (1 Peter 5:12-13). "Babylon" was probably a code name for Rome when Peter wrote this letter. Peter could not have been in ancient Babylon since it was uninhabited during the first-century AD. Due to possible persecution from the Roman authorities, Peter may have not wanted his real location revealed. Believers would have understood the word "Babylon" to represent whatever pagan city ruled the world at the time. Hence, believers would have known Peter meant Rome. Still, the Roman authorities, even if they intercepted Peter's letter, would not know where he was at the time.

Silvanus (also known as Silas) was Peter's secretary for this letter (1 Peter 5:12). Silas was an early church leader who attended the Jerusalem Council (49 AD) and accompanied Paul on his second missionary journey (50-52 AD; see Acts 15:22-40; 16:1-18:5). He may have been Paul's scribe or secretary for Paul's two letters to the Thessalonians (1 Thessalonians 1:1; 2 Thessalonians 2:1). The very precise and polished Greek of 1 Peter can be explained as due to the scribal work of Silas. This also reveals why the Greek of 2 Peter is rough and manifests a more Hebraic style (Thiede and D'Ancona, *Eyewitness to Jesus* 135).

John Mark was also with Silas and Peter when Peter wrote 1 Peter (1 Peter 5:13). We have already speculated that John Mark was probably with Peter in Rome in the early forties AD, and that he wrote his Gospel based on his remembrance of Peter's preaching after Peter departed Rome. However, Mark may have also been with Peter in Rome in the mid to late 60's AD towards the end of Peter's life. For, Paul, while in prison in Rome, sent for Mark just before he (Paul) was executed (see 2 Timothy 4:11). Since Peter was executed in Rome about the same time Paul was martyred in Rome, it is possible Mark may have been with Peter later in Peter's life. Since the a major theme of 1 Peter is to encourage believers to be willing to suffer for the cause of the Gospel (1 Peter 1:6-7; 3:13-4:1), it is likely that this letter was written when Emperor Nero was persecuting the church. Hence, 1 Peter was probably written around 65 AD (Thiessen, 284). Still, it is possible that Peter wrote this letter while in Rome in the early 40's AD since we know John Mark was with him at that time.

1 Peter was quoted from or alluded to by Clement of Rome in 70 AD (Lightfoot and Harmer, 31), and the Shepherd of Hermas in about 85 AD (313, 315, 316). This corroborates a date as early as 45 or 65 AD.

Again, differences in style and vocabulary between 1 Peter and 2 Peter can be explained by the fact that Silas was Peter's scribe for Peter's first epistle, but not for his second epistle. 2 Peter is alluded to very early in the Epistle of Barnabas (70's AD; Lightfoot and Harmer, 260, 284, 568; see also Geisler and Nix, 290) and the Epistle of Ignatius to the Philadelphians (107 AD; Chapter XI). Between 65 and 85 AD, other allusions to this epistle can be found in the *Shepherd of Hermas* and the *Didache* (Thiessen, 287).

Still, according to Thiessen, the internal evidence for the authenticity of this epistle is greater than the external evidence (287-289). The author of 2 Peter identifies himself as the Apostle Simon Peter (1:1). He speaks of witnessing the transfiguration (1:16-18), and says that the time of his death is near (1:13-15). He warns his readers about the false teachers who try to deceive believers (2:1-22), and informs his readers that this is the second letter he has written to them (3:1). He tells his readers to remember what the apostles have told them (3:2), and then warns them about the mockers who would come in the last days (3:3-7). He encourages his readers to be patient concerning the Lord's return (3:8-15). The author warns his readers concerning unstable individuals who pervert Paul's writings (3:15-16). He even refers to Paul's writings as "Scripture."

No forger would write such a letter—there is no hint of motive. The doctrine is consistent with the teachings of the apostles (Jude 17-18), and there is nothing to gain by forging a Christian document to promote Christian doctrine. The setting is true to the final days of Peter's life, and it makes sense that he would want to send out one last warning and one last reminder before he went to be with the Lord. Since Peter was executed during the reign of Nero around 67 AD, it is safe to date this writing to that time.

1, 2, 3 John

The consensus of the early church fathers identifies John the Apostle as the author of these letters. The style and vocabulary of these letters are also very close to the style and vocabulary of John's Gospel. John identifies himself as "the elder" in the prologue of 2 John and 3 John. Hence, this work may have been written after the age of the Apostles and during the age of the elders. John himself was an Apostle, but he lived longer than the other Apostles. He lived into and through the age of the elders—leaders in the church who were from Jesus' generation, but were not necessarily Apostles.

In 1 John, the author makes it clear that he was an eyewitness from the beginning of Jesus' ministry (1 John 1:1-3). In fact, he not only saw Jesus, but he also heard Him and touched Him. The author goes out of his way to refute an ancient heresy that eventually became known as "Docetism." Docetism acknowledged that Jesus was divine in some sense, but this false teaching denied that He genuinely became a man. Jesus only appeared to be human—He did not really have human flesh. John states that he touched, heard, and saw the Lord Jesus (1:1-3); he states that we are cleansed from our sins by Jesus' blood which He shed for us (1:7). John urges his readers to test the spirits because not all spirits are from God (4:1). The false prophets deny that Jesus had come in the flesh (4:1-3).

In 1 John, John also refutes heretics who deny that Jesus is the Christ (2:18-19, 22; 5:1). Apparently, these false teachers taught that the Christ is a spirit that came upon Jesus, but Jesus was not the Christ. Nor was Jesus God in the flesh. The author of 1 John encouraged his readers to love the brethren (3:23-24; 4:7-8). Those who do not love the brethren do not love God (1 John 4:20-21). The false teachers do not love the brethren. In fact, they have separated themselves from Christian fellowship (1 John 2:18-19). John also speaks out against the false teachers because they promote a license to sin (1:5-10; 2:4-5, 15-17; 3:4-10; 5:2-5, 18). John reminds his readers that true believers must obey the Lord's commands (2:3-6; 5:3). John also tells his readers that eternal life comes to all who believe in Jesus, the Son of God (5:1, 5, 10-13).

In 2 John, the author (who calls himself "the elder") tells his readers to love the brethren (vs. 5), walk in truth (vs. 4), and obey Jesus' commands (vs. 6). Again, John seems to be combatting Docetism as he identifies the deceiver and antichrist as anyone who refuses to acknowledge that Jesus Christ has come in the flesh (vs. 7). John warns his readers to not allow these false teachers into their homes or churches (vs. 10-11).

In 3 John, the author (who again identifies himself as "the elder") writes to a believer named Gaius (a common first-century name). The author rejoices that his spiritual children are walking in truth (vs. 3-4).

He commends Gaius for accepting and supporting travelling preachers who are in good standing with John and the elders (vs. 5-8). But, John warns Gaius about the poor conduct of Diotrephes, a man who always wants to be first (vs. 9-11). Diotrephes refused to accept and support godly preachers sent from the elders. John closes the letter by recommending Demetrius to Gaius (vs. 12). Demetrius is probably a travelling preacher sent by the elders to Gaius' town.

It seems that 1, 2, and 3 John were probably written about the same time. But, when exactly were these three letters written? We cannot be totally confident as to exactly when these letters were written. John A. T. Robinson dates these letters as early as 60 to 65 AD (*Redating the New Testament* 352). But, if this was the case, then why would John identify himself as an elder and not as an Apostle? Is it possible that the age of the Apostles has passed and now John the Apostle identifies himself as an elder? John's letters seem to address a vacuum of leadership within the church—false teachers are more than willing to fill the gap. John has to remind his readers to accept teachers who are recommended by the elders, but to reject teachers who teach false doctrines. Could it be that the last of the Apostles (except for John) has died and many deceivers are trying to take advantage of the situation? If this is the case, then a post-70 ad date for these letters seems to make sense; however, a late 60's AD date is still not ruled out.

Another point is worth noting. The Apostolic Father named Ignatius (the Bishop of Antioch in Syria) wrote several letters in 107 AD refuting Docetism, the belief that Jesus only appeared to be human—He did not really become a man. When did the Docetist heresy come into being? We are not sure of how or when it had its origin. But, if Ignatius is still refuting Docetism in 107 AD, and no New Testament writers (besides John) dealt with it, then maybe John was writing his letters only a decade or two before Ignatius wrote his epistles. This would make an 80-90 AD date for John's three epistles seem preferable (Thiessen, 310-313; see also Carson, Moo, and Morris, 451).

It is possible that John A. T. Robinson went too far to date all twenty-seven New Testament books before the temple's destruction in 70 AD. Still, his arguments should be taken seriously. He is probably closer to the truth than are most New Testament scholars today. Still, it is possible that five of the New Testament books were written after 70 AD (i.e., 1 John, 2 John, 3 John, Jude, and Revelation), though it is also possible to make a case, as Robinson did, for pre-70 AD dates for these books. The *Shepherd of Hermas* may have quoted from 1 John 2:27 in 85 AD, and the *Didache* may have alluded to 1 John 4:18 in the 60's AD (Lightfoot and Harmer, 319, 222). If this is the case, then a pre-70 AD date for John's epistles would not be unreasonable.

Both the development of Christian theology and the development of heretical theology (ebionism, docetism, gnosticism, etc.) may not have taken as long as many liberal New Testament scholars believe. It is possible that docetism may have begun to spread in some parts of the Roman empire before 70 AD. If this is the case, John's epistles may have been written as early as the late 60's AD. This is confirmed by the *Didache* (a document written in the 60's AD) quoting from 1 John.

Jude

The author of Jude identifies himself as "Jude, a bond-servant of Jesus Christ, and brother of James" (vs. 1). This would make the author one of Jesus' half-brothers (Matthew 13:55). At one time he was not a believer and may have mocked His half-brother Jesus, but after Jesus rose from the dead he had become a believer and leader in the early church (John 7:3-5; Acts 1:13-14). His older brother James became the recognized leader in the Jerusalem church after Peter and

John had departed Jerusalem. It is highly unlikely that a forger wrote this letter and pretended to be James' brother Jude since Jude was not a prominent figure in early Christianity. Hence, Jude was the real author of this letter.

Jude wrote this letter to "those who are the called" (vs. 1). Hence, it appears that he writes this letter to a group of believers. It may have been an encyclical letter, a letter intended to be copied and read to churches throughout the Roman Empire. If Jude, like his older brother James, had been entrusted primarily with a mission to the Jewish believers, then his readers could be Jewish Christians throughout the Roman Empire (Galatians 1:9). Jude may have done some travelling and missionary work himself (1 Corinthians 9:5).

It seems that Jude writes either towards the end of the age of the apostles (60 to 70 AD?) or a decade into the age of the elders (about 80 AD?). At the time Jude writes his epistle, false teachers had infiltrated the early church (vs. 3-4). It is possible that these heretics were trying to fill the void left by the deaths of the apostles—new leaders in the church were needed and these false teachers were trying to take advantage of the situation.

In Jude's short epistle, he lists many characteristics of these false teachers. They teach a license to sin and deny the Lord Jesus Christ (vs. 4). They reject authority, possibly the authority of the colleagues of the apostles whom the apostles had left in charge of the church (vs. 8). These false teachers also revile angelic majesties—they do not respect the power of the angelic realm (vs. 8). These heretics cause divisions in the body of believers and they mock the things of God (vs. 18-19). Jude identifies these deceivers with the mockers that the Apostle Peter warned would come (2 Peter 3:3-4).

The key phrase, when it comes to identifying the approximate date of the composition of this letter, is when Jude tells his readers to "remember the words that were spoken beforehand by the apostles of our Lord Jesus Christ, that they were saying to you, 'in the last times there will be mockers, following after their own ungodly lusts'" (vs. 17-18). This passage appears to be either a quote or a paraphrase from 2 Peter 3:3. Since 2 Peter was written in 67 AD when Peter was about to be martyred, if this passage is a quote or paraphrase from Peter's second epistle, then this would mean that Jude could not have been written until after that date.

However, Jude refers to the "words that were spoken," not the words that were written. And, he does not say that only the Apostle Peter spoke these words; instead, Jude tells his readers that "the apostles" spoke these words. In other words, Jude is not quoting or paraphrasing from 2 Peter—he is quoting the oral teachings of the apostles (which would include Peter's preaching). Apparently, when Peter wrote that mockers would appear in the last days, he was writing something that the apostles regulary preached. Hence, Jude's epistle does not necessarily have to be dated after 67 AD.

Still, Jude does seem to be looking back to a time in the past when the apostles led the church. This could imply that Peter is already dead, as well as most of the other apostles. It could imply that the age of the apostles is gone—now the elders are leading the church. Hence, Jude's letter could be written after 70 AD. If this is the case, one would expect him to mention the destruction of the temple unless a decent amount of time has passed. If Jude wrote after 70 AD, he probably wrote this letter around 80 AD. If he wrote before 70 AD but after Peter's death, then a 68 to 69 AD date would make sense.

But, it is also possible that Jude wrote earlier than this. Maybe he is not writing after the age of the apostles. It is possible that he writes after the original apostles have left Jerusalem (around 44 AD, just before the death of Herod Agrippa I; Acts 12:1-23). However, Jude could be writing in the early 60's AD and saying "remember what the apostles (when they were in Jerusalem) used to say."

When Jude identifies himself as the "brother of James" does this mean James is still alive or already dead? James was martyred in 62

AD in Jerusalem. Jude does not say whether James is still alive or if he writes after his brother's death. Hence, Jude could have been written as early as 60 to 65 AD, or as late as 68 to 80 AD (if written after Peter's death). Jude was probably several years younger than Jesus and James (Matthew 13:55-56; he may have had four older brothers and some sisters who may have been older than him as well), so he may have still been alive in 80 AD. Unfortunately, it is difficult to be dogmatic about a precise date for Jude's letter. Thiessen dates Jude to 75 to 80 AD (Thiessen, 296), while Robinson dates Jude to 61 to 62 AD (Robinson, 352). If the *Didache* was written in the 60's AD (a date which we have argued for earlier in this chapter) then, since the *Didache* quotes from the Epistle of Jude, Jude would have to be dated, at the latest, in the 60's AD.

Revelation

The early church fathers almost universally acknowledged the Apostle John as the author of the Book of Revelation. Those who accepted the Apostle John's authorship of Revelation include: Justin Martyr (150 AD), Melito Bishop of Sardis (165 AD), Irenaeus (180 AD), as well as Tertullian, Hippolytus, and Origen of the early third century AD (Carson, Moo, and Morris, 468).

Still, John's authorship of Revelation was rejected by some. But, those who rejected John's authorship did so apparently for theological reasons. In 140 AD, the heretic Marcion rejected John's authorship. However, he rejected most of the New Testament, especially books like Revelation, which quoted from the Old Testament since he rejected the Old Testament being God's Word. Also, Dionysius (a third century bishop of Alexandria) refused to accept John's authorship of Revelation because he rejected premillennialism (the view that Jesus will literally reign on earth for 1,000 years; Revelation 20). But, apart from those who rejected John as the author of

Revelation for theological reasons, acceptance of John's authorship is almost unanimous (Carson, Moo, and Morris, 468-469).

The author of Revelation identifies himself only as "John" (Revelation 1:1, 4, 9, 22:8). He writes this letter to seven churches in Asia Minor (Revelation 1:11). It is unlikely that anyone but the Apostle John would write to seven churches in Asia Minor (where the Apostle John ministered) in the first century AD and identify himself only as "John." Clearly, the burden of proof rests solely on those who choose to deny the Apostle John as the author of Revelation—the evidence strongly favors the Apostle as the author.

There is more controversy when it comes to dating the Book of Revelation. Most scholars date Revelation to the reign of Emperor Domitian (81-96 AD). However, some scholars favor a pre-70 AD date for Revelation. Westcott, Hort, Lightfoot, and Salmon believed Revelation was written in the late sixties AD (Thiessen, 322; see also Carson, Moo, and Morris, 471). John A. T. Robinson dates Revelation to 68 to 70 AD (*Redating the New Testament* 221-253, 352).

The Book of Revelation was clearly written during a time when Christians in Asia Minor were being persecuted by both the Roman Empire and Jewish communities (Revelation 1:9; 2:9-10, 13; 3:8-10). Most scholars identify this time of persecution with the reign of Emperor Domitian (81-96 AD). Still, Robinson argues that the persecution described in Revelation more likely points to the persecution of the church perpetrated by Emperor Nero during his reign (*Redating the New Testament* 230-238).

Eusebius quotes ancient tradition saying that the Apostle John was exiled to the Isle of Patmos by Emperor Domitian, and then released by the next Emperor, Nerva (Eusebius, *The History of the Church* 81-82). This would place the date of the composition of Revelation to 95 to 96 AD. However, Robinson points out that Domitian, as a teenager, actually served as Emperor temporarily from 69 to 70 AD (*Redating the New Testament* 249-250; see also Grant, *The Twelve Caesars* 240-

241). Nerva, a future Emperor, was a lawyer who served in Vespasian's reign (Vespasian replaced Domition after Domition's first, temporary reign as Emperor). It is possible that Nerva, long before he became emperor, released the Apostle John from exile (Robinson, 250). If Robinson is correct, John may have written Revelation around 68 to 69 AD, rather than 95 to 96 AD. It is difficult to be dogmatic on a specific date for the Book of Revelation. Either it was written around 68-69 AD or it was written as late as 95 AD. Either way, there is no reason to doubt the authorship of the Apostle John.

Some strong support for the earlier date for the Book of Revelation can be found in the possible allusions to Revelation found in Clement of Rome (70 AD; Lightfoot and Harmer, 23), the *Epistle of Barnabas* (70's AD; Lightfoot and Harmer, 265), and the *Shepherd of Hermas* (85 AD; Lightfoot and Harmer, 307). More research is needed concerning the date of composition for the Book of Revelation.

Conclusion

The important thing to remember is not that the dates given above should be embraced in any dogmatic fashion. What is important is this: scholars should not assume the latest dates possible for each of the New Testament books. They should also be open to accepting the earliest possible dates, especially when the earlier dates make more sense. Far too much speculation by liberal New Testament scholars has presupposed that the development of the early church's theology occurred so slowly that certain New Testament books had to have been written late in the first-century or early in the second-century. But, this is obviously not the case. Paul began to write around 48 to 50 AD, and already his doctrines of Christ and salvation were very highly developed. Hence, the Christology (doctrine of

Christ) and soteriology (doctrine of salvation) found in the Gospel of John should not automatically rule out an early mid-first century date.

The below chart summarizes the dates of the New Testament books proposed in this chapter:

New Testament Book	Approximate Date of Composition	Author
Matthew	35-42 AD	The Apostle Matthew
Mark	45 AD	John Mark
Luke	45-50 AD	Luke
John	50-55 AD	The Apostle John
Acts	61 AD	Luke
Romans	56-58 AD	The Apostle Paul
1 Corinthians	55 AD	Paul
2 Corinthians	56 AD	Paul
Galatians	48-49 AD	Paul
Ephesians	61 AD	Paul
Philippians	61 AD	Paul
Colossians	61 AD	Paul
1 Thessalonians	51 AD	Paul
2 Thessalonians	51 AD	Paul
1 Timothy	64-65 AD	Paul
2 Timothy	67 AD	Paul
Titus	65 AD	Paul
Philemon	61 AD	Paul
Hebrews	68-69 AD	Barnabas, Luke, Apollos, or Silas?
James	45-48 AD	James, half-brother of Jesus

1 Peter	44 or 65 AD	The Apostle Peter
2 Peter	67 AD	Peter
1 John	60's AD or 80-90 AD	The Apostle John
2 John	60's AD or 80-90 AD	John
3 John	60's AD or 80-90 AD	John
Jude	60-65 AD or 68-80 AD	Jude, the half-brother of Jesus
Revelation	69 AD or 95 AD	The Apostle John

Though we cannot be dogmatic about some of these dates, it should be emphasized that students of the New Testament should be open to the earliest possible dates, rather than only entertaining the latest possible dates. Though we cannot date the New Testament books with certainty, it is hoped that this book will encourage discussion and a re-examination of the dates for the composition of the New Testament books. The assumption that the early church waited an entire generation before writing a Gospel is excatly that—an assumption. And, in the opinion of this author, it is an assumption that needs to be questioned. Once we take more seriously the statements made by the early church fathers, the early dates for the New Testament books do not seem unreasonable.

Chapter Eight
Is Jesus Just Another Myth?

Many critics of Christianity claim that Jesus is just another myth. These skeptics believe that the early church borrowed from ancient pagan myths—the early church was not really recording any reliable information about the true Jesus of history. Two Christian scholars who have effectively responded to this objection to Christianity are Ronald Nash (author of *The Gospel and the Greeks*) and J. P. Moreland (author of *Scaling the Secular City*). As we refute the myth hypothesis in this chapter, we will discuss the defense of the historicity of Jesus made by these two scholars.

Nash & Moreland's Refutation of the Myth Hypothesis

Nash and Moreland point out that there are numerous differences between the New Testament information about Jesus and the ancient myths. First, there is a long gap in time between the original recording of ancient myths and the time when that myth supposedly occurred. In fact, in most cases the subject of the myth is not even a historical person or event. In the case of the New Testament Jesus, the entire New Testament was written during a time when eyewitnesses who knew Jesus were still alive and leading the church. The entire New Testament should be dated to the first century AD. In fact, ancient creeds (Colossians 1:15-17; Philippians 2:5-11; Romans 10:9; 2 Corinthians 5:15; etc.) that speak of Jesus' deity, resurrection, and substituionary death probably go back to the decade in which Jesus died—the 30's AD. As the historian and expert on ancient mythology, A. N. Sherwin-White, has stated, legends or myths need at least two generations to get started and gain acceptance (*Roman Society*, 186-193). With the New Testament portrait of Jesus, there is simply not enough time for a myth to have developed—the Jesus of the Gospels is the true Jesus of history.

Second, usually myths that sound like forerunners of Christianity were actually written after the New Testament writings were complete. Hence, if borrowing occurred, it was probably pagan mythology that borrowed from Christianity. It is difficult, if not impossible, to identify pre-Christian myths that depict a full-blown incarnation, death, and resurrection of a savior-figure. When myths take on these ideas, it seems that they post-date Christianity (Moreland, *Scaling*, 182).

Third, the mystery religions were syncretistic—they liked to blend beliefs from other religions with their own beliefs. Christianity, on the other hand, like the Judaism from which it came, was very exclusive. The early church, like first century Judaism, did not borrow from other religions. The early church believed that all non-Christian religions were false and that salvation comes only through Jesus. In short, the early church was not inclined to borrow from the pagan religions and their myths. In fact, many Christians were persecuted and martyred because they refused to blend Christianity with pagan beliefs.

Fourth, J. P. Moreland points out that the similarities between the Gospels and the pagan myths are often exagerrated by skeptics (*Scaling*, 182). In fact, often the myths only look similar to the Gospel if we use Christian terminology to describe them or read Christian themes into these myths.

Fifth, the ancient mystery religions had more concern about the religious experiences or emotional states of their followers than for correct doctrine. Early Christianity, conversely, had a large emphasis on history and correct doctrine—its focus was not primarily on the subjective state of its adherents.

Sixth, the writers of the ancient myths did not write as if they expected their readers to take them literally. Yet, the Gospel authors wrote as if they were recording real history. They informed their readers concerning the identity of current leaders, the time of the year, descriptions of the location, and other key factors which would enable the reader to place the events in their proper historical, chronological, and geographical setting. This is not the case with the ancient myths (Moreland, *Scaling*, 182).

Seventh, the vast majority of the world's leading New Testament scholars no longer try to trace the origin of Christianity to pagan myths. It is now widely accepted by New Testament scholarship that the ancient Jewish Faith is the root of New Testament Christianity, not Greek and Roman mythology.

Two Important Points Made by C. S. Lewis

C. S. Lewis was open to the possibility that some of the ancient myths of a God-man Savior who dies and rises may predate biblical Christianity. But Lewis saw this, even if true, as no obstacle to Christian belief. Lewis believed the first preaching of the Gospel was found in the Garden of Eden just after Adam and Eve fell into sin. God promised that a man would be born of woman ("the seed of the woman") who would save mankind by defeating Satan (the one who spoke through the serpent), but would be bruised in the process (Genesis 3:15). Therefore, reasoned Lewis, all of ancient mankind had some remembrance of the promise of a coming, suffering Savior who would redeem mankind from the curse.

Also, Lewis appreciated God's revelation to mankind through nature. Hence, the four seasons may have been given to mankind as a hint of the coming Redeemer. In Winter nature dies, but it is reborn or resurrected in the Spring. Many of the ancient myths had to do with the seasons and the production of crops. Yet, God may have given ancient pagans hints about the coming Redeemer, so that when He came, died, and rose, He would fulfill the hope of many pagans who were living in the expectancy of a dying and rising God. Lewis viewed the ancient myths as "signposts" pointing to the day when God would become a man, die for our sins, and rise from the dead (Nicholi, 86-90, 232; Lewis, *Miracles*, 133-134).

Although Lewis viewed the incarnation (God the Son becoming a man) as the myth that came true, he also noted that the Gospels were written as if the authors were recording straightforward history, not mythology. In other words, as an expert on ancient mythology, Lewis realized that the Gospels were not even written in the genre (or literary style) of mythology. They were written as if the authors were recording ancient history (Nicoli, 86).

Conclusion

The Jesus found on the pages of the New Testament is not a myth, nor was He borrowed from ancient myths. The New Testament was written by reliable eyewitnesses who were sincere enough about their beliefs that they were willing to die for their beliefs. They were not telling stories. The Gospel writers did not borrow from ancient myths. They reported accurately what they saw and heard concerning Jesus. Men do not die for legends or myths; the apostles were willing to suffer and die for Jesus because they witnessed His miracles and His post-resurrection appearances. They saw Him fulfill numerous Old Testament prophecies of the coming Messiah. They believed His claims to be God, Messiah, and Savior. Hence they were willing to die for Jesus—the true Jesus of history, not a mythological, fairy-tale Jesus. Hence, Paul could make a clear distinction between such things as "sound doctrine" and "truth" on the one hand, and "myths" or fables of false teachers on the other hand (2 Timothy 4:3-4). As the Apostle Peter wrote, "For we did not follow cleverly devised tales when we made known to you the power and coming of our Lord Jesus Christ, but we were eyewitnesses of His majesty" (2 Peter 1:16).

Though a person is free to choose to reject the New Testament accounts, it is clear that the New Testament authors were not writing mythology—they claimed they were recording reliable history.

Chapter Nine
Refuting Bart Ehrman's Skepticism Concerning the Original Text of the New Testament

New Testament scholar Bart Ehrman argues for skepticism towards the original New Testament manuscripts. In his work *Misquoting Jesus: The Story Behind Who Changed the Bible and Why*, he states that there may be as many as 400,000 vaiants among the copies of the New Testament. He points out that this number is three times as high as the total number of words in the New Testament text (89-90)! Because of all these variants, implies Ehrman, we have no way to determine what the original manuscripts of the New Testament actually said. Ehrman adds that we have no second, third, or fourth generation copy of the original texts! If this is the case, then our confidence that we can reproduce what the original New Testament writings actually said should be extremely low. Ehrman implies that we should be highly skeptical concerning the original New Testament manuscripts.

But, is the situation concerning the original New Testament really that bad? One can agree with much of Ehrman's data, yet draw the entirely opposite conclusion. Ehrman's mentor, the late Princeton scholar Bruce Metzger, knew more about New Testament criticism than just about any other scholar. Yet he blieved the New Testament text to be about 99.5% accurate. Metzger was also a great defender of the inspiration and inerrancy of the Bible. Hence, we can question the radical conclusions drawn by Ehrman without questioning his scholarship.

An Evangelical Response to Bart Ehrman's Views

The first point we need to make is that the New Testament, based upon its manuscript evidence, is by far the most reliable of all ancient writings. No ancient writing has as many copies as does the New Testament. No other ancient writing has copies that date so close to when the originals were supposedly written. Even Ehrman admits we have in existence today over 5,700 hand-written Greek copies of the New Testament. There are also over 10,000 Latin copies of the New Testament. All total, the number of New Testament copies excedes 25,000. No other ancient writing even comes close to this. In fact, almost the entire New Testament can be reproduced merely from the quotations found in the early church fathers.

Also, we have some fragments of the New Testament that date back to within one or two generations removed from the originals. Hence, how does Ehrman know that none of these fragments or manuscripts are copies of the originals, or at least copies of copies of the originals? Even some of the third and fourth century manuscripts that still exist might have been copied from the originals or copies of the originals. In fact Tertullian wrote around 200 AD that "authentic writings" still existed in Jerusalem in his day. He may have meant that some of the original New Testament books were still in existence, kept in Jerusalem. Or, he may have meant that extremely trustworthy copies of the originals still existed at that time. Surely, the main church fathers of the second and third century must have had reliable copies of the original New Testament writings. The idea that the content of the original New Testament books is forever lost to us is simply not the case. Ehrman argues for far too much in his attempt to raise doubt about the reliability of the New Testament text we have today.

Though the claim that there may be as many as 400,000 variants among the New Testament copies sounds overwhelming, a closer look at those variants reveal that they should not cause us to lose confidence in the New Testament copies we have today. New Testament scholars Darrell Bock and Daniel Wallace point out that the vast majority of these variants are spelling errors, the use of the movable nu, synonyms, word order, and the use of the definite article (Bock and Wallace, 55-57).

Some of the copyists simply mispelled words—this presents absolutely no probably for translators. The mistake is easily recognized. The movable nu is the letter of the Greek alphabet equivilant to our letter "n." In New Testament Greek (i.e., koine or common Greek), when the ending of a third person plural verb comes before a vowel or at the end of a sentence a nu (the movable nu) is added to the end of the verb. Many of the variants deal with the copyist either adding or deleting a movable nu. Again, no change to the meaning of the passage occurs when this is the variant.

Sometimes scribes would take the liberty of replacing a word with a synonym. Again, the meaning of the passage is not changed. Also, the word order in Greek is much different than in English. In the Greek language the subject, object, and predicate are identified by their word endings, not the word order. Hence, the order of the words in a sentence can be selected for several diffferent reasons. For example, if the author wants to emphasize a word in the sentence, he may choose to place the emphasized word first. Sometimes the copyist changed the word order. Still, the English translation of the sentence would probably not change merely because the order of the words was different in the Greek.

Finally, the copyist might choose to insert or remove the definite article in the text. For instance, in the Greek, proper names can have the definite article ("the") before them. Whether the copyist added a definite article or removed one, the English translation would once again remain the same. The meaning of the passage is not influenced at all.

Hence, once the variants are examined and so few are shown to be critical, less than 1% of all the variants are still considered both meaningful (i.e., the variant reading actually changes the meaning of the passage in question) and viable (i.e., the variant is actually a viable option for the original reading). This is why Metzger considered the New Testament manuscripts to be 99.5% accurate. Even in the cases of the meaningful and viable variants, no essential doctrine of Christianity is called into question (Bock and Wallace, 57-58). Ehrman's skepticism about the content original New Testament manuscripts and his doubts about the historical Jesus are totally unwarranted.

A Closer Look at Some of the Key Variants

Bart Ehrman lists several key variants that are meaningful and viable. He implies that these variants should cause us to lose our faith in ever hoping to find what the original manuscripts actually said. But, this is not the case. At this point, we will look at the key meaningful and viable variants.

John 7:53-8:11 recounts a story of Jesus forgiving an adultress woman brought to Him by the Jewish religious leaders. This passage is found in the vast majority of New Testament manuscripts, but it is not found in any of the oldest New Testament manuscripts. Many evangelical scholars do not believe this passage belongs in the Bible. Hence, it is usually bracketed out in modern translations, and a footnote informs the reader of the lack of textual support for this passage. Those evangelical scholars who favor the majority of the manuscripts believe this passage belongs in the Bible. Either way, the Christian's view of Jesus would change in no way if this passage were removed.

The last twelve verses of Mark's Gospel are also missing in the oldest existing manuscripts. Even without this passage, Mark's Gospel still ends with the empty tomb and the announcement that Jesus has risen from the dead and will appear to His disciples. Again, the absence of this passage does not change any core Christian doctrine.

1 John 5:7-8 is not represented in the oldest manuscripts. This passage says that "there are three that bear witness in heaven: the Father, the Word, and the Holy Spirit; and these three are one." Those translators who favor the majority text include this passage in the text of their Bibles (i.e., the King James Version and the New King James Version). Translators who favor the oldest manuscripts over the majority of the manuscripts either remove this passage or demote it to a footnote (i.e., New American Standard Version and the New International Version).

Whatever the case, Ehrman exaggerates the significance of this passage (1 John 5:7-8) by implying that the doctrine of the Trinity (i.e., that the one true God exists throughout all eternity as three equal Persons) is based solely on this passage. It is not. Numerous passages teach that there is only one God (Isaiah 43:10; 44:6; 46:9; 1 Timothy 2:5, etc.). The Bible teaches that the Father is God (Galatians 1:1; 1 Peter 1:1-2; etc.), the Son is God (John 1:1, 14; 5:17-18; 8:58-59; 10:30-33; Philippians 2:6; Romans 9:5; Colossians 2:9; Titus 2:13; 2 Peter 1:1, etc.), and the Holy Spirit is God (Acts 5:3-4; 1 Corinthians 3:16, etc.). But, the Bible also teaches that the Father, Son, and Holy Spirit are three distinct Persons (Matthew 3:16-17; John 14:16, 26; 15:26, etc.). Ehrman knows that systematic theology pulls together the teachings of different passages to produce coherent doctrines based in the Bible. No Trinitarian scholar ever based his entire biblical case for the doctrine of the Trinity on this one passage. Regardless of whether a Christian believes this passage belongs in the Bible or not, the doctrine of the Trinity remains intact.

Mark 1:41, in most translations, says that Jesus healed a leper because He was "moved with compassion." But, Ehrman points out that there is excellent manuscript evidence that the passage should read "moved with anger." If it turns out that Ehrman is right, it changes nothing. For, it doesn't make a difference if Jeus healed the leper because of compassion or anger. Whether Jesus healed the leper because he was angry (possibly at the unbelief of others), or if He healed the leper because He felt compassion towards him, our portrait of Jesus remains the same.

In short, none of the meaningful and viable textual variants changes any core doctrine of the Christian Faith. Virtually all the variants that Ehrman emphasizes are already noted in the footnotes of modern translations of the Bible. Evangelical scholars have openly discussed these textual variants for generations. Ehrman is right to point out these variants. But, the radical conclusions he draws from the data do not logically follow. In no way is any core doctrine of Christianity changed. Even with the presence of these variants, and the debate about whether they are authentic or not, Jesus Christ is still "the same yesterday, today, and forever" (Hebrews 13:8).

It seems that Ehrman is using his vast knowledge of textual criticism in an attempt to destroy the faith of Christians. Ehrman claims that the many textual variants should destroy our confidence in what the actual manuscripts actually said. But, this is not the case. Evangelicals may debate whether we should accept the oldest manuscripts or the majority of manuscripts. Either way, the risen Jesus of the Bible remains; the faith once for all delivered to the saints is unshaken.

Chapter Ten
The Apostolic Oral Tradition Behind the Four Gospels
By Kyle Larson

According to Dr. Bart Ehrman, between the written narratives about Jesus we have today and the original events lies a web of unreliable oral transmission. However, when conservative New Testament scholars discuss the reliability of the four Gospels, a period of *oral* transmission rarely comes up. Why? Conservative scholars assume that either an eyewitness wrote the Gospel account or a scribe of an eyewitness edited together the first-hand accounts of an Apostle or eyewitness. This view is espoused in the writings of the early church fathers. Textual analysis of existing texts and ancient fragments also promote the eyewitness basis for the Gospels.

Despite this, in his well received 2009 book, *Jesus Interrupted*, Dr. Bart Ehrman not only assumes a period of oral transmission for the Gospel texts, but he also provides arguments to support his theory that the Gospel narratives were corrupted in the process. He makes several assertions in his book concerning the supposed oral tradition. Although each assertion has a measure of truth to it in terms of how oral tradition worked in the first century, the conclusions in no way affect the reliability of the Gospel narratives we have today.

Dr. Ehrman begins his discussion by asking: How was the Gospel spread in the first century (Ehrman, *Jesus Interrupted* 146)? He asserts that the Gospel narratives were spread mainly by people who had no connection with Jesus or the Apostles (Ehrman, *Jesus Interrupted* 146). Thus, Dr. Ehrman assumes that the earliest Christians were forced to invent stories about Jesus to get people to believe in this new, mysterious savior. As these stories about Jesus were told over and over again, they became embellished with each retelling (Ehrman *Jesus Interrupted* 147). Eventually the original, historical message was almost completely lost. Dr. Ehrman uses the "telephone game" example to show that, as stories are passed on from person to person, they became more and more unreliable.

As one assesses Ehrman's view of the supposed oral traditions behind the four Gospels, even if we assume that there was an oral transmission period, it becomes obvious that he has an incomplete view of how oral transmission worked in the early Church. The first century was a world of spoken and memorized words. With literacy rates low and writing tools either expensive or overly cumbersome, such things as family histories, popular literature, religious texts and cultural traditions were generally passed among the common people via stories.

The earliest Church was no exception. What both the Jews and non Jews received from the Apostles was most likely at first memorized. That does not mean they were any less concerned with keeping an accurate historical account of the stories they received concerning their savior, Jesus. As a matter of fact, Paul is consistently found to be our earliest witness (if we assume later dates for the four Gospels), and he goes to great lengths to show the importance of having accurate information about Jesus.

In several of his epistles, Paul uses several standard Greek terms for the receiving and passing on of accurate traditions. New Testament scholar Richard Bauckham discusses several instances of this (*Jesus and the Eyewitnesses* 264-265). Bauckham relates that Paul speaks about "receiving a tradition" (*paralambano*). This Greek word for "receiving a tradition" is found in 1 Corinthians 15:1, Galatians 1:9, Colossians 2:1, Thessalonians 2:3, 1 Thessalonians 4 :1, 2 (264). As we read in 1 Corinthians 11:12, Paul also believed that once a tradition is "received", it needs to be "handed on" (*paradimomi*). Paul also speaks about "faithfully retaining or observing a tradition" (1 Corinthians 11:2; 2 Thessalonians 2:15; 3:6).

Bauckham defines *tradition* as: ". . . one hands over something to somebody so that the latter possess it" (264-265).

Paul is again a prime example of how the traditions about the life of Jesus were both received and then faithfully passed on to others. Now, Paul claimed to have received the Gospel message directly from Christ. However, for the sake of argument, if we assume that Paul learned what he knew from the Apostles, the knowledge he received was from more than one first hand source. If one made a mistake another would correct it. He spent two weeks with Peter and James (Jesus' half brother) confirming both the gospel message and the accounts of Jesus' earthly ministry (Galatians 1:18; Bacukham 266).

Paul firmly believed that the traditions he received went back to the time of Jesus himself and represented an accurate account of His life and teachings (Bauckham 268). He then faithfully passed on these traditions to the churches he founded (1 Corinthians 11:23, 15:1-3; Bauckham 267). More specifically, Paul also says that he entrusted the traditions he received to specific teachers within the congregation (Romans 12:7; 1 Corinthians 12:28-29; Galatians 6:6; Ephesians 4:11; Bauckham 269).

Of course, how can we tell if these traditions were received properly by those in future generations? Maybe between what Paul gave and what future generations received legends and myths found their way into the Gospel narratives? Do we have proof that the stories were not embellished and eventually corrupted?

We know from history that the Apostles did exactly what Jesus had told them to do: *Go and make disciples.* A generation later (assuming the Gospels were written late), we have texts written by these disciples. Some of these converts went on to lead the early church after the Apostles' deaths. These students of the Apostles became Bishops of early congregations in the late first and early second century. In most cases we know that it was the Apostles themselves who gave them these appointments.

Had the Apostles done their job well? Did this next generation of Christians pass on an embellished Gospel to future generations of Christians? Fortunately, we have both the writings of the Apostles in the New Testament and of many early church fathers to compare. After examination, the writings authored by the Apostles' students, from the late first and early second century, does reflect the same Gospel message.

For example, we have the writings of Irenaeus, a bishop in Lyons, France. He lived in the middle to late second century. Because he was trained by Polycarp, a man discipled by the Apostle John himself, Irenaeus could be called a "spiritual grandson" of the Apostles. In his five volume work entitled "Against Heresies," Irenaeus gives some brief glimpses into the lives of those who knew the Apostles and faithfully transmitted what the Apostles taught to the rest of the church. Because Polycarp was Irenaeus' immediate teacher, we will begin with Polycarp.

Polycarp of Smyrna. Irenaeus states in several places in his writings that his teacher, Polycarp, knew the Apostles and was appointed a Bishop in Smyrna (present day Turkey) by the Apostle John. We have two quotes from Irenaeus concerning Polycarp, his spiritual teacher, and his associations with the original twelve Apostles.

The first quote comes from *Against Heresies*, which was written about 180 AD:

> But Polycarp also was not only instructed by apostles and conversed with many who had seen Christ, but was also, by apostles in Asia, appointed bishop of the Church in Smyrna, whom I also saw in my early youth, for he tarried [on earth] a very long time, and, when a very old man, gloriously and most nobly suffering martyrdom, departed this life, having always taught the things which he had learned from the apostles, and

> which the Church has handed down, and which alone are true. To these things all the Asiatic Churches testify, as do also those men who have succeeded Polycarp down to the present time, a man who was of much greater weight, and a more steadfast witness of truth, than Valentinus and Marcion, and the rest of the heretics (*Against Heresies* 3:3:3; *Ante Nicene Fathers*, vol. 1, pg 416 CCEL Internet Library).

The second reference from Irenaeus concerning Polycarp comes from a letter that Irenaeus had written to a boyhood friend, Florinus, who had left the faith and embraced the heresy known as Gnosticism. This letter has been preserved by Eusebius in his work *Church History*. Irenaeus wanted to remind his friend Florinus that the heresy he is embracing does not come either from the Apostles or from those whom the Apostles directly taught. Irenaeus states that Florinus needs to remember the teachings of Polycarp, who himself was taught by the Apostles.

In the letter to Florinus, of which we have spoken, Irenaeus mentions again his intimacy with Polycarp, saying:

> These doctrines, O Florinus, to speak mildly, are not of sound judgment. These doctrines disagree with the Church, and drive into the greatest impiety those who accept them. These doctrines, not even the heretics outside of the Church, have ever dared to publish. These doctrines, the presbyters who were before us, and who were companions of the apostles did not deliver to you. For when I was a boy, I saw you in lower Asia with Polycarp, moving in splendor in the royal court, and endeavoring to gain his approbation. I remember the events of that time more clearly than those of recent years. For what boys learn, growing with their mind, becomes joined with it; so that I am able to describe the very place in which the

> blessed Polycarp sat as he discoursed, and his goings out and his comings in, and the manner of his life, and his physical appearance, and his discourses to the people, and the accounts which he gave of his intercourse with John and with the others who had seen the Lord. And as he remembered their words, and what he heard from them concerning the Lord, and concerning his miracles and his teaching, having received them from eyewitnesses of the 'Word of life' [1 John 1:1], Polycarp related all things in harmony with the Scriptures (Eusebius, *Church History* 5:20; *Nicene and Post Nicene Fathers*, vol. 1, pg 238-239, CCEL Internet Library).

These are two extremely important quotes by Irenaeus regarding his connection with Polycarp. Polycarp taught Irenaeus what the Apostles, and specifically, what the Apostle John, had taught him. Ehrman completely ignores both of these quotes from Irenaeus concerning Polycarp and his connections with the twelve Apostles. These two specific quotes do not appear in *Jesus Interrupted.*

Ehrman also leaves the reader wondering who Irenaeus was. He simply states that Irenaeus was alive in 180 AD, and thus he is too late in time to be able to give us any accurate information about the early church or who may have written any of the four Gospels. Ehrman does not acknowledge that Irenaeus was a "spiritual grandson" of the Apostles, and thus was in an excellent position to know what the Apostles taught and also what they wrote (Ehrman, *Jesus Interrupted* 111,122).

Clement of Rome. Irenaeus gives us some very interesting information concerning Clement, the Bishop of Rome. He writes:

> Clement was allotted the bishopric. This man, as he had seen the blessed apostles, and had been conversant with them, might be said to have the preaching of the apostles still

> echoing [in his ears], and their traditions before his eyes. Nor was he alone [in this], for there were many still remaining who had received instructions from the apostles (*Against Heresies* 3:3:3 *Ante Nicene Fathers*, vol. 1, pg 416, CCEL Internet Library).

Again, both Polycarp and Clement knew the Apostles around the late first century. Clement tells us specifically that whenever the Apostles evangelized an area, they would appoint Bishops and deacons to lead the new Christian congregation in that area (*1 Clement* 42). This is a key refutation to Ehrman's assertion that the Gospel was never spread through eyewitnesses. The Apostles were the eyewitnesses who then passed on the Gospel to men who could continue this process of handing on the Gospel that they themselves had received.

Tertullian, another important leader in the early church, gives further information on how both Clement of Rome and Polycarp became Bishops:

> For this is the manner in which the apostolic churches transmit their registers: as the church of Smyrna, which records that Polycarp was placed therein by John; as also the church of Rome, which makes Clement to have been ordained in like manner by Peter. In exactly the same way the other churches likewise exhibit (their several worthies), whom, as having been appointed to their episcopal places by apostles, they regard as transmitters of the apostolic see (*Prescription Against Heretics* 32, *Ante-Nicene Fathers* vol. 3, pg 258, CCEL Internet Library).

The Churches that were originally established by the Apostles kept records of those who continued in the leadership of the churches after the Apostles had passed away. After Polycarp and Clement died, new bishops were elected to replace them.

Ignatius of Antioch. There are also two bishops who had friends who knew the Apostles. The first of these was Ignatius, the Bishop of Antioch. The evidence does not definitively show that Ignatius personally knew the Apostles, but that he knew of Polycarp, a student of the Apostles. Thus, if Ignatius wanted to know what the Apostles had actually taught about Jesus, he could inquire of Polycarp, who had personally known the Apostles. Still, it is possible that Ignatius may have known some of the Apostles since he died in 107 AD. He had been the Bishop of Antioch of Syria (the church that commissioned Paul and Barnabas for their missionary journeys) for several decades before his martyrdom.

Papias. Papias was the Bishop of Hierapolis during the first half of the second century (Bauckham 12). The evidence cited below shows that Papias knew disciples of two of the last living eyewitnesses to the ministry of Jesus. These last two living eyewitnesses were Ariston and the Apostle John. These last two eyewitnesses had disciples who passed on to Papias what they were teaching about Jesus.

Papias wrote *Expositions of the Sayings of the Lord* between 110 and 140 AD. In it, he tells how he gathered information about the Lord from eyewitness sources. We gain much information about Papias by reading Eusebius' *Church History*. Papias lived at a time when there was only one generation between himself and the generation of the Apostles (Bauckham 13).

Ehrman is content to leave Papias as some mysterious figure with no historical connections to the early church. Ehrman simply calls Papias "an enigmatic figure." This is simply not true. Ehrman does not mention that Ariston and John, two of the last living eyewitnesses of Jesus, their immediate disciples, or Papias were all alive at the same time in the late first century. Ehrman does not mention that

Papias was a Bishop in the early second century. He does not mention the area over which he presided as Bishop—Papias was Bishop of Hierapolis, which was a cross roads town where information passed freely. Bauckham quotes the following passage from Bartlet on the importance of the city of Hireapolis:

> Hireapolis of which he (Papias) became "bishop" or chief local pastor, stood at the meeting point of two great roads: one running east and west, between Antioch in Syria and Ephesus , the chief city of "Asia". The other south-east to Attalila in Pamphylia and north-west to Smyrna. There Papias was almost uniquely placed for collecting traditions coming direct from the original home of the Gospel before his own day and during it, as well as from Palestinian Christian leaders settled in Asia (a great center of the Jewish Dispersion; Bauckham 15).

Thus, Hireapolis was a real city in a real geographic location, and Papias was the Bishop of the city. Ehrman mentions none of this important information in connection with Papias, the Bishop of Hireapolis. We will return to Papias when we look at the origins of the four Gospels.

In summary, it can be shown that the leadership of the church of the late first century and into the early second century was personally directed by the Apostles themselves. The Apostle Peter specifically appointed Clement as Bishop of Rome and the Apostle John appointed Polycarp as Bishop of Smyrna. Both Clement and Polycarp knew the rest of the Apostles besides Peter and John. The Apostles taught Polycarp and Polycarp taught Irenaeus the Faith. Certainly both Peter and John would have expected Clement and Polycarp to faithfully pass on the Gospel that they had been taught. Both the Apostle John and Polycarp lived to be very old men. This is why there are only two generations between Jesus and Irenaeus. Thus, Irenaeus is an extremely good position to tell us who wrote the four Gospels.

The evidence indicates that the early church of the first and second centuries strove to preserve the words and deeds of Jesus. The next question that needs to be asked is: how accurately was this historical information about Jesus transmitted in the early church? Ehrman discounts oral tradition of any kind as simply being unreliable. He believes that ancient people in general and the Apostles specifically simply could not pass on accurate information by word of mouth. Yet much scholarly work has been done on the accurate transmission of oral tradition in ancient cultures. Was the passing on of oral tradition in ancient cultures done as carelessly as Ehrman maintains?

Forms of Oral Tradition

Scholars have identified three main forms of oral tradition in ancient cultures. As these three models of oral tradition are explained, it should become evident that Ehrman has an overly simplistic understanding of ancient oral tradition and how it works. He mentions one form of oral tradition because it suits his purpose despite its lack of historical merit. The oral traditions behind the four Gospels are, in Ehrman's view, unreliable, and thus the four Gospels themselves are unreliable.

The first model sees the oral tradition (which supposedly formed the basis for the written Gospels) as a mixture of fact, fiction and legend. Some parts of the tradition are factual while other parts are not (Blomberg 51). Rudolf Bultmann believed that the early church was not interested in preserving historical information concerning the life of Jesus, but rather with the pressing day to day concerns of the churches. If a problem arose in the church, someone came along and "made up" a saying of Jesus to solve the problem (Bauckham 244;

Blomberg 50). This type of free floating oral transmission is still found in the Middle East today (Bauckham 253). This is Ehrman's "telephone game."

Ehrman sees all oral transmission of information as unreliable. He believes that people are just not able to remember large amounts of information over time. Ehrman, in mentioning this type of oral transmission, fails to note the other two major forms of oral transmission from the first and second century. Scholars recognize that both of these other methods of oral transmission are more accurate in passing on historical information in ancient oral societies. So which method is more plausible?

There are some very strong reasons why the early church would want to remember the words and deeds of Jesus. Rainer Riesner gives five basic reasons on why the Disciples would have carefully preserved the teaching of Jesus.

First, The Disciples recognized that the teachings of Jesus were authoritative. In the early Church they were placed on the same level as the Old Testament Prophets; both were considered the Word of God. So it only makes sense that the original disciples, who had heard Jesus themselves, would have been careful to preserve their master's words.

Second, the disciples believed that Jesus was the Messiah. Would the words of the long awaited savior be quickly forgotten? Rather, the teachings of someone so revered in first century Jewish culture would have been carefully remembered.

Third, Jesus was a good Rabbi. His teachings were in easy to memorize, poetical forms. They were intended to be shared from the moment they left Jesus' mouth.

Fourth, there are passages in the Gospels where Jesus commands his disciples to remember his words (Luke 6:7-13; Luke 10:1-17; Mark 15:28). If they truly believed Jesus to be God and Messiah, would they have disobeyed Him by altering His sacred teachings by replacing them with invented legends and false lessons? It seems unlikely that this would be the case.

Fifth, the first century Jewish culture was an oral culture. Educated Jewish boys memorized large sections of the Torah. In the same way, Jesus had encouraged the disciples to remember His words.

Finally, it was a common practice in the first century for religious and philosophical teachers to gather bands of disciples who were committed to remember their teacher's words (Blomberg 56-57).

The second form of oral tradition is called "formal controlled tradition." The main scholars who advanced this type of oral tradition are Main Reisenfeld, Gerharsson, and Reisner. Both Harold Risenfield in *The Gospel Tradition and its Beginning* and the Swedish scholar Binger Gerhardsson in *Memory and Manuscript: Oral Tradition and Written Transmission in Rabbinic Judaism and Early Christianity* write that Jesus, being a good Jewish rabbi, had his disciples memorize his teaching in a very strict and rigid word for word form. This understanding of oral tradition has people remembering the exact wording of a tradition (Blomberg 55, 56).

This view holds that Jesus adopted the common methods employed by first century rabbis by teaching his disciples to memorize his teachings. Even to this day, some cultures still use this method. Two contemporary examples of this include young Muslims memorizing the Koran and Eastern Orthodox Priests memorizing, word for word, long and complex Eastern Orthodox liturgies (Bauckham 254).

The third form of oral tradition and that which closely models what is found in the Gospels is called "informal controlled transmission." This form of oral tradition is a flexible transmission within a fixed limit. Scholars A. B. Lord and Jan Vansina have noted that in this form of oral tradition, the community makes it its job to ensure that the oral tradition being repeated sticks to the basic outline of the known historical facts (Bauckham 256).

There were many eyewitnesses to the ministry of Jesus who continued on in the early church. When others retold to their listeners what these original eyewitnesses experienced, the important point was not to memorize what the eyewitnesses said in a strict word for word way, but to tell the basic stories of Jesus with some variation in the wording but with keeping the main historical outline of what happened historically intact (Bauckham 256).

The scholarly work of Lord and Vansina present a middle of the road understanding of oral tradition between the "make it up as you go along" type of oral tradition (Ehrman's understanding) and a "strict and stringent having to memorize everything exactly word for word" type of oral tradition.

The work of these two scholars shows that the tradition of Jesus was carefully preserved, though not in a strict word for word way. A. B. Lord's work on Yugoslavian folk singers illustrates how these singers were able to memorize long, epic stories (about 100,000 words in length). Though these folk singers had great memories, they never used the exact same wording in telling the same basic stories. These folk singers made different additions and omissions to the stories, but never changed the basic contents of the story.

According to the research, there was about a ten percent to forty percent variation in the telling of the stories, but again, the same basic outline of these epic stories remained the same. Bauckham reminds us that this ten to forty percent variation in the words used in these Yugoslavian folk tales is about the same percentage in the word variation of the first three Gospels in the telling of the stories of Jesus. In both the cases of the stories being told by folksingers and the Gospels, the stories remain the same, but a strict word for word retelling is not necessary (Blomberg 58-59).

Bauckham reminds us that anthropologist Jan Vasina makes a distinction between oral tradition (tradition that goes past the lifetimes of the original eyewitnesses) and oral history—traditions that are passed on while the original eyewitnesses are still living (Bauckham 30-33). Other Specialists in oral tradition have found that within an orally based community, there were specially designated people who were given the charge to accurately pass on the community's oral traditions.

The twelve Apostles and other eyewitnesses to the ministry of Jesus felt a holy and solemn obligation to pass on accurately what they saw and heard of Jesus (Boyd and Eddy, *Jesus Legend* 273). The early church valued the testimony of those who had actually been with Jesus throughout his 3 ½ year ministry. These eyewitnesses continued to be active in both the church and the general population for a good part of the first century. A lot of scholarly work has been done concerning how oral traditions are passed on in an orally based culture, yet Ehrman conveniently disregards the work of these scholars.

The earliest Church was Jewish and she believed that she had received a new covenant from God through Jesus the Messiah. In the Torah, bearing false witness was a serious crime (Exodus 20:16). Also in the Torah, a claim had to be substantiated on the basis of eyewitness testimony (Deuteronomy 17:6-7; Numbers 35:30).

The Gospels affirm this principle of having multiple eyewitnesses to establish a claim (Mark 14:56.59; John 5: 31-32). The principle of multiple witnesses became the foundation for discipline in the early church (Matthew 18:16; 2 Corinthians 13:1; 1 Timothy 5:19; Boyd, *Jesus Legend,* 287). It has been recognized by scholars that much of the teachings of Jesus in the Synoptic Gospels was in easy to remember poetic form. Jesus wanted his teaching to be remembered, especially by the twelve Apostles who would carry on the work after He was gone (Blomberg 56).

Even before the birthday of the Church on Pentecost, the main criteria for taking over the apostolic ministry of Judas was that a person had to be an eyewitness to Jesus from the baptism of Jesus by John to his post-resurrection appearances (Acts 1:21-22; Bauckham 114). Peter says basically the same thing in Acts 10:36-42 (Bauckham 115).

The Greek word for eyewitness used by Luke in his Prologue means "firsthand observers." The Greek words "from the beginning" in Luke 1 carries the same meaning as the above scriptures (i.e., Acts 1 and Acts 10); they indicate "a claim that the eyewitnesses had been present throughout the events from the appropriate commencement of the author's history onwards" (Bauckham 116-117).

In conclusion, it is overly simplistic for Ehrman to use the "telephone game" as a way to show that, if the gospels were in fact transmitted orally before being committed to the pen, these oral traditions behind the Four Gospels are unreliable. Ehrman has not discussed the work of noted anthropologists who have conducted numerous studies into how the passing on of oral traditions occurred in ancient cultures. He seems to suggest that because modern contemporary people do not have the adequate memory abilities to remember large amounts of oral tradition, that this is true for all people in all times and cultures. This assumption is simply not based on the facts of history. There were too many safe guards in place to prevent distortion of the apostolic oral traditions about Jesus. The earliest eyewitnesses were very careful to preserve the words and deeds of Jesus until finally they were written down in the canonical four Gospels that are currently in the New Testament.

It should also be noted that, by the late first-century AD, the Gospels were already being quoted or alluded to by the apostolic fathers. Hence, it is apparent that Ehrman's entire thesis crumbles. Though current studies concerning the careful passing on of oral information argues in favor of the reliability of the four Gospels, the evidence clearly shows that the four Gospels were already being circulated in written form by the late first century AD (while many eyewitnesses were still alive). In short, the "oral tradition period" (the period between the ascension and when the Gospels were written) was probably much shorter than contemporary scholarship admits.

Chapter Eleven
Bart Ehrman's View of the Four Gospels
By Kyle Larson

Now that we've debunked the myth of an unreliable oral tradition between the original events depicted and the writing of the Gospel texts, we need to look at establishing the authorship of the Gospels. Were they truly written by the traditional authors? Or, are some, in whole or in part, merely apocryphal accounts fabricated by some well meaning, overzealous believer? Dr. Bart Ehrman, in his book, very plainly denies that the Gospel accounts we have today are based on eyewitness testimony. This leaves us with the impression that the Gospels are, to at least some extent, not based on actual history.

There are several reasons why he believes this. First, Dr. Ehrman claims that the Apostles were probably illiterate; if illiterate, they could not have possibly written any of the four Gospels themselves (Ehrman, *Jesus Interrupted* 106). Second, he doubts the accuracy of the external evidence concerning the testimony of the church fathers. Dr. Ehrman believes that the church fathers' testimony comes too late. In his view, so much time had passed between the writing of the Gospels and the time of the church fathers that the church fathers couldn't accurately ascertain who wrote the Gospels (107). Third, Ehrman further states that no one really knew who wrote the Gospels because the Gospel writers, in fact, wrote anonymously (111).

Ehrman makes the following statement concerning the supposed illiteracy of the twelve Apostles:

> The Original 12 Apostles could not read or write, therefore, they could not have authored any of the Four Gospels. Nothing in the Gospels or Acts indicates that Jesus' followers could read, let alone write. In fact, there is an account in Acts

> in which Peter and John are said to be unlettered (Acts 4:15) - the ancient word for illiterate. As Galilean Jews, Jesus' followers, like Jesus himself, would have been speakers of Aramaic. As rural folk, they probably would not have had any knowledge of Greek, if they did, it would have been extremely rough, since they spent their time with other illiterate Aramaic speaking peasants trying to eke out a hand to mouth existence. In short who were Jesus' disciples? Lower class illiterate Aramaic speaking peasants from Galilee (Ehrman, 106).
>
> Illiteracy was widespread throughout the Roman Empire. At best of times, maybe 10 percent of the population was literate. And that 10 percent would be the upper classes—upper class people who had the time and money to get an education (and their slaves and servants taught to read for the benefit of such services to their masters). (Ehrman, 105).

The Apostles were not Illiterate

There is a measure of truth to Dr. Ehrman's claim of partial or complete illiteracy of Greek. Peter and John were fishermen. They did *"eke out"* a living in that trade. In addition, they may never have received a formal education in Greek or Aramaic like the Rabbis (Boyd, *Jesus Legend* 249-250).

On the other hand, the Apostle Matthew was a tax collector for Rome. Literacy would have been a prerequisite to carrying out these duties (Mark 2:14; Matthew 9:9; 10:3; Boyd, *Jesus Legend* 250). The church father Papias indicated that Matthew could both read and write and was the author of a Gospel in Hebrew (Boyd, *Jesus Legend* 250). Another church father, Eusebius, says that a man named Mark, acting as scribe, faithfully recorded the preaching and teachings of Peter about Jesus (Boyd, *Jesus Legend* 250). It was he, then, that edited together the Gospel bearing his name (i.e. The Gospel of Mark).

Of course, the issue of the illiteracy among of the Disciples raises the larger issue of illiteracy among the general population of the first century Roman world. Was it as low as Dr. Ehrman claims? Could only a small fraction of Jesus' contemporaries in Judah and Galilee read and write—even in their own language? To the contrary, there is actually evidence that literacy was much more wide spread.

According to Gregory Boyd and Paul Eddy, people on all social levels—soldiers, slaves and even many common laborers were, to some extent, literate in at least one language. Inexpensive writing materials, such as clay and pottery shards, were readily available to even the lowest classes of Roman society. The words found written on them by later archaeologists testify to this. This means that a much larger segment of society was able to both read and write in at least a rudimentary way (Boyd, *Lord or Legend?* 68).

For example, writing materials were discovered at a Roman fort in England dated to about 100 AD (Boyd, *Jesus Legend* 243). Could some of those unschooled Roman soldiers really have been literate? Later, more writing materials were also found at this same site. Apparently, some of Roman soldiers had the ability to read and write (Boyd, *Jesus Legend* 243).

As another example, public notices have been discovered in ancient Roman cities. This seems to assume some degree of literary among the masses—otherwise, why post the notices (Boyd, *Lord or Legend?* 68)?

Taking a look at first century Judaism, it was obviously based on the Law of Moses—a text written and available in Greek, Aramaic and Hebrew. Being central to their religion, many Jewish males immersed themselves in reading the law (Boyd, *Lord or Legend?* 68). As a matter of fact, the first century synagogues in Palestine served as both a school and a place of worship. Young Jewish boys had their basic educational needs met in the synagogues. Learning to read was essential to studying the Law of Moses (Boyd, *Jesus Legend* 246).

Apparently, there is some good evidence that illiteracy wasn't as widespread in first century Palestine as Dr. Ehrman claims in his book. So even given a high level of illiteracy, enough people could write, whether by scribe or by their own hand. Hence, we are well justified in believing that eyewitness testimony is the basis for all four Gospel accounts. Professor Ehrman quite simply overstates his case.

The Church Fathers on the Four Gospels

The second objection that Ehrman raises has to with the testimony of the church fathers. If nearly a century exists between the Gospels' original authorship and the church fathers' authorship claims, can we trust their possibly second or third hand information? Dr. Ehrman believes we simply have no reliable early testimony about who authored the Gospels; early church leaders simply took "wild guesses" based on rumors and popular lore about who wrote the each of the four Gospels.

This unusual view is rare in modern New Testament scholarship, not because Dr. Ehrman has some unique insight, but rather because he is mistaken from the start. Now, there is a time gap between the original authorship of the Gospels and the church fathers. However, this gap isn't nearly as wide or empty as Ehrman claims. We do, in fact, have early testimony from church leaders who knew one or more of the Apostles personally. Being in such close in proximity in time to the Apostles, their testimony, as related by their disciples, was based on much more than mere "wild guesses" or popular hearsay. On the contrary, this provides near first hand information as to who the authors of the four Gospels were.

The church father Papias had access to both Ariston and John the Apostle, two of the last living eyewitnesses to the ministry of Jesus, through their immediate disciples at the close of the first century.

Eusebius gives us the following quote from Papias as to how he collected early traditions concerning what the Apostles said and did:

> "I shall not hesitate to furnish you, along with the interpretation, with all that in days gone by I carefully learnt from the presbyters and I have carefully recalled for I can guarantee its truth. Unlike most people, I felt at home not with those who had a great deal to say, but with those who taught the truth: with those who appeal to commandments given by the Lord to faith and coming to us from truth itself. And whenever anyone came who had been a follower of the presbyters. I inquired into the words of the presbyter, what Andrew or Peter had said or Phillip or Thomas or James or John or Matthew or any other disciple of the Lord and what Ariston and the presbyter John, disciples of the Lord were still saying. For I did not imagine that things out of books would help me as much as the utterance of a living and abiding voice (Eusebius, *Church History* 3:39:3-4; *Nicene and Post Nicene Fathers* Series 2 Vol 1. Pg. 170-171. CCEL Online library).

In many ways, Papias followed the same investigative method that Luke did in his Gospel and in the book of Acts. Both Luke and Papias wanted to go back, as close as possible, to the earliest eyewitness sources for the ministry of Jesus (Bauckham 29). Papias names the specific authors for two the Gospels. He states that the Apostle Matthew wrote the Gospel that bears his name (Eusebius, *Ecclesiastical History* 3.39.16 Series 2 *Ante Nicene and Post Nicene Fathers* Volume 1, pg 173). Papias also states that Mark, a companion of Peter, wrote the Gospel of Mark (Eusebius, *Church History* 3.39.14-15, *Nicene and Post Nicene Fathers* Series 2, Vol 1, pg 172-173 CCEL Online Library).

Again, Papias got this information from Ariston and John, who were two of the last living eyewitnesses to the ministry of Jesus. Their disciples traveled through the area where Papias was bishop and told him what Ariston and John were saying about the origins of the Gospels of Matthew and Mark.

Irenaeus, a pupil of Polycarp, who knew the Apostle John, gives us the same information regarding the authorship of both Matthew and Mark. In two specific places in his writings, Irenaeus says Matthew wrote the Gospel of Matthew (*Against Heresies* 3.1.1, *Ante Nicene Fathers* Vol 1. pg 414; Fragments of the Lost Writings 29 *Ante Nicene Fathers* Vol. 1 pg 573 CCEL Online library). Irenaeus also agrees with Papias that Mark, a companion of Peter, wrote the Gospel bearing his name.

Internal Hints for Eyewitness Testimony within the Gospels

Aside from external testimony, the Gospel texts themselves contain hints to their authorship. The Gospel of Mark, for example, contains suggestions that it is based on the eyewitness testimony of the Apostle Peter. Bauckham, in his book, *Jesus and the Eyewitnesses*, lists several indications that this is indeed the case. First, as you would expect from a disciple of Peter, Peter is mentioned more times in the Gospel of Mark than in any of the other three Gospels (Bauckham 125-126). Peter is also the first named disciple in his Gospel (Mark 1:16) and the last as well (Mark 16:7; Bauckham 124-125). This type of name preference and book ending seems to suggest both a preference for Peter's account and his perspective in the Gospel narrative.

Second, Peter's personal actions and words appear many times throughout the traveling ministry of Jesus. More so than the other disciples, he appears very active as he follows Jesus throughout his journeys as recorded in the Gospel of Mark. These details point to someone who knew Peter personally. And, assuming that Peter did not give every detail of every account, these details also point to someone who had access to several accounts of Peter's testimony.

Third, Bauckham further notes that Mark uses a "first person" literary device to highlight how close Peter is to Jesus throughout his ministry in Galilee. Bauckham cites an important study on the Gospel of Mark by Culbert Turner written back in 1925. Turner wanted to show that the Gospel of Mark gives Peter's eyewitness testimony. According to his research, the Gospel of Mark was written in such a way that it appears to be Peter's eyewitness testimony from his perspective. Concerning Turner's conclusion regarding this much overlooked literary device used by Mark, Bauckham states:

> … the natural and obvious explanation is that we have before us the experience of a disciple and apostle who tells the story from the point of view of an eyewitness and companion who puts himself in the same group with the Master … Matthew and Luke are Christian historians who stand away from the events and concentrate their narrative on the central figure (Turner in "Markan Usage," quoted in Bauckham 158).

Fourth, a number of word for word quotes from Mark's Gospel are found in both the Gospels of Luke and John. This may reveal that both incorporated differing amounts of material from Mark's Gospel directly into their own. Thus, they apparently considered Mark to be both a very reliable and valuable account. Considering that John was also an eyewitness, this heavily suggests that Mark's Gospel was held in the same regard. Otherwise, if Mark's Gospel was found unreliable or partially fabricated, they would certainly not have used it as one of their sources (Bauckham 126-127).

The Gospel of Luke

Two leading church fathers state that Luke, a companion of the Apostle Paul, wrote the Gospel that bears his name. Irenaeus wrote: "Luke also, the companion of Paul, recorded in a book the Gospel preached by him" (*Against Heresies* 3:1:1 *Ante Nicene Fathers* Vol 1. pg 414). Irenaeus got his information from Polycarp, who got it from the Apostle John himself. Considering this direct chain of transmission, Irenaeus could hardly have been wrong in attributing this Gospel to Luke.

The church father Tertullian also writes concerning the authorship of the Gospel of Luke:

> Of the apostles, therefore, John and Matthew first instill faith into us; whilst of apostolic men, Luke and Mark renew it afterwards. These all start with the same principles of the faith, so far as relates to the one only God the Creator and His Christ, how that He was born of the Virgin, and came to fulfill the law and the prophets (*Against Marcion* 4:2, *Ante Nicene Fathers* Vol. 3. Pg 347 CCEL online library).

Later in the same work Tertulian states:

> The same authority of the apostolic churches will afford evidence to the other Gospels also, which we possess equally through their means, and according to their usage—I mean the Gospels of John and Matthew—whilst that which Mark published may be affirmed to be Peter's whose interpreter Mark was. For even Luke's form of the Gospel men usually ascribe to Paul. And it may well seem that the works which disciples publish belong to their masters (*Against Marcion* 4:5, *Ante Nicene Fathers*, Vol. 3. pg 350).

The Internal Eyewitness Evidence For Luke

Luke opens his Gospel with a quick discussion on his procedure for gathering first hand sources for the writing of his Gospel (Luke 1:1-4). In this passage, the Greek word for "eyewitness" means "first hand observers of the event" (Bauckham 117). As a comparison, two contemporary historians also used this term: Polybius and Josephus. Their works indicate that eyewitness testimony of actual events was only considered accurate historical writing if the eyewitness was present from the beginning to end of the events recounted in the story (Bauckham 119). For example, Josephus himself could claim personal participation in the Jewish War between 66-70 AD (Bauckham 120).

Since Luke was not an eyewitness to the ministry of Jesus, he needed to find several eyewitness sources when writing his Gospel account. As stated before, there is strong evidence that Mark's Gospel was one of his primary sources. If he considered it a reliable reflection of Peter's eyewitness testimony, he must have found agreement between its record and those of other eyewitnesses. So when Luke drew on other sources for writing his Gospel each must have been found reliable as an eyewitness. Among these, studies of the text show that Luke drew on a source shared by the Apostle Matthew (giving its reliability strong support) but not by Mark or John. Thus, Luke drew on independent sources not shared by the other Gospel writers.

Surprisingly, Luke's Gospel appears to draw heavily from the first-hand accounts of women who followed Jesus. Luke's account records more than just the twelve male apostles going out to preach the Good News of the Kingdom (Luke 6:17, 8:1-3, 10:1-20). Luke's Gospel also singles out Joanna and Suzanna (Luke 8:3). How did he know that they had supported Jesus and his disciples out of their own means unless they told him? How did he know that these two women were present, along with the twelve, when Jesus gave his prediction that He would die and rise again in Jerusalem? Luke names these women at the empty tomb (24:10). The angel at the tomb asked these women to remember what Jesus had previously said to them concerning the prediction of his death and resurrection (Luke 24:6, 7; Bauckham 130). Internal textual evidence indicates that Luke most certainly got at least some of the history recorded in his account from these two women (Bauckham 129-131).

Keener on Luke's Prologue

The majority of New Testament scholars agree that Luke's Gospel is attempting to write a history Jesus' life in the ancient Greco-Roman tradition (Keener 87). Several technical Greek words that Luke uses in Luke 1:1-4 indicate to his readers that he is attempting to write an accurate history of Jesus. Setting the story against the backdrop of imperial Rome also indicates that Luke intended to write an accurate, Greco-Roman style, historical account of Jesus' life and ministry (Keener 88).

For Greek and Roman historians, personal investigation of the facts was a prerequisite; writing could not begin until a complete story emerged. Luke, being an educated Greek, most likely followed the example of two other prominent Greek historians: Thucydidides and Polybius. They followed this practice of carefully investigating the facts before writing the account. For this reason, it seems reasonable to believe that Luke followed this method (Keener 89).

Greek and Roman historians made it a practice to become thoroughly familiar with their sources before committing it to writing. In the same way, it is reasonable to assume that Luke used this process with his Gospel account. Luke, as well as Greek and Roman historians, made every effort to include first hand eyewitness testimonies in their histories (Keener 91). Since these eyewitnesses had to have been actual participants in the events to be used as sources, we can once again conclude that Luke searched diligently for reliable, first-hand accounts of the life of Jesus.

External Evidence for the Gospel of John

Irenaeus tells us that he learned from Polycarp that the Apostle John wrote a Gospel (*Against Heresies* 3:1:1 *Ante Nicene Fathers* Vol 1. pg 414). The church father, Tertullian, agreed:

> Of the apostles, therefore, John and Matthew first instill faith into us; whilst of apostolic men, Luke and Mark renew it afterwards. These all start with the same principles of the faith, so far as relates to the one only God the Creator and His Christ, how that He was born of the Virgin, and came to fulfill the law and the prophets (*Against Marcion* 4:2, *Ante Nicene Fathers* Vol. 3. Pg 347 CCEL online library).

> The same authority of the apostolic churches will afford evidence to the other Gospels also, which we possess equally through their means, and according to their usage—I mean the Gospels of John and Matthew—whilst that which Mark published may be affirmed to be Peter's whose interpreter Mark was. For even Luke's form of the Gospel men usually ascribe to Paul. And it may well seem that the works which disciples publish belong to their masters (*Against Marcion* 4:5, *Ante Nicene Fathers*, Vol. 3. pg 350 CCEL online library).

Despite the existence of the Gospel, the main Christian writers of 2nd century did not quote extensively from John's Gospel in the way they did from the synoptic Gospels. Church father Justin mentions John 3:3-5 briefly in his *First Apology*. *The Gnostic Basilides* quoted from John 1:9 in support of a heretical distortion of the faith. The Gnostic, apocryphal Gospels of Thomas and Phillip also use material from John. We can be assured, at least then, that the Gospel existed in the second century.

The church father Irenaeus gives us the most information concerning the Gospel of John in the second century. Irenaeus writes that a Gospel was written by John, ". . . the disciple of the Lord, as the one who leaned against Jesus breast at the last supper." He further claims that John wrote his Gospel while living in Ephesus (*Against Heresies* 3.1.1). Irenaeus did use the Gospel of John on several occasions to refute the rising, second century Gnostic heresy. In other places in his writings, he calls this John, who "is a disciple of the Lord," an Apostle. Based on these statements by Irenaeus, it had been generally accepted throughout church history that John, the Son of Zebedee, wrote the Gospel that bears his name (Blomberg *Historical Reliability of John's Gospel* 24, 25).

It is not until the fourth century, with the writings of Eusebius, that the authorship of the Gospel of John is called into question. Eusebius quotes from Papias about a "John the Elder" who might have written the Gospel instead of John the Apostle.

Internal Evidence for the authorship of the Gospel of John—John of Zebedee

Well respected New Testament scholar B. F. Wescott wrote about five clues from the text that gives us an idea who the author was:

1. The Author is Jewish

Whoever wrote the Gospel of John was very familiar with Jewish temple customs prior to the destruction of Jerusalem by the Roman army in 70 AD. This suggests that the author was an adult before 70 AD and a Jew living near enough to the temple at Jerusalem to visit it regularly. The fact that the author was also aware of both the political Jewish sects around Jerusalem and the Jewish rituals of

Jesus' day further supports this claim. Evidence from the Dead Sea Scrolls confirms much of the Jewish culture and ritual during the time in which Jesus lived. Thus, the evidence supports a Jewish author living within reach of Jerusalem in the mid to early first century. On the other hand, it does not support an author steeped in Greek traditions or one coming to adulthood in the late first century (Blomberg, *Historical Reliability of John's Gospel* 27).

2. The Author Lived in Palestine

The number of geographical details and topographical references found in the Gospel of John clearly point to an author who lived in or had lived in Palestine. Some examples of these details include: the discovery of the Pools of Bethseda (John 5:2) and Siloam (9:11), Jacob's well at Sychar (4:5-6) which still remains to this day, and the discovery of Pontius Pilate's stone pavement where he pronounced the final sentence on Jesus (19:13). These places, some of which were lost for centuries, show an author familiar with Jerusalem before its destruction.

The Gospel includes many Aramaic terms which only Jews living in first century Palestine would have both known and understood. It also shows an understanding of the nuances of first century Jewish legal code; this is the same legal code about which Jesus and the religious leaders regularly argued. In the same vein, the author was at least passively familiar with the theology of the Samaritans as well (Blomberg, *Historical Reliability of John's Gospel* 27). This everyday understanding of both the theology and laws of first century Judaism and Samaritan theology indicates an author who spent a lot of time in the vicinity of both Samaria and Jerusalem.

3. The Author Was an Eyewitness

This is the most difficult of Westcott's five points for authorship. We have no confirmatory evidence to support certain aspects of the Gospel of John. For example, the speeches that Jesus gave in this Gospel sound very different from those in the synoptic Gospels. For this reason, the question of the eyewitness testimony behind John's Gospel remains open in the minds of some.

4. The Author Was One of the Twelve Apostles

Wescott further noted that the Gospel of John itself claims to be written by one of the twelve Apostles. The *"Beloved Disciple"* is said to have written it (21:24). This *"Beloved Disciple"* appears at: The Last Supper (13:23-25), the crucifixion (19:26-27, 34-35), the empty tomb (20:2-5, 8), and fishing with other Apostles when the 153 fish were caught (21:1-7).

5. Only "John the Baptist" is Called "John" in the Gospel

The synoptic Gospels refer to John the Baptist as simply, John the Baptist. If the Gospel of John was not written by John, the Son of Zebedee, then a second possibility is that it is written by one of the two anonymous disciples mentioned in John 21:2.

This leaves us with three main possibilities as to who wrote the Gospel of John. These three possibilities are: John the son of Zebedee, one of the two anonymous disciples mentioned in John 21:2 or the mysterious John the elder (Blomberg, *Historical Reliability of John's Gospel* 40). It must be noted that whichever of these three possibilities one accepts, the account was written at a time when eyewitnesses could still be questioned and what they knew about the ministry of Jesus recorded (Blomberg, *Historical Reliability of John's Gospel* 40-41).

Third objection by Ehrman: The Gospels were written anonymously.

Dr. Ehrman insists that since none of the four Gospels record the author's identity in the actual text, that we can't know the authors for certain. As far as he is concerned, all four Gospel writers wrote anonymously. Of course, this is simply not the case for two reasons: the early church would have rejected an non-attributable text and early Roman writing techniques generally placed the author's name at the end of the text or apart from the text itself on a tag.

Tertullian, the great church Father, defended the Gospels against the heretic, Marcion. Marcion had created his own canon of scripture that differed from the accepted one. He included only the books that agreed with his own theology. This led Marcion to reject of the Gospels of Matthew, Mark and John. He kept the Gospel of Luke, even publishing his own version, but only after cutting out its Jewish elements. Tertullian takes Marcion to task for doing this. Tertullian writes:

> Marcion, on the other hand, you must know, ascribes no author to his Gospel, as if it could not be allowed him to affix a title to that from which it was no crime (in his eyes) to subvert the very body. And here I might now make a stand, and contend that a work ought not to be recognized, which holds not its head erect, which exhibits no consistency, which gives no promise of credibility from the fullness of its title and the just profession of its author (*Against Marcion* 4:2, *Ante Nicene Fathers*, Vol. 3 pg 347 CCEL online library).

Clearly, the churches of his day, being founded by the Apostles, would never accept the obviously fraudulent "cut and paste" Gospel created by Marcion. Marcion didn't even bother give his creation a title. Would other gospels be accepted if they were, in fact, on the same level, lacking a title or clear authorship?

In his book, Dr. Ehrman seems to completely ignore ancient publishing practices in his assessment of the Gospels' authorship. Ancient works were identified in the Roman world with attached titles or ending credits. If I gave you a history book today, could you tell who the author was if you only read the text and didn't see the cover or the cover pages?

In his online article, "Evidence for First Century Publishing", New Testament literature expert Dr. Ron Jones states:

> In the first century A.D. books were written and published with the title and name of the author placed at the end of the papyrus roll on which they were written or copied and on a tag attached to the outside of the papyrus roll called in Greek, a "sillybos" and in Latin a "titulus." This was the normal custom of identifying the author of a book in the Roman world in the first century. Sometimes it would also be placed in the front of the papyrus roll. The author did not normally identify himself in the text itself, but like today's title page, his name was placed along with a title in a location on the document but outside the main text.

Jones then gives some scholarly quotes to show that this was indeed the practice in the First Century:

> "Romans stored rolls either vertically in containers like umbrella stands or horizontally on shelves. The identification of the contents of the rolls was made easier by attaching a protruding tag (sillybos) to the outside top edge of the papyrus to identify the contents, just like the spine of a modern book. Many such tags are extant, often detached from scrolls now

> lost…The last sheet of the roll sometimes contained an end-title, so that, if some lazy reader neglected to rewind the book, both beginning and end of a roll could identify title and author (David Sider, The Library of the Villa Dei Papyri at Herculaneum, Los Angeles, Getty Publications 2005, p.28-30).

Dr. Ron Jones also gives a very important quote by Kathryn J. Gutzwiller on how the authorship of ancient documents was identified.

> "A tag with author's name and the title, called a syllybos, was glued to the back of the rolled papyrus, for ease of finding a text in storage bins or on shelves. This information was also written at the end of the text, the most interior and protected position on the book roll, and sometimes also at the beginning on the front or back of the first papyrus sheet. The beginning of the roll was the place where damage was most likely to occur, so that information about author and title was often lost, as has happened in the new papyrus collection of epigrams attributed to Posiddipus. (Kathryn J. Gutzwiller, *A Guide to Hellenistic literature*, Wiley-Blackwell, 2007, p.44).

Thus, to sum up, when a Roman style document was completed in the first century, the author would identify himself in two places. The first place was on a tag attached to the outside of the document. The second place where the author identified himself was at the end of the document. Dr. Ehrman mentions none of this in his discussion of the Four Gospels.

Just because we don't have extant first century scrolls, complete with tags and title pages identifying the authors, doesn't mean these documents never existed. We have good reasons to believe that the church fathers, writing in the second and third centuries, did in fact have access to these original documents (or at least copies of the originals). Thus, the traditionally attributed authors are most likely the actual authors.

Chapter Twelve
Bart Ehrman and the Deity of Jesus Christ

By Kyle Larson

Bart Ehrman believes that Jesus himself never claimed to be God, but that his early followers put words into his mouth to make it appear that Jesus claimed to be God. Before delving into this objection, we must first take a very brief look at what 20th century scholarship has said concerning what Jesus believed about himself, as well as what the earliest church believed about Jesus.

It is important to discuss 20th century scholarship on Chistology, because, when one reads some of Ehrman's statements on the subject, one might get the idea that all scholars hold to his understanding of the claims of Jesus. Ehrman would try to paint the picture that only evangelicals believe that Jesus claimed to be God; this is clearly not the case.

Twentieth Century Discussions on the Identity of Jesus of Nazareth

As one surveys the scholarly trends in Christology over the last 100 years, five views on the claims of Christ appear:

1) *Non-scholarly conservatism*—this was the view of the Christian Church for the first 1700 years of her history. This is a very direct approach to Christology by simply saying "If Jesus said he was God via the pages of the Gospels, end of conversation." Christians had believed during those 1700 years that the Gospel writers wrote down, in a strict word for word way, what Jesus actually said. Yet, scholars argued that if this is the case that the Gospel writers wrote exactly what Jesus said about himself, why then are there even minor

differences at all, even among the synoptic Gospels, not to mention what Jesus says about himself in the Gospel of John (Brown 7, 8).

2) *Non-scholarly liberalism*—this second view among scholars simply states that Jesus' earliest followers were simply mistaken in thinking that Jesus was God. Jesus came simply as a teacher of ethics, and his followers turned him into God. A vast number of scholars hold this view (Brown 10).

3) *Scholarly Liberalism*—in a very similar way to non-scholarly liberalism, this perspective states that Jesus' earliest followers made a simple mistake in saying that Jesus was God. Jesus never said He was God, but his overly enthusiastic followers turned him into God in the flesh anyway. Different groups of early Christians had different levels of elevation for Jesus. No one form of understanding who Jesus was dominated the Church. Christians believed that only through making Jesus more and more into God could the memory of Jesus remain throughout the ages (Brown 11-13). Bultmann was an example of a scholar who believed there was a gradual rise among of early Christians which turned Jesus from an ethical teacher into God. Jesus did not believe or teach that He was God, but early Christians said people should believe it anyway in order to give them a greater understanding of what God was doing in the world (Brown 13, 14).

4) *Scholarly Moderate Conservatism*—a group of non evangelical scholars exists who still see that Jesus claimed more for Himself than just being a good ethical teacher. This group of scholars would be divided on whether Jesus made explicit or implicit claims concerning his identity. Jesus gave hints during his lifetime as to who he was, and the earliest Christians filled in the lines explicitly on what Jesus had said implicitly during his lifetime. Scholars such as Jeremias, Dodd and Fuller are examples of scholars in this non evangelical scholarly moderate conservatism.

This brief survey of 20th century scholarly discussions on Christology is important because Ehrman portrays evangelicals, who are supposedly ignorant because they believe that Jesus claimed to be God, in a very negative light. Ehrman believes the "real scholars" are those who say with certainty, based on their extensive research, that Jesus never claimed to be God.

Ehrman says that nowhere in the Gospels of Matthew, Mark, or Luke does Jesus ever claim to be God (Ehrman, *Jesus Interrupted* 141, 246). According to Ehrman, it is only in the Gospel of John, where Jesus is said to have claimed He to be God.

When the Gospel writers wrote their Gospels, they used earlier oral and written sources about Jesus. Bart Ehrman admits that the Gospel writers used earlier sources of information about Jesus, and that they included these earlier sources when they wrote their Gospels. Ehrman explains that he believes the Gospel of Mark was the earliest of the four Gospels to be written. He further explains that the authors of both Matthew and Luke used Mark as a source when they wrote their Gospels. Matthew and Luke also shared another source known as the "Q" document. This now lost document was probably a very early listing of the sayings of Jesus (if it existed at all). This "Q" document is not totally lost because it has been included in the Gospels of Matthew and Luke. This shared material might be found in different places throughout Matthew and Luke, with different chapter and verse numberings, but the shared material in Matthew and Luke is still there for all to see. Ehrman also states Matthew adds additional material in his Gospel that is found only in his Gospel. This information used only by Matthew is known as "M" document. The Gospel of Luke includes material that is found only in Luke. This is known as "L" material (Ehrman, *Jesus Interrupted* 152-153). Though many New Testament scholars believe in the existence of these earlier sources, the theory itself is highly speculative and very subjective. Still, this type of thinking is very descriptive of much of current New Testament scholarship.

Ehrman gives a listing of historical rules that historians use to determine what is historical and what is not historical (Ehrman, *Jesus Interrupted* 152-155). What Ehrman does not seem to realize is that, when one uses these "historical rules" and applies them to the claims of Jesus in the first three Gospels, the results shows that Jesus had a very "high view" of Himself. One does not have to read the Gospel of John in order to show that Jesus claimed to be God. There are many examples in the synoptic Gospels to show Jesus' high view of himself.

A Summary of Christology in the Synoptic Gospels

1) *Jesus proclaimed the Kingdom of God and believed that he was the central figure to bring in that Kingdom.* The announcing of the Kingdom of God was Jesus' central message. Jesus believed that He was the key pivotal person to bring in God's kingdom to the world.

The many parables of Jesus describe the nature of the Kingdom of God that He believed He was bringing in during his ministry. One of the parables of Jesus concerns a man who found buried treasure in his field and sold everything he had in order to keep the treasure (Mark 13:44-36). Jesus was teaching, in this parable, that the Kingdom of God is as valuable as the hidden treasure in the field.

In another parable, Jesus spoke of Himself as the Bridegroom (Mark 2:19). The Bridegroom in an ancient Middle Eastern wedding was the central person in the marriage celebration. Thus, Jesus was putting himself in the center of everything that goes on. Jesus called people to share in the blessings of the Kingdom. Some will accept this invitation to join the kingdom and some will not. Jesus will not allow anyone to sit on the fence concerning this invitation to be a part of the Kingdom of God. Jesus does warn that those who refuse his invitation of the Kingdom will be cast into the outer darkness (Matthew 22:1-14, Luke 16:16-24; Brown 67-68).

Jesus gives two other parables concerning a person's possible response to His preaching of the Kingdom of God. In the parable of the workers in the vineyard, Jesus indicates that no matter when a person realizes the validity of Jesus' preaching of the Kingdom, all will be equally welcomed (Matthew 20:1-16). Humility is a key requirement to entering God's Kingdom. Pride shuts the door from entering into the Kingdom of God (Luke 18:9-14).

In all these parables, Jesus preaching of the Kingdom and His central role for letting people into the Kingdom is the key point. The question must be honestly asked, who does Jesus think He is to paint Himself as the central figure of God's Kingdom (Brown 67-68)?

2) *Jesus believed that His healings and exorcisms were two of the primary signs that the Kingdom of God had arrived.* Jesus saw His miracles as the sign that God's Kingdom arrived on earth. Jesus declared that His exorcisms of demons is a key sign that the Kingdom of God had arrived on earth (Matthew 12:28, Luke 11:20). Jesus saw his miracles in these two cities as the "in breaking" of God's kingdom into the lives of citizens of the village. The villagers saw them merely as nice little acts of kindness and nothing more. These miracles were an opportunity for the people of Chorazin to repent and turn to God, but they declined. Thus, Jesus pronounced judgment on these two towns. How one responds to Jesus determines one's eternal destiny before God. Jesus saw Himself as the final and complete revelation of God (Witherington 167).

3) *Jesus believed he had the right to lay down the conditions for a person to enter the Kingdom of God, and also the right to warn people of the consequences of rejecting Him.* Jesus believed that entrance into the Kingdom of God required that a person put himself or herself under the personal discipleship of Jesus (Matthew 7:21, Luke12:32, Luke 22:29; 23:4 2). Jesus believed that people's eternal destiny depended on how they respond to Jesus and his ministry (Matthew 11:21, Luke 10:13; Witherington 166-167).

4) *Jesus believed that his words were superior to the Law of Moses.* He believed he had the right to give the final ultimate interpretation of the Law of Moses (Witherington 68, Marshall 50). There are many ways in which Jesus asserted his belief in his own authority above the Law of Moses. In the Sermon on the Mount (Matthew chapters 5 to 7), Jesus quotes from the Law of Moses, and then gives his own authoritative commentary on the Law of Moses.

Jesus believed that he had the right to make authoritative statements on the Jewish Sabbath. Jesus was in constant turmoil with the Pharisees who were sticklers for the Law of Moses. Jesus claimed that He was Lord even over the Sabbath (Mark 2:23-28; Witherington 66-67). How can this be when God Himself instituted the Sabbath? Jehovah alone is Lord of the Sabbath. Yet, Jesus believed He had the authority and freedom from God to heal people on the Sabbath regardless of how the Pharisees interpreted the oral or written law. Jesus saw Himself as standing above the Law of Moses (Witherington 69). This alone would constitute blasphemy in the eyes of the Jewish leadership with the result of the death penalty against Jesus.

5) *Jesus' Use of "Amen," Jesus' solemn preface before giving authoritative teaching.* When Jesus would give a teaching, He would preface it with the word "Amen," which is translated "But I say to you" (Marshall 45). Jesus believed that what He said on a manner was the final word on the subject. By giving this solemn preface before giving his own teaching, it is evidence that Jesus is speaking on his own authority. In the Sermon on the Mount, Jesus quotes the Torah, and then proceeds to give His own supreme interpretation on the Law of Moses. He was not speaking only on the Father's authority, but His own authority (Witherington 188). Jesus was claiming that His words over rode the words of the Old Testament. Jesus believed that His words were greater than the words of the OT Prophets (Witherington 188). He acted and spoke as if he believed his interpretation of the Old Testament was infallible.

6) *"Abba" used by Jesus to express his unique relationship with God.* Jesus used the word "Abba" in describing his relationship with God. The Aramaic form of the term "Abba" is the most intimate term a son can use in addressing his Father. Jesus used this term in addressing God. No Jewish man would ever dare to address God in such intimate terms. Most scholars believe that Jesus used this term to describe his deep intimate relationship with God (Marshall 46; Brown 86, 87). Jeremias did a extensive scholarly work on this term "Abba," as used by Jesus (Witherington 216). Jesus' use of the term "Abba" is a claim that He had a special exclusive relationship with God that no one else had. Jesus claimed that a person could only address God as "Abba" by being one of Jesus' followers.

While Jesus called God "My Abba" and told the disciples they could call God "Our Abba," He never put himself in the same company as the disciples by corporately addressing God as "Our Abba." Jesus claimed to have exclusive knowledge of God that no one else had (Matthew 11:27; Luke 10:22; Witherington 220, 221).

7) *Jesus and the Twelve Apostles.* In Matthew 19:28, Jesus promised that the 12 apostles would sit on twelve thrones and judge the 12 tribes of Israel. The formation of the 12 disciples was the formation of the 12 new tribes of Israel, which would form the church. Jesus would rule over the twelve disciples (Witherington 128-129). Since God was the founder of the "old Israel," Jesus is implying equality with God by claiming to be the founder of the "new Israel."

8) *Jesus claimed to have the authority to forgive sin.* Jesus believed He had the authority to forgive sin (Mark 2:1-10; Luke 7:48; Marshall 50). Jesus ate with sinners and thus was offering them forgiveness (Matthew 11:19; Luke 7:36-50). Yet, only God has the authority to offer forgiveness to a sinner. Thus, Jesus was acting in the place of God (Witherington 73; Marshall 50).

9) *Jesus made the demand for people to follow him.* Sacred religious duties such as burying the dead is secondary to a person's

decision to follow Jesus (Luke 9:59-60; Brown 68). A person's loyalty to Jesus must take precedence over one's loyalty to his family (Luke 14:26: Matthew 10:37; Brown 68). Jesus pronounced judgment on those towns where he preached but rejected his message (Matthew 11:20-24).

Based on these nine examples found in the Synoptic Gospels, it is difficult to see how Bart Ehrman can maintain that Jesus never claimed to be God. Ehrman is simply wrong to maintain that's it is only the Gospel of John that gives a "high Christology" to Jesus.

The Earliest Jewish Christians' View of Jesus

The next major issue that must be addressed is: what did the earliest Jewish Christians believe about Jesus? Ehrman states that the earliest Jewish Christians believed Jesus was simply a man who was adopted as Son by God at the resurrection. The Jewish Christians accepted that Jesus was the Messiah, but still only a man, and not God incarnate (Ehrman, *Jesus Interrupted* 195, 247).

The Church began in Jerusalem about 33 AD. The four Gospels were written between 60 AD and 100 AD (if we accept the later dates). This would be between 30 to 70 years after the life and death of Jesus. Do we have any information about Jesus between 33 AD when Jesus died and 60 AD, when many critics believe the Gospel of Mark was written?

Paul was the earliest window into the earliest church in Jerusalem. He wrote his letters in the 50's AD after about a decade of missionary work among the Gentiles in the 40's AD. Paul became a Christian about 34 to 36 AD as a result of an appearance of the risen Jesus on the road to Damascus. This was less than 3 years after Jesus died. Paul became very familiar with the Church in Judea before he went on his missionary journeys. He mentions the Judean Church in Galatians 1:22-23, with the passing reference to "the churches of

Judea in Christ." In fact, throughout Galatians 1 and 2, Paul talks about his conversion and his ongoing respect for the Church in Jerusalem. He lists major leaders in Jerusalem, including Peter, James, and John as the pillars of the church. Paul recognized the special role of the Church in Jerusalem (I Corinthians 15:7; Galatians 1:19).

Paul took up a special collection for the Church in Jerusalem among his Gentile congregations (Galatians 2:20; 1 Corinthians 16:1-4; 2 Corinthians 8-9; Romans 15:25-27). He mentions again the Church in Judea in I Thessalonians 2:14-15 (Hurtado, *Lord Jesus Christ* 157-159).

The historical evidence shows that both Paul and the earliest Church in Jerusalem agreed that Jesus was God in human flesh. There are several areas of agreement that existed between Paul and the Jerusalem Church concerning Jesus. Both Paul and the earliest Jewish Christians believed that Jesus is "the Christ. The term "Christ" is Greek for the Jewish term "Messiah" which is specifically what the earliest Jewish Christians were calling Jesus. Paul's Gentile converts also called Jesus "the Christ." Both Jewish and Gentile Christians were united in their belief that Jesus is "the Christ" (Hurtado, *Lord Jesus Christ* 98-100).

The second main title of Jesus that both Paul and the earliest Jewish Christians attributed to Jesus is "the Son of God" (Hurtado, *Lord Jesus Christ* 102). When Paul called Jesus "the Son of God" he meant it in a Jewish sense, and not in a pagan sense. The term "Son" that the early Christians used for Jesus was grounded in the previously written Jewish scriptures.

Both Paul and the earliest Jewish Christians believed that Jesus is "Lord." The Greek word for "Lord" (Kyrios) has linguistic equivalents in both Hebrew and Aramaic and both refer to God as "Lord." The term "Kyrios" was used to refer to Jehovah God of the Old Testament by Greek speaking Jews (Hurtado, *Lord Jesus Christ*

109). Paul uses the term "Lord" to refer to Jesus in the same way that Orthodox Jews would call God, "Jehovah" (Hurtado Lord Jesus Christ 108-110).

Paul uses the term "Lord" 200 times in 7 of his epistles. Out of the 200 usages of the term "Lord," 180 of them refer to Jesus. Yet Paul also refers to God the Father as "Lord." For Paul, the term "Lord" can also mean the name "Yahweh." Paul always meant "God" when he used the term "Lord" (Romans 4:8; Psalm 32:1-2; I Corinthians 3:20; Psalm 94:11).

Paul used direct Old Testament passages where "Lord" refers to God, and applies them to Jesus (Romans 10:13; Joel 2:32; I Corinthians1:31; Jeremiah 9:23-24). Additional uses of the term "Lord" that Paul applied to Jesus are as follows: "Jesus Christ our Lord" (Romans 1:4, 5:21), "Our Lord Jesus Christ" (Romans 5:1, 11; 16:20; Gal 6:18), and "The Lord Jesus" (Romans 14:14; 1 Corinthians 11:23; 1:26; Psalms 24:1). Paul also uses Old Testament allusions as a way of referring to Jesus (1 Corinthians 10:21 and Malachi 1:7, 12; 1 Corinthians10:22 and Deuteronomy 32:21; 2 Corinthians 3:16 and Exodus 34:34; Philippians2:10-11 and Isaiah 45:23-25; see Hurtado, *Lord Jesus Christ* 112).

Paul specifically says that his Christian beliefs are the same beliefs shared with the earliest Jewish Christian community in Jerusalem (1 Corinthians 15:11). Paul and the earliest Jewish Christians shared the same worship practices. Both addressed prayer to Jesus (Hurtado, *Lord Jesus Christ* 138-139). Several studies have indicated that both Paul and the Jewish Christians addressed "The Father "in prayer. This thanksgiving to the Father is usually found at the beginning of Paul's letters (1 Thessalonians 1:2-3; 1 Corinthians 1:4, 5; Romans 1:8; Hurtado, *Lord Jesus Christ* 139).

Both Paul and his Gentile congregations united with the earliest Jewish Christians in praying in the name of Jesus. Paul unites with Jewish Christians on the importance of baptism (1 Corinthians 6:11;

Hurtado, *Lord Jesus Christ* 143). Paul and the earliest Christians also believed in the importance of observing the Lord's Supper (1 Corinthians 11:23-27; Hurtado, *Lord Jesus Christ* 144-145).

The Book of Acts Declares that Jesus is God

Ehrman says that nowhere in the book of Acts is Jesus called God. The earliest Jewish Church in Jerusalem never thought that Jesus was God. He was just a man adopted by God at his Resurrection (Ehrman, *Jesus Interrupted* 246, 247). When going through the book of Acts, one sees that the Apostles used various titles for Jesus. When speaking to their fellow Jews, the Apostles always referred to Jesus as "The Christ," meaning Messiah (Acts 2:36; 5:42; 9:22; 18:5). This was only natural that the Apostles would want their fellow Jews to see that Jesus is the Messiah because the eventual coming of the Messiah (whether Jesus or someone else) was a long standing hope and promise that God gave to the people of Israel. The Apostles wanted to show specifically that the Jewish Messiah had actually come in the person of Jesus (Longnecker 135). Yet, the Apostles went beyond even the title of "Messiah" in describing who Jesus was. Jesus is called "LORD" many times throughout the book of Acts. In several places in Acts, the Apostles will take an Old Testament passage that talks about "The Lord," meaning Yaweh or Jehovah, and apply it to Jesus the Son. By doing this, the Apostles were stating that Jesus is God in a similar way that the Father is "God." Jesus was seen as having an equal status with the Father since both share the attributes of "God."

We will now examine some examples of this in the book of Acts. In Acts 2:17-21, Peter alludes to Joel 2:28-32. Throughout Peter's first sermon in Acts 2, he connects the idea of Jesus being "Lord" with references in the Old Testament of Jehovah being "LORD." In several instances in Peter's sermon, he connects Jesus to many several passages in the Old Testament. For instance, Peter, when speaking of Jesus' resurrection, quotes from Psalms 16. In Psalms 16, David says that God will not abandon His "Holy One" to the grave. All of earliest Christianity, Pauline and non-Pauline, were united in calling Jesus "Lord." This was especially true of Aramaic and Greek speaking Jewish Christians in Jerusalem (Hurtado *Lord Jesus Christ* 180-182).

In conclusion, it can be shown from the epistles of Paul and the book of Acts that both Paul and the earliest Jewish Christians believed that Jesus was much more than just a man. Contrary to the wild speculation of Bart Ehrman, the early church believed that Jesus was God in human flesh.

Chapter Thirteen
Responding to the Bauer-Ehrman Thesis

By Kyle Larson

Ehrman, for the sake of political correctness, advances a theory that was first proposed by Walter Bauer in the early 20th century. In its simplest form, it states that during the first century, there were many forms of Christianity (Ehrman, *Jesus Interrupted* 215). According to Ehrman, the first century included many types of esoteric forms as well as "Jewish" forms of Christianity (*Jesus Interrupted* 195). All forms of Christianity claimed the Apostles had originally endorsed their particular brand of Christianity. Ehrman says that each of these early forms of Christianity had their own unique understanding of who Jesus was. No two forms of Christianity could agree on the identity of Jesus (*Jesus Interrupted* 252-253). Thus, Ehrman believes that the form of Christianity that we know today was simply one of these many forms of Christianity that were trying to promote their own version of the faith. At this same time, other versions of the Christian faith were also trying to promote their own version of Christianity.

Ehrman believes that Jesus and His Apostles were never specific on what constituted correct doctrine for a Christian (*Lost Christianities* 168). He says that the Christian beliefs that we have today came long after Jesus and the Apostles (170). Ehrman states that there was no right or wrong form of Christianity in the first century. Two of the many early forms of Christianity, according to Ehrman, were the Judaizers and the Gnostics. Another form of Christianity was advocated by the Apostle Paul; yet, according to Ehrman, none of these forms was more or less authentic than any other form of Christianity (177). Ehrman believes the Judaizers, who later continued under the name of "Ebionites," were the original form of Apostolic Christianity, and that Paul had misrepresented the teachings of Jesus and his original twelve Apostles (*Jesus Interrupted* 192, 258; *Lost Christianities* 182-184).

The Gnostics also claimed that they were descended spiritually from the apostles. They said that the original form of the Gospel had nothing to do with Jesus dying as a substitute for humanity's sin. Jesus never really died—it was only the "outer shell" of Jesus that appeared to have died, but the true inner "spiritual Jesus" could not die (*Jesus Interrupted* 195).

The form of Christianity that we know today is called by Ehrman "proto orthodox" (*Jesus Interrupted* 197). Ehrman says the "proto orthodox" developed creeds long after Jesus and the Apostles lived. Ehrman states that these creeds do not express what Jesus and the Apostles originally taught (215). Many other scholars, though in the minority, agree with Ehrman and Bauer's theory that there were many legitimate forms of Christianity, and no one form was more right or wrong over any other form (Kostenberger 28-29).

REFUTATION OF THE BAUER-EHRMAN THESIS

There were several initial scholarly reactions to Bauer's work. There are four main objections that kept coming up in early reviews of Bauer's thesis. First, Bauer made many of his conclusions based either on insufficient evidence that was available at the time or no evidence at all. Second, Bauer never took seriously the evidence for the New Testament being descriptive of the earliest Christianity and, instead, he thought looking at second century evidence was enough to make an accurate determination of the state of Christianity in the first century. Third, he made too many sweeping and overly simplistic conclusions about the state of the first century church. Last, Bauer ignored the possibility that there were standard doctrines in the first century church (Kostenberger 33).

Jesus specifically appointed twelve Apostles who could be trusted with carrying on his work after he had gone back to heaven (Matthew 10:1-4; Mark 3:13-15; 6:7-13; Luke 6:13; 9:1-2). Jesus commanded these men to preach the Gospel to the whole world (Matthew 28:18-20; Luke 24:45-48; John 20:21-22; Acts 1:8). The earliest Jewish Christians devoted themselves to the teaching of the Apostles (Acts 2:42). The early church strove to be in strict doctrinal continuity with Jesus himself (Kostenberger 75). Scholarship has shown that several oral confessions circulated in the early church before any of the books of the New Testament were written. Several of these creeds speak of Jesus as "Lord" in the same Jewish sense that non-Christian Jews spoke of Yahweh as being "Lord" (Philippians 2:6-11; Colossians 1:15-20; Romans 10:9). These creeds also give other lofty titles to Jesus (Habermas, *Historical Jesus* 168).

Even within the first century Apostle-led Church, the emergence of a collection of apostolic sacred writings was starting to be formed (2 Peter 3:16; 1 Timothy 5:18; Luke 10:7; Kostenberger, 127- 130). Public reading, in the churches, of the New Testament took place before the end of the first century (Colossians 4:16; 1 Thessalonians 5:27; 2 Corinthians 10:9). The public reading of the New Testament in the early Christian congregations is similar to the public reading of the Old Testament in the Jewish synagogues before Christ (Kostenberger, 133).

The Canon and the Apostolic Fathers

Clement was appointed bishop of Rome by Peter (*Against Heresies* 3.3.3.). Clement wrote a letter to the church in Corinth to encourage them in the faith. In this letter, he commends Paul's earlier letter to them (1 Clement 47:1-377). Clement recognizes the apostolic authority of Paul and urges the Christians in Corinth to do the same.

Clement also recognizes the Pauline authorship of Romans, Galatians, Philippians and Ephesians (Kostenberger, 136).

Polycarp was the Bishop of Smyrna. Polycarp's disciple Irenaeus stated that Polycarp knew the Apostle John and other eyewitnesses of Jesus. Polycarp quotes more from the New Testament than he does from the Old Testament. He also recognized the apostolic authority of Paul and mentions several of Paul's letters as found currently in the New Testament. Polycarp also quotes from the four canonical Gospels (Kostenberger, 143).

Ignatius was the Bishop of Antioch. He also recognized the apostolic authority of Paul in his letter to the Ephesian church (Ignatius, *Letter to the Ephesians* 12:2; Kostenberger 141). Ignatius acknowledged the supreme authority of the writings of the Apostles. The writings of the Apostles were the final court of appeal in doctrinal and practical matters for the early church (Kostenberger, 141). Ignatius also stated that the Apostles handed down "decrees" for the whole church to follow. These Apostles included Paul, Peter, James, John and the other Apostles. Ignatius also cited many times from the four Gospels (141).

A Brief History of the Nazarenes and the Ebionites

It is at this point that one must carefully follow Ehrman's line of thinking. He gives hints in his writings, especially in his book, *Jesus Interrupted,* that the Jewish "Christian" group, known as the Ebionites, were the rightful spiritual heirs of the Jerusalem church as described in the book of Acts. Ehrman believes that both the first century Jerusalem church in Acts and the later Ebionite group were one and the same, and that they were united in their belief that Jesus was not God, but only a human messenger who spoke on God's behalf. Ehrman believes that Jesus never claimed to be God; thus, the earliest church never claimed that Jesus was God.

An examination of both what Jesus taught concerning Himself and what the earliest church in Acts believed about Jesus has already been shown to indicate that Jesus claimed to be God and the earliest church followed Jesus' teachings and also taught that Jesus is God. Further research shows Ehrman's overly simplistic picture of first and second century Jewish Christianity. The first thing that must be kept in mind is that one of the earliest names of the Jewish followers of Jesus was the "Nazarenes" (Acts 24:5; Pritz 14, 15). They were called this because Jesus grew up in Nazareth, so His later followers were called "Nazarenes." Beginning in 60 AD, when Gentile Christianity started to spread rapidly throughout the Mediterranean world and into Europe until the 470's AD, the Nazarenes were known by several Gentile Church Fathers.

Irenaeus stated that there existed a group of Jewish Christians who claimed to go back to the Apostles but who considered Jesus to be a mere man who was simply chosen by God for a special mission. These are Ehrman's Ebionites (*Against Heresies* 1,26, 2). Eusebius, the church historian, mentions two specific heretical Jewish Christian groups who denied the Deity of Jesus and insisted on keeping the Law of Moses in order to be saved. One type of "Jewish Christian" view was that Jesus was merely a good and righteous man who obtained His righteousness by observing the Jewish Law. This same group said that we need to do the same thing and strive to keep the Jewish Law in order to be saved. According to this heretical group, faith in Jesus was not enough for a person to be saved. They also denied the virgin birth of Christ (Eusebius *Church History*, 3,27:2; Pritz 23-24).

The other heretical Jewish Christian group accepted the virgin birth but denied that Jesus was God in the flesh, said that the keeping of the Law of Moses was necessary for salvation, and rejected Paul as an apostate from Judaism. They had their own "Gospel of the Hebrews." They kept Sunday as well as Saturday observances (Eusebius *Church History,* 3,27:3-6). Thus, there were at least two heretical Jewish-Christian groups mentioned by Eusebius that did not stem from the original Jerusalem Church under the leadership of the Apostles. Eusebius and Ehrman have a clear disagreement on the apostolic roots of either of these forms of Jewish Christianity.

Justin Martyr gives us some information concerning the Nazarenes. In his *Dialogue with Trypho,* Justin states that a Jew can be saved by believing that Jesus is the Messiah. A Jewish Christian may continue to follow the Law as an observant Jew, provided that he does not insist that Gentile Christians must keep the Jewish Law in order to be saved (*Dialogue with Trypho* 47; Pritz 19). Justin seems to indicate that this group of Jewish Christians stemmed from the original Jerusalem Church. This is what was decided by the Jerusalem church in Acts 15 at the famous Jerusalem Council. Gentile Christians were not required to keep the Jewish Law in order to be saved.

Justin also stated that Jewish Christians who obey the Law of Moses, yet put their faith in Jesus for salvation, deserve the continued fellowship of Gentile Christians. Faith in Jesus is the key for salvation, not the observing of the Law (*Dialogue* 47; Pritz 20). Justin also mentioned Jews who keep the Law of Moses and see Jesus as the Christ, but not as God incarnate, do not stem from the original Apostolic Church in Jerusalem. Again, these are Ehrman's Ebionites of the second century *(Dialogue with Trypho* 48). Thus, as far as Justin is concerned, a Jewish Christian group can only be a legitimate heir of the apostolic heritage if it agrees with the Apostles in proclaiming Jesus as God. Any group that sees Jesus as only a man, a prophet, or the Messiah, but rejects Jesus' deity, does not have a legitimate claim to apostolic origin.

As the Gentile Christian Church expanded throughout the Mediterranean area, all forms of Jewish Christianity were rejected and despised. This included the Nazarenes, the one Jewish Christian group that can be shown to have come from the Apostles and who agreed with the Gentile Church in proclaiming Jesus as God incarnate.

The Church Father Epiphanus declared a "curse" on the Nazarenes simply because they chose to continue in their Jewish tradition in following the Law of Moses, even though Christologically, they were totally orthodox (Panarion 29, 9:1; Pritz, 34). Thus, the Gentile Church painted all Jewish-Christian groups with the same theological brush instead of taking each Jewish Christian group on a case by case basis based on their view of Jesus.

Ehrman has not made the careful distinctions among the various Jewish Christian groups of the second century. Thus, he uses the Bauer thesis to support his view that there was no standard orthodoxy in the first century church. But, he has failed to make his case. Ehrman's inaccuracies and over-simplifications destroy his case against orthodox Christianity.

Bibliography for Chapter Thirteen:

Kostenberger, Andreas J. and Michael J Kruger. *The Heresy of Orthodoxy: How Contemporary Culture's Fascination with Diversity Has Reshaped Our Understanding of Early Christianity.* Wheaton, Illinois: Crossway Books, 2010.

Pritz, Ray. *Nazarene Christianity.* (All Pritz citations comes from the online article "The Mysterious Relationship of The Early Nazarene and Rabbinic Judaism" by William F. Dankenbring; experientialism.freewebspace.com/dankenbring.htm.)

The Ante Nicene Fathers: Translations of the writings of the Fathers down to A.D 325, A. Roberts, J. Donaldson and A.C. Coxe Oak Habor, Ore Logos Research Systems 1997.

Chapter Fourteen
Identifying the Canon: Which Books Belong in the Bible?

How do we know which books belong in the New Testament? What if the early church got it wrong? Dan Brown, the Jesus Seminar, Bart Erhman, and Elaine Pagels are just a few of those petitioning for a new canon, claiming that the New Testament we have today does not necessarily contain the books that most accurately depict the true Jesus of history.

Many argue that books like *The Gospel of Thomas*, *The Gospel of Philip*, and *The Gospel of Mary* belong in the New Testament, or at least offer a glimpse into the true Jesus of history. Some scholars even claim that *The Gospel of Judas* depicts the historical Jesus as accurately as any of the New Testament Gospels. This chapter will deal with this question—which books belong in the New Testament? I will argue that the early church was right to select the twenty-seven books we have in our New Testament today.

The *canon* is the list of the books that belong in the Bible. How do we know the early church got the canon right? In this chapter, we will look at the tests for New Testament canonization, the history of canonization (how it occurred), why the New Testament books were accepted, and why the Gnostic texts were rejected.

The Evangelical Position

Evangelicals believe that Bible is the inerrant, inspired Word of God. Therefore, evangelicals should not be overly concerned by contemporary attacks on the New Testament canon. This is because if God went through the trouble to write an inerrant book (i.e., the Bible), then He would also go through the trouble of guiding the early church to find the books that belonged in the Bible. It makes no sense for God to inspire a Bible totally without error, but then not see to it that those books, and only those books, be recognized and acknowledged by His people (the church).

Six biblical doctrines are interrelated on this point: revelation, inspiration, inerrancy, illumination, canonization, and preservation. We will look at these doctrines, one at a time, showing how they logically relate to one another. The point we are making is this: if God wrote a book (actually He wrote 66 books), He also saw to it that this book would be recognized as His Word by His followers.

The first doctrine we will examine is called *revelation*. In this context, revelation means that before God guided human authors to record His Word, He had to reveal His Word to them. This does not mean that God dictated His Word to the human authors. God used their minds, their vocabularies, and their personalities to produce His perfect Word in written form. In some cases, God even used the research of the author (i.e., Luke 1:1-4).

Inspiration is the second doctrine we will look at. This doctrine teaches us that, after revealing His perfect Word to the New Testament authors, God guided them to record His Word in written form totally without errors. This is why Evangelical Christians call the Bible the Word of God. Though human authors recorded His Word, it was His Word they were recording. This is what Evangelicals call the *dual authorship* of the biblical books.

Third, the doctrine of *inerrancy* declares that the Bible, in the original manuscripts, is totally without errors. This logically follows from the doctrine of inspiration. If God decided to oversee human authors in the writing of His Word, then He saw to it that no errors were allowed in the original manuscripts.

The fourth doctrine is called *illumination*. This doctrine tells us that the Holy Spirit must enlighten our hearts and minds to receive truths from God's Word. This is not because God's Word was written in some type of secret code or that it is beyond human understanding.

It is because humans are sinful and we pervert that which is true and just. We have the natural tendency to pervert God's perfect revelation in His Word just as we pervert God's revelation of Himself in nature. Only through the power of the Holy Spirit can we rightly interpret the Word of God.

Canonization is the fifth doctrine we will discuss. Since Evangelicals believe that God actively wrote a book for His church, it make no sense to believe that He would leave it to chance as to whether or not His church would be able to identify the contents of that book. If God wrote a book that He wanted His church to read throughout the centuries (and Evangelicals believe He did), it only makes sense that He would see to it that His church correctly identify the writings that belong in that book and reject the writings that do not belong there. Hence, the Holy Spirit guided the early church to properly identify which books belong in the Bible.

The sixth and final Evangelical doctrine, relevant to this discussion, is called *preservation*. Since God went through the trouble of writing a perfect book and wanted it to be read by His people throughout the centuries, then it logically follows that He would see to it that accurate copies of His Word would be preserved throughout the centuries. We do not have the original manuscripts, but we have accurate copies of the originals. The New Testament has the greatest manuscript evidence in its favor when compared with any other ancient writing. The well over twenty-thousand handwritten copies still in existence today are in agreement 99.5% of the time. This means that only five words out of every one-thousand are called into question. And, with well over twenty thousand copies, textual critics can identify the true text without tremendous difficulty.

After examining these six doctrines, we should see that the doctrine of canonization logically flows from the doctrine of inspiration. If God wrote a book, He would see to it that the early church recognize which writings belong in that book. The evangelical doctrine of inspiration makes no sense without the doctrine of canonization.

Tests for Canonization

The early church had three tests to tell if a book should be canonized (i.e., recognized as a book that should be added to the Bible). The first test was *apostolic authorship or authority*. Was the book or letter written by an apostle or a close colleague of an apostle? New Testament books had to be written by one of Jesus' authoritative pupils (i.e., the apostles) or at least accepted by the authority of His authoritative pupils. A case can be made that all twenty-seven New Testament books can be traced back to the authority of the apostles (i.e., Matthew, Peter, Paul, John, and Jesus' brothers—James and Jude) as shown in the chapter on New Testament reliability. Mark's Gospel was accepted because he was an associate of the Apostle Peter. Luke's Gospel and his Book of Acts were recognized as canonical due to Luke being a colleague of the Apostle Paul. Though Paul was not the author of Hebrews (Hebrews 2:3-4), the author of Hebrews knew Paul's theology and he knew Timothy (Hebrews 13:23). Thus, the author of Hebrews was probably a colleague of the Apostle Paul as well. Hence, the early church acknowledged the canonization of the twenty-seven New Testament books due to their apostolic authority or authorship.

A second test for canonization was that *the book had to be edifying or profitable for the entire church*. We know that Paul wrote at least four letters to the Corinthians, yet only two of these letters were canonized. Apparently, the Corinthian believers, moved by the Holy Spirit, recognized that the two letters of Paul to the Corinthians found in our New Testament today would be edifying to the entire church. Therefore, they not only read these letters to their churches in Corinth, but also copied them for other ancient churches. The two letters of Paul to the Corinthians not found in the New Testament were apparently not considered material that would be edifying for the entire church. Hence, they were not copied and circulated throughout the ancient church.

The third test for canonization was that *the writng had to be in agreement with previous revelation* (both the Old Testament and whatever New Testament books were already written). The early church knew that God would not contradict Himself; His truth is non-contradictory. If a writing contradicted the Old Testament (or an accepted New Testament book already written), it was rejected.

How Canonization Occurred

The first stage of canonization was what I call *canonization by addition.* Canonization by addition was completed by the close of the first century AD. By this I mean that the New Testament books were accepted as the authoritative and inspired Word of God as soon as they were received by the readers (the local church or the person to whom the letter was written). In other words, the New Testament books were acknowledged as God's Word as soon as they were written or at least received by the recipients. All the New Testament books were written in the first century; hence, canonization by addition was complete by the close of the first century AD. This is why twenty-five of the twenty-seven New Testament books were already being quoted or alluded to as authoritative by just three of the apostolic fathers (Clement of Rome, Polycarp, and Ignatius) by 110 AD (Barnett, *Is the New Testament Reliable?* 40-41). Hence, the great nineteenth-century biblical scholar Theodor Zahn viewed canonization as a selection process and argued for its completion by the close of the first century AD (Metzger, *The Canon*, 23-24).

Even after this first stage of canonization, problems occurred. This was due to the fact that not all churches throughout the Roman

Empire had copies of all twenty-seven of the New Testament books. Also, bogus books claiming to be authored by apostles, or others who knew Jesus, were being written and circulated in the latter half of the second century AD. Some early church leaders were fooled by these pseudo-writings and read them to their churches as if they belonged in the canon. This led to what I call *canonization by subtraction*—the process of removing the spurios books from the canon.

Canonization by subtraction was completed by the close of the second century AD. Spurios second-century books like *The Gospel of Thomas* and *The Gospel of Judas* were exposed as frauds by the early church fathers in their writings. Pastors of local churches were advised to refrain from reading these books to their congregations. This is why another nineteenth century biblical scholar Adolph Harnack placed the date of completion for the New Testament canon at the close of the second century AD (Metzger, *The Canon* 24). He was dealing with what I called *canonization by subtraction*.

Many of the early church fathers got somewhat over-zealous during the stage of canonization by subtraction. New Testament books such as Hebrews (no one at that time knew the author's identity), 2 Peter, 2 John, 3 John, James, Jude, and Revelation were almost dropped from the canon by orthodox leaders. But, by the close of the second century, all twenty-seven books were regaining the acceptance they once had during the age of the apostolic fathers. An example of this is the Muratorian Fragment, dated to about 170 AD, which lists almost all the New Testament books. (Only Peter's letters, James, and Hebrews are ommitted.)

Though differing church fathers continued to question the canonicity of some of the New Testament books, most agreed with the assessment of Athanasius and Jerome by the close of the fourth century (Metzger, 211; 234-238). They acknowledged only the twenty-seven books we have in the New Testament today. These twenty-seven books were confirmed in the Council of Hippo (393

AD) and the two councils held in Carthage (397 AD and 419 AD). The Holy Spirit had guided His church to recognize His voice in these twenty-seven books.

Why the New Testament Books were Accepted

The New Testament books were, in the end, acknowledged as canonical because they were first-century AD documents written by the apostles or their closest colleagues. These writings were accurate depictions of Jesus' life, death, resurrection, and teachings. These writings did not contradict the Old Testament (previous revelation); in fact, these writings brought the Old Testament to its fulfillment—the coming of Messiah. Also, the early church considered the New Testament books edifying for the entire church. Just as the Holy Spirit guided members of the early church to write the New Testament, the Holy Spirit also guided the early church to recognize those writings and include them in the canon.

Why the Gnostic Texts were Rejected

The Gnostic writings were rejected by the early church for numerous reasons. First, the Gnostic writings (i.e., the Gospel of Judas, the Gospel of Thomas, the Gospel of Philip, the Gospel of Mary, etc.) were written much too late. The earliest date given to one of these books (i.e., the Gospel of Thomas) is about 140 AD, over one-hundred years after Jesus' death and resurrection. Hence, these books lacked apostolic authority and did not come from eyewitnesses or anyone who personally knew the eyewitnesses. Hence, the information was written far too late to contain reliable information about Jesus and His teachings.

Second, these writings were deceptive. They are often classified as pseudopigrapha—they were forgeries. The unknown authors were not the person they claimed to be. No New Testament critic, not even the liberal critics of the Jesus Seminar, believes that these books were actually written by Judas, Thomas, Philip, or Mary Magdalene. The authors were lying; they claimed to be someone they were not.

Third, the Gnostic writings were considered heretical by the early church, and therefore could not be added to the canon. The Gnostics rejected salvation through faith in Jesus and instead taught salvation through secret knowledge. (The word "Gnosticism" comes from the Greek word "gnosis," which means knowledge.) The ancient Gnostics rejected the Old Testament as an evil book written by an evil god. They taught that matter is totally evil and the spiritual realm is totally good. Since the Old Testament God created the material universe, the Gnostics deemed Him to be an evil god. Whereas biblical Christianity has always considered itself to be the completion or fulfillment of the Jewish Faith (i.e., the Old Testament), the Gnostics were opposed to the teachings of the Old Testament and the God of the Jewish Faith. Hence, the early church rejected the Gnostic writings as being heretical; these writings were not in agreement with previous revelation. Hence, as heretical works, the early church believed the Gnostic texts were not edifying for true believers.

Further Questions to Think About

Two further questions need to be asked when dealing with issues of the canon. First, what if we find other books written by New Testament authors—should we add these to the canon? Second, the Gnostic writings were clearly written too late to be included in the canon. But, what if we find first century heretical works, or, worse yet, first century forgeries?

First, if we find other writings written by recognized New Testament authors, we should not add them to the New Testament canon. We must trust in the Holy Spirit on this point. If a first-century

AD document, proven to be a writing of an apostle, is ever found, it should be held in high esteem if it is consistent with the Bible. But, it should not be added to the canon. If the Holy Spirit inspired Paul (or any other New Testament author) to write extra books that He wanted to be included in the Bible, He would have guided the early church in identifying these books. Since the early church did not canonize any other books, the canon should be considered closed.

Second, it is possible we may find first century heretical works, even first-century AD forgeries. Paul seemed to imply that he may have known about the existence of such forgeries as early as the mid-first-century. He clearly states this in 2 Thessalonians 2:1-3. We must remember that the age of the documents is not the sole test for canonicity. Many writings were authored in the first-century AD that are not included in the New Testament. If a first-century AD heretical work is ever found, it is still heretical and has no place in the canon of the Bible. When we say that the Gnostic writings were written too late to be added to the canon, that is true. But, we must remember that there are other reasons why these writings were rejected—they contradicted earlier, proven revelation and were not edifying for the church.

Therefore, if we have confidence that the Holy Spirit inspired authors to record His Word without errors, then we should also be confident that the Holy Spirit aided the early church to correctly recognize which books belong in the New Testament. Hence, Christians have no reason to doubt the authority and inspiration of the twenty-seven books in today's New Testament.

Chapter Fifteen
Did Jesus Rise From the Dead?

A person should not reject a miracle claim simply because it does not fit into his world view. The evidence for and against a particular miracle claim must be weighed. This chapter will examine the historical evidence for the bodily resurrection of Jesus from the dead.

The importance of Christ's resurrection should not be overlooked. The apostle Paul considered belief in Christ's resurrection to be necessary for salvation (Romans 10:9). Paul stated:

> . . . and if Christ has not been raised, then our preaching is vain, your faith also is vain. . . and if Christ has not been raised, your faith is worthless; you are still in your sins (1 Corinthians 15:14, 17).

Paul was quick to point out that if Christ could not raise Himself from the dead, then faith in Him would be worthless. Therefore, Christianity stands or falls on the resurrection of Christ. If the resurrection really happened, then Christianity is true and Jesus is the only Savior. However, if the resurrection never occurred, then Christianity is just another false religion, promoting a false messiah.

Christ's Resurrection was a Physical Resurrection

Before examining the evidence for Christ's resurrection, the nature of that resurrection must be discussed. Throughout the centuries the Christian Church has recognized that Christ's resurrection was bodily (Geisler, *Battle for the Resurrection* 51). Despite this fact, many today deny that Jesus rose bodily from the dead. The Jehovah's Witnesses are a non-Christian cult which denies Christ's bodily resurrection. Their literature states:

> On the third day of his being dead in the grave his immortal Father Jehovah God raised him from the dead, not as a human Son, but as a mighty immortal spirit Son, with all power in heaven and earth under the Most High God (*Let God be True*, 43).
>
> Jesus was the first one to rise from the dead. . . This firstborn one from the dead was not raised out of the grave a human creature, but was raised a spirit (*Let God be True*, 272).

Unfortunately, the denial of the bodily resurrection of Christ is no longer limited solely to non-Christian cults. Even evangelical scholar Murray Harris once denied that Jesus rose in the body which was crucified (*Raised Immortal* 126). To make matters worse, many evangelical scholars, rather than refuting his heresy, came to Harris' defense when he was confronted by Christian apologist Norman Geisler (Geisler, *Defense of the Resurrection* 8-13).

If Christ did not rise bodily, then there would be no way to verify the truth of the resurrection. Presumably, His corpse would have been rotting in the tomb when the apostles were proclaiming Him as the risen Savior. Although those who hold to a spiritual resurrection of Christ usually invent an additional miracle through which Christ's corpse dissappears, it seems more reasonable to conclude that either Jesus rose bodily or His corpse remained in the tomb. Since the New Testament records that the tomb was empty, it implies that the resurrection was bodily. A few passages of Scripture will suffice to show that Christ's resurrection, according to the apostles, was bodily:

> He is not here, for He has risen, just as He said. Come, see the place where He was lying (Matthew 28:6).

> Jesus answered and said to them, "Destroy this temple, and in three days I will raise it up." . . . But He was speaking of the temple of His body (John 2:19, 21).

> And after eight days again His disciples were inside, and Thomas with them. Jesus came, the doors having been shut, and stood in their midst, and said, "Peace be with you." Then He said to Thomas, "Reach here your finger, and see My hands; and reach here your hand, and put it into My side; and be not unbelieving, but believing" (John 20:26-27).

> And while they were telling these things, He Himself stood in their midst. But they were startled and frightened and thought that they were seeing a spirit. And He said to them, "Why are you troubled, and why do doubts arise in your hearts? See My hands and My feet, that it is I Myself; touch Me and see, for a spirit does not have flesh and bones as you see that I have." And when He had said this, He showed them His hands and His feet. And while they still could not believe it for joy and were marveling, He said to them, "Have you anything here to eat?" And they gave Him a piece of broiled fish; and He took it and ate it before them (Luke 24:36-43).

The apostles were eyewitnesses of Christ's post-resurrection appearances. Their testimony revealed several important points. First, the tomb was empty. Second, Christ appeared to them on several occassions. Third, they thought He was a spirit. Fourth, Jesus proved to them that He was physical by inviting them to touch His body and by eating with them. Fifth, His pierced side, hands, and feet showed that His resurrection body was the body which was crucified. Therefore, it is clear that the apostles taught that Christ rose bodily.

The debate about whether Christ's resurrection was bodily is usually based upon this passage:

> So also is the resurrection of the dead. It is sown a perishable body, it is raised an imperishable body; it is sown in dishonor, it is raised in glory; it is sown in weakness, it is raised in power; it is sown a natural body, it is raised a spiritual body. . . (1 Corinthians 15:42-44).

The Spiritual Body

Many people misunderstand the phrase "spiritual body." They mistake this phrase for signifying some type of immaterial spirit. However, this is not the case. In the Greek, the phrase is "soma pneumatikon." The word soma almost always refers to a physical body. Still, in this passage this physical body is somehow described as being "spiritual" (pneumatikon). But, the spiritual body is contrasted with the natural body. The natural body refers to the physical body before physical death. The Greek words for natural body are "soma psuchikon." Literally, this phrase means a "soulish body." The word soul usually carries with it the idea of immateriality, but, in this passage, it cannot. It is referring to the human body before death, and, the human body is of course physical, despite the adjective "soulish." Therefore, if the "soulish body" is physical, then there should be no difficulty viewing the "spiritual body" as also being physical. The soulish body is sown (buried) at death, but, this same body is raised as a spiritual body; it receives new powers. It is no longer a natural body; it is a supernatural body. The body is changed, but it is still the same body. For, the body that was sown (buried) is the same body that will be raised. Gary Habermas discussed Christ's spiritual body in the following words:

> . . . the Gospels and Paul agree on an important fact: the resurrected Jesus had a new spiritual body. The Gospels never present Jesus walking out of the tomb. . . when the stone is rolled away, Jesus does not walk out the way He does in apocryphal literature. He's already gone, so He presumably exited through the rock. Later He appears in buildings and then disappears at will. The Gospels clearly say that Jesus was raised in a spiritual body. It was His real body, but it was changed, including new, spiritual qualities (Habermas and Flew, *Did Jesus Rise from the Dead?* 58).
>
> Paul is using the term spiritual body to contrast it with the natural body. He is making the point that Christ's body after the Resurrection (and ours too) has different characteristics to it than it did before. . . But the point is made very clearly that what is being talked about is the same body, the contrast here is not between physical body and spiritual body, but rather between the same body in different states or with different characteristics (Habermas and Flew, 95).

Walter Martin, the foremost authority on non-Christian cults during his lifetime, also discussed Christ's spiritual body in his greatest work, *Kingdom of the Cults*:

> However, Christ had a "spiritual body" (1 Corinthians 15:50, 53) in His glorified state, identical in form to His earthly body, but immortal, and thus capable of entering the dimension of earth or heaven with no violation to the laws of either one (86).

Therefore, Christ rose in the same body in which He lived and died. However, His body had been changed in the "twinkling of an eye" (1 Corinthians 15:50-53) so that His mortal body (a body capable of death) was glorified and became immortal (incapable of death). In His spiritual body, He can apparently travel at the speed of thought, unhindered by distance. The Bible teaches that in the first resurrection all believers will receive glorified bodies. Believers' bodies will be changed into glorified and immortal bodies. The presence of sin will be totally removed from them (1 Corinthians 15:50-53).

There are several good arguments that Jesus' resurrection was bodily—it was not merely a spiritual resurrection. First, as the British New Testament scholar N. T, Wright points out, the Greek words for resurrection (anistemi, anastasis, eigero, etc.), in the first century AD, always meant a reanimation of a corpse, the raising back to life of a dead body. Even those who denied the reality of resurrection always used these words to refer to bodily resurrection when denying the reality of resurrection (*The Resurrection of the Son of God* 31, 147-148).

Second, Paul was a Pharisee (Philippians 3:5). The Pharisees believed in the concept of physical resurrection—they believed that the children of God would be bodily raised from the dead on the last day. A non-bodily resurrection is an oxymoron.

Third, Paul believed in life after death, and that life after death started immediately following death for the believer (2 Corinthians 5:8; Philippians 1:23). But, resurrection is something that occurred *after* life after death. For instance, the creed of 1 Corinthians 15:3-8 states that Jesus died, was buried, and then was raised "on the third day" (vs. 4). So, as N. T. Wright says, resurrection is "life after life-after-death." The difference between "life after death" and "life after life-after-death" is that the former is non-bodily existence, while the latter is bodily existence. Hence, the first-century ad concept of resurrection was bodily (Wright, *Resurrection* 31).

Fourth, the Old Testament concept of resurrection (Daniel 12; Ezekiel 37; Isaiah 26:19), which was inherited by the early church, was clearly that of bodily resurrection. Fifth, Paul's writings reveal that when he spoke of resurrection he meant bodily resurrection (1 Thessalonians 4:13-18; Philippians 3:21). Sixth, 1 Corinthians 15:42-44, speaking about the resurrection body, says that that which is sown or buried is that which is raised—the same thing that is buried (i.e., the body) is the same thing that is raised (i.e., the body). Seventh, if Paul denied the bodily resurrection and was trying to proclaim a spiritual resurrection, why not say "it is sown a soma (body), but it is raised a pneuma (spirit)?"

And, finally, the Gospel accounts of Jesus post-resurrection appearances, according to N. T. Wright, are not very theologically developed. These accounts are certainly much less theologically developed than Paul's discussions of Jesus' resurrection in his letters. Paul draws a lot of theological data from Jesus' resurrection—this implies he thought deeply about the theological implications of Jesus' resurrection. This is not the case with the Gospels—the resurrection and appearances are merely reported as historical incidents. Wright argues that this shows that the resurrection accounts in the Gospels predate Paul's writings. Since Paul began to write around 50 AD, the Gospel accounts of Jesus' resurrection and appearances must predate 50 AD (Flew, *There is a God* 202-209). Yet, in these early accounts, Jesus is reported to have bodily appeared to His disciples. He still had the scars in His hands, feet, and side. He encouraged the apostles to touch Him; He even ate food with them (John 20:26-29; Luke 24: 36-43). Together, these eight points make it clear that the early church proclaimed and believed that Jesus bodily rose from the dead.

Therefore, the apostles claimed that Jesus rose bodily from the dead. Since the resurrection occurred in the physical realm it could be verified; it could be proven true or false. Therefore, in reference to Christ's resurrection, only four options exist: 1) the resurrection accounts may be legends, 2) the accounts may be lies, 3) the apostles may have been sincere but deceived, or 4) the apostles were telling the truth. The remainder of this chapter will determine, by process of elimination, which of these four options best explains the available evidence.

The Resurrection Accounts were not Legends

The resurrection accounts were not legends. The evidence presented in the last several chapters clearly shows that the resurrection accounts predate even the New Testament itself. Legends usually take centuries to evolve (Craig, *Apologetics* 197). But, as chapter six has shown, the earliest known written resurrection accounts date back to less than twenty years after Christ's death. These accounts were ancient creeds and hymns of the first generation church (1 Corinthians 15:3-8; Romans 10:9; etc.). There is simply no way that a resurrection legend could receive universal acceptance (in order to become a hymn or creed) in the church while the apostles themselves led the church. If the resurrection account was merely a legend, the apostles would have refuted it. If the apostles chose not to refute a ficticious resurrection story, then they would have purposely perpetrated a falsehood. In that case, however, the resurrection accounts would not be legends; instead, the apostles would be liars.

Also, the Apostles were not likely candidates to borrow from Roman and Greek pagan myths. They had their background in Old Testament Judaism, and Judaism did not borrow from other religions. It was an exclusivistic faith. It is also unlikely that the apostles would have been willing to die for a myth.

The apostles knew Jesus personally. They were eyewitnesses of the events of His life and the things He taught. The apostles also led the early church. They were the authoritative witnesses to the facts concerning Christian doctrine, history, and practice. No legend could gain wide acceptance in the first generation church with the apostles in positions of authority. Since it can be shown that the resurrection accounts were not legends, some have concluded that the apostles were liars.

The Apostles were not Liars

Skeptics sometimes accuse the apostles of fabricating the resurrection accounts. One theory suggests that the apostles stole the body of Jesus from the tomb (Craig, *Apologetics* 179-180). In fact, this was the first attempted refutation of Christ's resurrection (Matthew 28:11-15).

Though it would be ludicrous to suggest that the apostles overpowered the Roman soldiers who guarded Jesus' tomb, this point will not be argued here. For many skeptics reject the apostolic witness concerning the guards at the tomb. Apart from the debate over whether or not the tomb was guarded, it can still be shown that the apostles were not liars. The apostles claimed that they saw Jesus risen from the dead, and, they were willing to suffer and die for for their testimony. It is clearly against human nature for men to die for what they know to be a hoax.

Death by martyrdom is probably a more accurate way to determine if someone is telling the truth than even modern lie-detector tests. William Lane Craig describes the horrible sufferings that the first generation Christians endured for their faith:

> One of the most popular arguments against this theory is the obvious sincerity of the disciples as attested by their suffering and death . . . Writing seventy years after Jesus' death, Tacitus narrates Nero's persecution about thirty years after Christ,

> how the Christians were clothed with the skins of wild beasts and thrown to the dogs, how others were smeared with pitch and used as human torches to illuminate the night while Nero rode about Rome in the dress of a charioteer, viewing the spectacle. The testimonies of Suetonius and Juvenal confirm the fact that within thirty-one years after Jesus' death, Christians were dying for their faith. From the writings of Pliny the Younger, Martial, Epictetus, and Marcus Aurelius, it is clear that believers were voluntarily submitting to torture and death rather than renounce their religion. This suffering is abundantly attested in Christian writings as well (175-176).

Foxe's Book of Martyrs lists the deaths of eight of the twelve original apostles. James (John's brother) was put to death with the sword by order of Herod Agrippa I. The apostle Philip was crucified. Matthew (who wrote one of the Gospels) was beaten to death with an axe-shaped weapon. Andrew (Peter's brother) was crucified on an X-shaped cross. Peter (author of two epistles) was crucified upside down by order of Nero. Bartholomew was crucified. Thomas was killed when a spear was thrust through him. Simon the Zealot was crucified (6-13).

Foxe's Book of Martyrs also discusses the deaths of other New Testament authors. James (a half-brother of Christ and author of the epistle bearing his name) was beaten and stoned to death. Jude (another half-brother of Jesus and author of the epistle bearing his name) was crucified. Mark (author of the Gospel bearing his name) was dragged to pieces in Alexandria. Paul (who wrote thirteen or fourteen epistles) was beheaded in Rome. Luke (who wrote the Gospel named after him and Acts) was hanged on an olive tree (6-13).

The apostles claimed to have seen Christ risen from the dead. They were willing to suffer and die for this claim. It is against human nature for one to die for what one knows to be a lie. Therefore, the apostles did not steal the body. They were not lying.

They were sincere. They believed that they had really seen the resurrected Lord. Hence, they were either sincere but deceived, or they were telling the truth.

The Apostles were not Deceived

Most of today's New Testament scholars recognize that the apostles were sincere in their belief that they had seen Jesus risen from the dead. Therefore, in an attempt to explain away the resurrection, some of these scholars accept one of several theories devised to explain how the apostles were decieved into thinking they had seen the risen Lord. It is interesting to note that these theories have all been refuted by other skeptics (Habermas and Flew, *Did Jesus Rise* 20-21).

The swoon theory suggests that Christ never actually died on the cross. Instead, He only passed out but was mistaken for dead. Christ then, according to this view, revived in the tomb. When He visited the apostles, they mistakenly proclaimed Him as risen from the dead (Habermas, *Ancient Evidence* 54-58). The swoon theory is easily refuted. The apostle John recorded in his Gospel strong evidence for Christ's death on the cross:

> The Jews therefore, because it was the day of preparation, so that the bodies should not remain on the cross on the Sabbath (for the Sabbath was a high day), asked Pilate that their legs might be broken, and that they might be taken away. The soldiers therefore came, and broke the legs of the first man, and of the other man who was crucified with Him; but coming to Jesus, when they saw that He was already dead, they did not break His legs; but one of the soldiers pierced His side with a

> spear, and immediately there came out blood and water (John 19:31-34).

Death by crucifixion was a horrible ordeal. To prolong the sufferings of the crucified person, a wooden block was placed under the feet to give him leverage to straighten up in order to breathe. When the Jewish authorities wanted to quicken the deaths of the victims so that they would not be on the cross during their feast days, they would have the Roman soldiers break the legs of the crucified victims. Being unable to straighten up in order to breathe, the victim would quickly die (Stevenson and Habermas, *Verdict on the Shroud* 178-179).

In Christ's case, the Roman soldier saw that He was already dead. Still, being a good soldier who was conscientous about his job, he confirmed his view that Christ was dead by thrusting his spear into Christ's side. In this way, if the soldier was mistaken and Christ was actually alive, the spear wound would be fatal. The soldier, an expert in mortal combat, was surely trained in how to deliver a death blow to an enemy. Therefore, if Christ had been alive, the piercing of His side would have certainly killed Him.

Another detail in this passage provides evidence that Christ did in fact die. The apostle John reported a flow of "blood and water" coming from Christ's side as a result of the spear wound. Today, medical science has shown that this phenomenon proves that Christ was dead prior to the spear wound (184). The flow of "blood and water" could only occur if the wound was inflicted upon a corpse. It should also be noted that this medical knowledge was unknown in John's day. Therefore, he had no knowledge that his reporting of this detail was irrefutable proof of death. Hence, he could not have fabricated this event in an attempt to prove Christ's death (184).

The evidence, therefore, clearly indicates that Jesus died on the cross. Still, even if He did survive the cross, imminent death would follow due to His injuries from the scourging and crucifixion. Furthermore, even if He survived these injuries, there is no way in His battered condition He would have been able to convince His disciples that He had conquered death for all mankind (184). The evidence declares that Jesus did die.

Some skeptics have proposed the *wrong tomb theory*. This view holds that everyone went to the wrong tomb and thus proclaimed Christ as risen (McDowell, *Evidence that Demands a Verdict* 255). However, this theory also has many problems. It offers no explanation for the apostles' claim to have seen the risen Christ on several occassions, and the apostles' willingness to die for their testimony. Also, the Jewish religious authorities would have searched every tomb in the Jerusalem area in an attempt to produce the rotting corpse of Christ. They had both the means and the desire to do so. Had they produced the corpse, Christianity would have been dealt a death blow while still in its infancy. The fact that the Jews did not produce the corpse of Christ is itself evidence of the empty tomb (255). Again, any claim that the disciples stole the body offers no explanation as to how they could have been willing to die for what they knew to be a hoax.

Other skeptics have proposed the *hallucination theory*. This theory states that the apostles did not really see the resurrected Christ; instead, they only hallucinated and thought they saw the risen Lord (Habermas, *Resurrection of Jesus* 26-28). However, psychologists inform us that hallucinations occur inside a person's mind. It is therefore impossible for two people—not to mention 500—to have had the same hallucination at the same time. Since many of the reported appearances of the risen Christ were to groups of people, the hallucination theory fails to explain the resurrection accounts (McDowell, *Evidence* 249).

Another attempt to explain away the resurrection is the *hypnotic theory*. This highly speculative view suggests that the witnesses of

Christ's post-resurrection appearances were all hypnotized. They did not actually see the risen Lord. Today, modern hypnotists deny this possibility (Morris, *Many Infallible Proofs* 94).

Christian scholar Gary Habermas sums up the failure of skeptics to explain away the resurrection of Christ:

> One interesting illustration of this failure of the naturalistic theories is that they were disproven by the nineteenth-century older liberals themselves, by whom these views were popularized. These scholars refuted each other's theories, leaving no viable naturalistic hypotheses. For instance, Albert Schweitzer dismissed Reimaru's fraud theory and listed no proponents of this view since 1768. David Strauss delivered the historical death blow to the swoon theory held by Karl Venturini, Heinrich Paulus, and others. On the other hand, Friedrich Schleiermacher and Paulus pointed out errors in Strauss's hallucination theory. The major decimation of the hallucination theory, however, came at the hands of Theodor Keim. Otto Pfleiderer was critical of the legendary or mythological theory, even admitting that it did not explain Jesus' resurrection. By these critiques such scholars pointed out that each of these theories was disproven by the historical facts (Habermas and Flew, *Did Jesus Rise?* 20-21).

Conclusion: The Apostles were Telling the Truth (Confirmed by Accepted Facts)

The failure of these theories shows that the apostles told the truth. Jesus did rise from the dead. Further evidence for Jesus' resurrection can be found when one examines the historical data accepted by nearly all New Testament scholars today. Christian apologist Gary Habermas lists ten facts accepted as historical by "virtually all scholars who study this subject" (Habermas, *Resurrection of Jesus* 25). These facts include: 1) Jesus' death by crucifixion, 2) Jesus' burial, 3) the disciples' loss of hope due to Jesus' death, 4) the empty tomb, 5) the disciples' experiences in which they believed they saw appearances of the risen Jesus, 6) the disciples' transformed lives and martyr's deaths due to these experiences, 7) the disciples' preaching of the resurrection in Jerusalem shortly after Jesus' death, 8) the Church began at that point and grew rapidly, 9) Sunday became the primary day of worship for the new Church, and 10) a few years later, Paul became a Christian after seeing what he believed to be an appearance of the risen Jesus (25-28).

Habermas then goes on to argue that no naturalistic explanation can account for these ten facts. Habermas adds that using only four of these facts is enough to prove Christ's resurrection and disprove all naturalistic attempts to explain away the resurrection. The four cour historical facts pointed to by Habermas are: 1) Jesus' death by crucifixion, 2) the disciples' experiences in which they believed they saw the risen Jesus, 3) the transformed lives of the apostles because of these experiences, and 4) Paul's transformed life due to what he believed was an appearance to him by the risen Jesus (38).

Christian philosopher William Lane Craig defends Jesus' resurrection from the dead in a manner similar to that of Habermas. He solidifies his case for the resurrection by listing the names of forty-four of the world's leading New Testament scholars who acknowledge the historicity of the empty tomb (*The Son Rises* 85).

Using this line of argumentation, I will argue for Jesus' resurrection based upon historical data accepted by nearly all New Testament scholars, even those who do not trust in Jesus for salvation. First, many scholars acknowledge that Jesus' half-brother James, though at first not a believer but a mocker of his brother's ministry, became a believer and leader of the Jerusalem church. Apart from the post-resurrection appearance of Jesus to James (as recorded in 1

Corinthians 15:7) there is no explanation for James' conversion and changed life.

Second, the Apostle Paul was originally a persecutor of the early church, yet his life was transformed dramatically so that he became the most outspoken defender of the Christian Faith. Paul credits a post-resurrection appearance of Jesus with changing his life.

Third, the Apostle Peter went from a man who denied Jesus three times on the night Jesus was betrayed to a courageous leader of the early church who was willing to suffer and die for Christ. Again, anything short of an appearance of the risen Christ would fail to explain this transformed life. It should be noted that the early church had no incentive to invent the account of Peter's denials. They reported his denials only because it really happened, for fabricating Peter's denials would have been horrible public relations for the founding of the infant church.

Fourth, the empty tomb, as noted above, is being accepted by more and more New Testament scholars, for if the tomb had not been empty the Jewish religious leaders would have produced the rotting corpse of Christ to disprove the preaching of the apostles. Since this did not happen, the evidence favors the tomb being empty.

Fifth, the Gospel accounts of women being the first witnesses of the empty tomb and the resurrected Christ is further confirmation of Christ's resurrection. In the first century AD a woman's testimony was not accepted in a court of law. If the apostles made up this account, they would have made the first witnesses males, and most likely, the apostles themselves.

Sixth, Jesus was buried in the tomb of a well-known Pharisee and member of the Sanhedrin—the Jewish ruling Council—named Joseph of Arimathea. Since the members of the Sanhedrin were well-known in the Jewish community and numbered only seventy, the apostles would not have been able to invent him. Therefore, Joseph of Arimathea really did exist, and, since he existed, the apostles would not have been able to lie about Jesus being buried in his tomb (Copan, 26-27). Joseph, as a public figure, would have been easily accessible to the masses—he could have easily refuted the story about Jesus' burial if it were not true.

Seventh, the apostles were sincere enough about their beliefs to die horrible martyrs' deaths. Eighth, the apostles sincerely believed they saw Jesus alive numerous times after His death. For instance, Paul quotes an ancient creed in 1 Corinthians 15:3-8 in which he gives a summary list of Christ's post-resurrection appearances. The list includes two appearances to the original apostles, an appearance to Peter, as well as appearances to James and Paul. New Testament scholars are nearly unanimous in accepting Paul as the author of 1 Corinthians in the mid 50's AD. Therefore, the creed predates the writing of that letter. Some scholars date the composition of this particular creed to the early to mid 30's AD. No leading New Testament scholar would dare to call Paul a liar. Paul also records meetings with Peter, James, and John in the thirties and forties AD. Therefore, he was familiar with their beliefs concerning Christ's post-resurrection appearances. Hence, the apostles sincerely believed they had seen Jesus risen from the dead.

Ninth, the earliest sermons preached by the apostles in Jerusalem proclaimed Christ's resurrection. This is accepted by most leading New Testament scholars today. This means that the resurrection accounts found in the Gospels were not legends, but eyewitness accounts. And since Jesus was buried in a tomb near Jerusalem, the resurrection claims would have been easy to disprove if the resurrection accounts had not actually been true.

Tenth, the apostles and leaders of the early church changed their primary worship day from Saturday (the Sabbath) to Sunday (the day Jesus rose and the day of most of His appearances). Since the apostles were traditional Jews and the Sabbath Day was established by God for the Jews to commemorate God's work of creation, there must have been a good reason for the change. Anything less than Christ's reusurrection would not be a sufficient explanation for this change.

Eleventh, the rapid growth of the early church in Jerusalem is universally accepted by New Testament scholars and historians today. However, a Messianic movement with a dead Messiah would die out, for the Jews expected the Messiah to rescue them from their Gentile enemies—the Romans. Only the resurrection of Jesus could revitalize the Messianic movement that centered on Him. Many Jews claimed to be Messiah, but when they died, so did their movement. But after Jesus' death, His movement grew at a faster rate than during His life. The resurrection is the only way to adequately explain this phenomena.

When we look at these eleven factors, all naturalistic attempts to explain away the resurrection of Jesus fail. In fact, as Gary Habermas has pointed out, just a few of these factors are enough to prove Jesus' resurrection from the dead.

The evidence for Christ's resurrection is overwhelming. The empty tomb stands as a monument to Christ's victory over death, a monument that, though attacked throughout the ages, remains standing and unmoved. The empty tomb is not a silent witness: the echoing of the angel's voice can still be heard coming from it, "He is not here, for He has risen, just as He said. Come, see the place where He was lying" (Matthew 28:6).

Chapter Sixteen
Is Jesus God?

The deity of Christ is hard to accept for many people. For a person to admit that Jesus is God in the flesh is to admit that he owes Him complete allegiance. Recognition of Jesus' Godhood calls for the abandonment of one's autonomy. Therefore, many people refuse to worship Jesus as God and consider Him to be merely a great human teacher. Mohandas K. Gandhi said of Christ:

> It was more than I could believe that Jesus was the only incarnate son of God. And that only he who believed in Him would have everlasting life. If God could have sons, all of us were His sons. If Jesus was like God . . . then all men were like God and could be God Himself (*Mahatma Ghandi Autobiography* 170).

The internationally respected theologian, John Hick, also denied Christ's deity:

> Now it used to be assumed—and in some Christian circles is still assumed—that this Jesus, who lived in Palestine in the first third of the first century AD, was conscious of being God incarnate, so that you must either believe him or reject him as a deceiver or a megalomaniac. "Mad, bad, or God" went the argument. And of course if Jesus did indeed claim to be God incarnate, then this dilemma, or trilemma, does arise. But did he claim this? The assumption that he did is largely based on the Fourth Gospel, for it is here that Jesus makes precisely such claims. He says "I and the Father are one," "No one comes to the Father, but by me" and "He who has seen me

> has seen the Father." But it is no secret today, after more than a hundred years of scholarly study of the scriptures, that very few New Testament experts now hold that the Jesus who actually lived ever spoke those words, or their Aramaic equivalents. They are much more probably words put into his mouth by a Christian writer who is expressing the view of Christ which had been arrived at in his part of the church, probably two or three generations after Jesus' death. And it is likewise doubted whether the few sayings of the same kind in the other gospels are authentic words of Jesus. How, then, did this Christian deification of Jesus—which began within the first decades after his death and was essentially completed by the end of the first century—take place? Such a development is not as hard to understand in the ancient world as it would be today... (Hick, *The Center of Christianity* 27-28).

It is interesting that Hick admits that the New Testament quotes Jesus as claiming to be God. Second, he acknowledges that the deity of Christ was being taught within a few decades of Christ's death. (In fact, what Hick ignores is that the ancient creeds in the New Testament indicate that the early church embraced Jessu as God in the early 30's AD—shortly after the resurrection.) And, third, Hick at least recognizes that the deity of Christ was completely established as church doctrine by the end of the first century AD. (Again, Hick ignores an important fact: Paul began writing in the late forties or early 50's AD. Yet, he does not argue for Christ's deity—he merely assumes it as if the early church already agreed that Jesus of Nazareth is God.)

However, by admitting these three facts, Hick is inadvertently conceding that all the available evidence points to the authenticity of Christ's claims to be God. Surely the apostles would have stopped this heresy (if indeed it was a heresy) when it started just decades after Christ's death (assuming it started that late—the ancient creeds teach otherwise). The Apostle John would also have opposed this teaching as it was being established as church dogma at the end of the first century AD.

Contrary to what John Hick believes, true scholarship bases its decisions on the evidence, not on mere speculation. All the available evidence points to the fact that Christ did claim to be God. The eyewitnesses who heard these claims died horrible deaths refusing to deny their validity. No liberal scholar has ever proposed an adequate explanation as to how a legend that Jesus claimed to be God could develop while the original apostles (those who personally knew Christ) were still alive and leading the new church. Legends take centuries to develope into dogma (Wilkins and Moreland, *Jesus Under Fire* 154). Any attempted origination of legends cannot get started while honest eyewitnesses are still alive (especially if these honest eyewitnesses hold positions of authority in the church).

Therefore, liberal scholars like Hick can believe what they wish. However, to deny that Christ claimed to be God is to simply ignore all the available evidence. Liberal scholars throw out any passages of the Bible that do not agree with their anti-supernaturalistic biases, but this is not true scholarship. True scholarship examines the evidence; it does not speculate as to how the evidence can be explained away.

The 1985 World Book Encyclopedia is an example of the high regard in which many people esteem Jesus, while stopping short of calling Him God:

> Jesus Christ was the founder of the Christian religion. Christians believe that He is the Son of God who was sent to earth to save mankind. Even many persons who are not Christians believe that He was a great and wise teacher. He has probably influenced humanity more than anyone else who ever lived (vol. 11, page 82).

It is not wise to call Jesus merely a great man and teacher since He claimed to be God. For no merely great man or wise teacher would claim to be God. If Jesus claimed to be God, then we must view Him as either a liar, insane, or God. There are no other alternatives, and no ignoring of the evidence will help.

Jesus Claimed to be God

Earlier in this work, it was shown that the message found in the New Testament is one and the same as the message of the first generation church. The ancient creeds found in the New Testament predate the New Testament and represent the teachings of the apostles themselves (Moreland, *Scaling the Secular City* 148-149). Several of these ancient creeds teach the deity of Christ (Philippians 2:5-11; Romans 10:9-10; 1 Timothy 3:16). Therefore, there is no reason to doubt that Jesus claimed to be God. The leaders of the first generation church taught that Jesus is God, and they were willing to die for their testimony. Hence, there is no reason (apart from an a priori bias against miracles) to reject the claims of deity made by Christ in the New Testament.

The Jews of Jesus' day understood that Jesus was claiming to be God:

> But He answered them, "My Father is working until now, and I myself am working." For this cause therefore the Jews were seeking all the more to kill Him, because He not only was breaking the Sabbath, but also was calling God His own Father, making Himself equal with God (John 5:17-18).

Whenever Jesus spoke of a unique Father-Son relationship between God the Father and Himself, the Jews understood Him to be claiming equality with God the Father. Jesus spoke to the Jews in their language. He communicated to them on their terms. They understood Jesus to be claiming to be deity. If Jesus never meant to claim to be God, then He was one of the poorest communicators who ever lived. If Jesus was misunderstood by His listeners, He should have clarified His words. A clear and articulate representation of His words would have been in His best interest; yet, He was executed for blasphemy (Mark 14:60-64). Hence, He did clearly claim to be God.

Jesus taught that He deserved the same honor that the Father deserved:

> For not even the Father judges anyone, But He has given all judgment to the Son, in order that all may honor the Son, even as they honor the Father. He who does not honor the Son does not honor the Father who sent Him (John 5:22-23).

Since the Father is God, the honor due Him is worship. Therefore, Jesus taught that He also deserved to be worshiped. Despite the fact that the Old Testament Law forbid the worship of any being other than God (Exodus 20:1-6), Jesus accepted worship on numerous occassions (Matthew 2:11; 14:33; 28:9; John 9:38; 20:28-29). Jesus also stated:

> You are from below, I am from above; you are of this world, I am not of this world. I said therefore to you, that you shall die in your sins; for unless you believe that I am He, you shall die in your sins. . . . Truly, truly, I say to you, before Abraham was born, I am (John 8:23-24; 58).

The Jewish religious leaders understood Jesus' claim to deity in this passage: "they picked up stones to throw at Him" (John 8:59). The comments of J. Dwight Pentecost are helpful:

> Christ affirmed, "Before Abraham was born, I am!" (v. 58). "I AM" was the name of the Self-existing God who had revealed Himself to Moses at the burning bush (Exod. 3:14). Jesus Christ was claiming to be "I AM", the Self-existent God. He was claiming eternity. To the Jews this was blasphemy (*Thye Words and Works of Jesus Christ* 288).

Merrill C. Tenney also elaborates on this specific claim of Christ:

> In actuality the phrase "I am" is an assertion of absolute, timeless existence, not merely of a personal identity as the English equivalent would suggest. A comparison of the use of the phrase, "I am" with self-revelation of Jehovah in the Old Testament shows that much the same terminology was employed. God, in commissioning Moses (Ex. 3:14), said: "Thus shalt thou say to unto the children of Israel, I AM hath sent me unto you." When the Jews heard Jesus say, "Before Abraham was born, I am," they took the statement to mean not priority to Abraham, but an assertion of deity. To them it was blasphemy, and they picked up stones to cast at Him (Tenney, *John, The Gospel of Belief* 150).

It is important to note two things about this passage. First, Jesus did not say, "Before Abraham was, I was." This would have been merely a claim to have preexisted Abraham. Though this would be a bold claim in itself, Christ actually said far more than this. Jesus was claiming that His existence is always in the present tense. In other words, He was claiming eternal existence for Himself. He was declaring himself to have absolutely no beginning. He was claiming that He was not bound by time. He was declaring Himself to be the eternal God. Second, Christ probably spoke these words in Aramaic (the common language of the Hebrews of his day). Therefore, He probably did not use the Greek words "ego eimi" for "I AM." Rather, He would have used the Hebrew "YHWH." This was the title for the eternal God. Out of reverence for God, the Jews never spoke this word. So here, Christ was not only be speaking the unspeakable title of God (YHWH), but He was using it to refer to Himself. Properly understood, this was probably Christ's most unambiguous claim to deity. The Jews clearly understood this, and for this reason they attempted to stone him. Another clear claim to deity made by Christ is the following passage:

> "I and the Father are one." The Jews took up stones again to stone Him. Jesus answered them, "I showed you many good works from the Father; for which of them are you stoning Me?" The Jews answered Him, "For a good work we do not stone You, but for blasphemy; and because You, being a man, make yourself out to be God" (John 10:30-33).

Concerning this passage, Merrill F. Unger wrote, "Jesus asserted His unity of essence with the Father, hence His unequivocal deity. . . and the Jews understood Him" (*Unger's Bible Handbook* 555). In this passage, Jesus clearly claimed to be equal with God the Father. Christ said that His nature is identical to that of the Father. The Jews understood Him to be calling Himself God. They later sentenced Him to death for these claims to deity.

Jesus also made other claims to deity. He said that, "He who has seen Me has seen the Father" (John 14:9). In this passage, Jesus was claiming to perfectly represent the Father. This implied that He considered Himself to be God-incarnate.

When He prayed to the Father, He asked the Father to return to Him the glory which He and the Father shared before the universe was created (John 17:5). In this one statement, Jesus makes two claims to deity. First, He claimed to already have personal existence before the universe was created. Only a divine Person could truthfully claim this. Second, He claimed to share God's glory with Him before creation. But, the Old Testament clearly teaches that God does not share His glory with anyone else (Isaiah 42:8). Hence, Jesus was claiming to be God.

Many of Jesus' claims to be God are found in the Gospel of John. John Hick dismisses this Gospel as being a very late composition. However, we have already given strong evidence for a pre-70 AD date for John's Gospel. James Charlesworth of Princeton dates John's Gospel to the 50's AD. Even a critical scholar like Richard Baukman admits that John's Gospel was written by an eyewitness who personally knew Jesus. Hence, John's testimony is eyewitness testimony—it represents what Jesus really said about Himself.

As Hick admits, Jesus also claims to be God in the other three Gospels as well. Jesus forgave sins (Mark 2:5-7) and accepted worship (Matthew 28:9). Jesus called Himself the bridegroom of Israel, knowing that the Old Testament calls Yahweh the bridegroom (Matthew 9:15). Jesus called Himself "the Lord of the Sabbath," knowing that God issued the Sabbath command (Matthew 12:8).

The apostles were Jesus' closest associates. They were more familiar with the teachings of Christ than anyone else, and they called Jesus God (Matthew 1:23; John 1:1; John 20:28; Philippians 2:6; Colossians 2:9; Titus 2:13; 2 Peter 1:1). This is further confirmation that Jesus did in fact claim to be God.

Considering the strong evidence for the reliability of the New Testament, Christ's claims to deity cannot be considered mere legends. The teaching that Jesus is God predates the New Testament (as shown in the ancient creeds), and is best explained by attributing the source of this doctrine to Jesus Himself. It must be remembered that the apostles were not liars. They were sincere enough about their beliefs to die for them, and they recorded unambiguous statements made by Christ attributing deity to Himself.

The case for Jesus' deity based on His explicit claims (as mentioned above) is strong. Still, since many New Testament scholars throw out these explicit claims (for less than good reasons), we will now build a case for Jesus' deity on Jesus' implicit claims. Most New Testament scholars accept the statements below as authentic sayings of Jesus. However, these implicit claims of Jesus confirm His explicit claims; for, His implicit claims also show that Jesus considered Himself to be equal with God.

Larry Hurtado, a New Testament scholar who teaches at the University of Edinburgh, showed in his work *The Lord Jesus Christ* that when Paul began writing his letters in 49 or 50 AD, he already had a "high Christology." He already referred to Jesus as "the Lord Jesus Christ." He already equated Jesus with Yahweh—the God of the Old Testament. Yet, Paul mentioned Jesus' deity in passing—he did not argue for it. Hurtado observes that Paul liked to debate. If there was any debate in the early church concerning the deity of Christ, Paul would have made the case for Jesus' deity. But, he does not. Instead, Paul assumes his readers (or any Christians in the 50's AD) already accepted Christ's deity. Hurtado then notes that Paul claimed he taught the same gospel message that Peter, James, and John taught (Galatians 1 and 2; see also 1 Corinthians 15:1-11). Hurtado then refers to ancient creeds and ancient sermons to solidify his case. He concludes that the early church, from its inception in the early 30's AD, engaged in "binitarian worship." In other words, before the early church figured out the role of the Holy Spirit and the doctrine of the Trinity, they came to realize Jesus' deity and began to worship Him as deity alongside the Father. The early church was monotheistic—they believed in only one God. But, they acknowledged that, though Jesus was a distinct Person from the Father, He was also equally God—He shared the divine nature with the Father. Hence, Hurtado makes a strong case that the worship of Jesus as deity goes back to the early 30's AD—the start of the church (Hurtado, *The Lord Jesus Christ* 101, 128-129, 131-133, 174-176, 650).

Many New Testament scholars acknowledge the "Son of Man" sayings as authentic sayings of Jesus. This is because of the critical principle called "discontinuity." This principle says that a saying attributed to Jesus in the Gospels was probably actually uttered by Jesus if it was dissimilar to what first-century AD Jews taught, and dissimilar to what the early church taught. The reasoning of critical scholars is that if the early church taught something, then they would place those words on Jesus' lips to give authority to their beliefs. But, this cannot apply to the "Son of Man" sayings. For, though the phrase comes from Daniel chapter seven, it was not in common use by the Jews of the first century AD. Also, the church almost never used the title of Jesus, not even in New Testament times. Yet, it was the most common title Jesus used of Himself. Hence, the principle of discontinuity shows that the "Son of Man" sayings were probably uttered by Jesus Himself (Habermas, *Risen Jesus and Future Hope* 100-106). But, when we look at the Son of Man sayings, we see several things that Jesus taught about Himself. Jesus predicted His death and resurrection numerous times (Mark 8:31; 9:31; 10:32-34). He claimed to be equal to God and have the power to forgive sins (Mark 2:5-12). Also, He claimed to be the Son of God and the Jewish Messiah, and He said that He would return to judge the world (Mark 14:61-64). He also claimed He came to earth to die "to give His life a ransom for many" (Mark 10:45).

When Jesus called God "Abba," He claimed to have a closeness or intimacy with the Father that no one else had (107). When He claimed that God was His "Abba" (something as intimate as "daddy," yet more respectful), the Jews understood Jesus to be claiming to be "the Son of God" and equal to God (John 5:17-18).

Some modern critics reject the passages where Jesus called Himself the Son of God. But, it is hard for New Testament critics to deny the authenticity of Mark 13:32. For, in this passage, Jesus, while calling Himself "the Son," admits that, in His human nature, He did not know the day or the hour of His return. This is an excellent example of the principle of embarrassment. The Apostles would never place these words on the lips of Jesus if He did not actually say them, for they imply a limitation of Jesus' knowledge. Hence, Jesus did make this statement, and He did think of Himself as the Son of God.

Jesus viewed His interpretation of the Mosaic Law as holding as much authority as the Mosaic Law itself. He refused to quote from other rabbis for His authority, but instead (contrary to the common practice of His day) He went right to the Old Testament and interpreted it Himself. His prefacing His interpretations with "truly, truly, I say to you" shows that He considered His interpretation of God's Law as authoritative as God's Law itself. Jesus implied that His interpretation of God's Law was as much God's Word as the Old Testament was. This is why the crowds were astonished at the authority with which Jesus spoke (Matthew 7:28-29).

Paul's accepted writings, the Gospel of Mark, the supposed "Q" material (parallel passages found in both Matthew and Luke, but not in Mark), the ancient sermons of Acts chapters one through twelve, and the ancient creeds all paint a portrait of Christ as God incarnate. Yet, even liberal New Testament critics agree that these sources all predate 70 AD. Hence, all the ancient evidence from the first generation AD points to a fully divine Jesus, without denying His true humanity.

The deity of Christ is not a legend. All the early historical evidence shows that Jesus claimed to be God incarnate. Hence, one cannot consider Him to be simply a great man; for if a mere man claims to be God, we do not consider him great or good. Jesus claimed to be God. If Jesus is not God, then He was either a liar or insane. There are no other options.

Jesus was not a Liar

The absurd idea that Jesus was a liar who claimed to be God can be easily refuted. For Christ is considered, even by many who reject His claim to deity, to have taught the highest standard of morality known to man. His teachings have motivated such actions as the abolition of slavery, government by the consent of the people, the modern hospital system, education for all children, and charitable programs for the needy. A habitual liar could not have possibly encouraged these movements.

Christ has had a positive impact on mankind like no other person. It is extremely unlikely that so much good could come from a deceiver who led people astray by claiming to be God. The eyewitness accounts of the apostles display the tremendous love Christ had for people. It is not possible that a self-centered and egotistical liar could express genuine affection for his fellow man like that expressed by Christ. The question can also be asked, "Would a liar die for his lie?" It is doubtful that Jesus would lie and then suffer death by crucifixion as a consequence. A liar would admit his lie to save his life. Jesus was sincere in His claim to be God since He died for that claim.

It has already been shown that the resurrection of Jesus was a historical event and not a hoax. But, why would God raise a blaspheming liar from the dead? Christ offered His resurrection as proof for His claims to deity (John 2:18-21; Matthew 12:38-40). Therefore, His resurrection proves the validity of His claims to be God. He claimed to be God and then proved it by doing what no mere man could do—He rose from the dead.

Jesus was not Insane

Christ's claims to deity have been shown not to be legends or lies, but the possibility remains that Jesus may have been insane. Could it be that Jesus claimed to be God because He was mentally disturbed?

Often, people compare Jesus of Nazareth with other respected religious leaders. However, very few of these leaders (if any) claimed to be God in a unique sense. Some have claimed to be God, but then teach that we are all God. Jesus claimed to be God in a sense that no other man could claim to be God. Usually, when a religious leader makes a claim as bold as this, it is evidence that he is unbalanced. Charles Manson and David Koresh are two examples of this type of religious leader. The evidence for their instability is obvious. However, this is not so in the case of Jesus. He made bold claims to deity, but also backed these claims by the life He lived and the things He did. He, and He alone, lived a life consistent with His claim to be God.

Declaring Christ to be insane is not a common view. Nearly everyone admits that He was a great teacher, even if they reject His deity. However, insane people make lousy teachers. The teachings of Christ are not the teachings of a mad man. They are the greatest teachings ever taught by a man, and this man claimed to be God incarnate.

The miraculous life of Christ is also evidence that He was not insane. Christ gave evidence for His bold claims through His supernatural works. The apostles were eyewitnesses of these miracles. Even the enemies of Christ, the Jewish religious leaders of His day, did not deny His miracles. Instead, they stated in their Talmud that Jesus "practiced sorcery" (Habermas, *Ancient Evidence for the Life of Jesus* 98). Though they rejected Jesus' message, they were forced to admit that He did supernatural works. However, the powerful influence for good that Christ has had upon mankind declares His miracles to be from God and not from Satan. Therefore, Jesus' miracles show that He was not insane. They provide strong evidence to support His claim to be God.

Another piece of evidence that shows Christ was not insane is the fact that His life and works were prophesied hundreds of years before His birth. A small fraction of the prophecies He fulfilled are listed below:

1) -He was a descendant of Abraham (Genesis 12:1-3; fulfilled in Matthew 1:1-2 and Luke 3:34)

2) -He was from the tribe of Judah (Genesis 49:10; fulfilled in Matthew 1:3 and Luke 3:33)

3) -He was a descendant of Jesse (Isaiah 11:1; fufilled in Matthew 1:5-6 and Luke 3:32)

4) -He was a descendant of David (Jeremiah 23:5; fulfilled in Matthew 1:1, 6 and Luke 3:31)

5) -He was born to a virgin (Isaiah 7:14; fulfilled in Matthew 1:18-25 and Luke 1:34-35)

6) -He was born in Bethlehem (Micah 5:2; fulfilled in Matthew 2:1 and Luke 2:1-7)

7) -His birth announced by a star (Numbers 24:7; fulfilled in Matthew 2:1-2)

8) -His forerunner (Isaiah 40:3; fulfilled in Matthew 3:1-3 and Mark 1:2-4)

9) -The specific time of His first coming (Daniel 9:24-27 predicts that the Messiah would be executed before the temple would be destroyed. The destruction of the temple occurred in 70 AD. Matthew 27:1-2, 26 states that Jesus was crucified when Pilate was govenor of Judea. Pilate reigned as govenor in Judea from 26 AD to 36 AD.)

10) -His miracles (Isaiah 35:4-6; fulfilled in Matthew 11:1-6)

11) -His parables (Psalm 78:2; fulfilled in Matthew 13:3)

12) -He was rejected by the Jews (Isaiah 53; fulfilled in Matthew 23:37; 27:22-25; Romans 10:1-3; 11:25)

13) -He received a wide Gentile following (Isaiah 42:1-4; fulfilled in Romans 9:30-33; 11:11 and confirmed in the history of the church)

14) -He was betrayed for 30 pieces of silver (Zechariah 11:12-13; fulfilled in Matthew 26:14-16)

15) -He was forsaken by His disciples (Zechariah 13:7; fulfilled in Matthew 26:56)

16) -He enterred Jerusalem on a donkey while receiving a king's welcome (Zechariah 9:9; fulfilled in Matthew 21:1-11)

17) -He was silent before His accusers (Isaiah 53:7; fulfilled in Matthew 26:63; 27:14)

18) -He was crucified (Psalm 22:16; fulfilled in Matthew 27:35)

19) -Soldiers cast lots for His garments (Psalm 22:18; fulfilled in Matthew 27:35)

20) -His bones were not broken (Psalm 34:20; fulfilled in John 19:31-34)

21) -His side was pierced (Zechariah 12:10; fulfilled in John 19:34)

22) -He was buried in a rich man's tomb (Isaiah 53:9; fulfilled in Matthew 27:57-60)

23) -His resurrection from the dead (Psalm 16:10; fulfilled in Matthew 28:1-9)

24) -His ascension (Psalm 68:18; fulfilled in Acts 1:9-11)

25) -His position at the Father's right hand (Psalm 110:1; fulfilled in Hebrews 1:3)

As was noted earlier, these are just a few of the many prophecies that were fulfilled by Christ (McDowell, *Evidence tha Demands a Verdict* 141-177). Even liberal scholars admit that these prophecies were recorded hundreds of years before Christ's birth. Although they deny the traditional early dates of the Old Testament books, it is almost universally accepted that *the Septuagint* (the Greek translation of the Hebrew Old Testament) was completed two hundred years before Christ was born (144).

Most liberal critics do not consider some of the prophecies listed above as having been fulfilled by Christ. This is because these liberals a priori deny the possibility of miracles. Since they deny Christ's resurrection, they also deny that Christ fulfilled the Old Testament prophecy of the resurrection. Even if one removes the Old Testament predictions concerning the supernatural aspects of Christ's life, one is still left with the evidence from the fulfillment of prophecies of the non-supernatural aspects of Christ's life.

Norman Geisler has noted that the chances of Christ fulfilling just sixteen of these prophecies by mere coincidence are 1 in 10^{45} (a one with forty-five zeroes after it; Geisler, *Apologetics* 343).

In fact, three of these Old Testament predictions concerning the Messiah—Daniel 9:26; Isaiah 42:4; Isaiah 53—are enough to prove that only Jesus of Nazareth meets the messianic qualifications. Daniel 9:26 stated that the Messiah would be executed before the destruction of the temple (which occurred in 70 AD). Isaiah 42:4 teaches that the Gentile nations would expectantly await Christ's law. Isaiah 53 declares that the Jews would reject their Messiah. Jesus of Nazareth is the only person in history who has fulfilled all three of these prophecies. He claimed to be the Jewish Messiah and was crucified around 30 to 33 AD (approximately forty years before the temple was destroyed), the Jews rejected Him, and He received a wide Gentile following.

The life of an insane man would not be prophesied. It is also unlikely that these predictions would refer to an insane man as the Messiah (God's annointed one) and "the mighty God" (Isaiah 9:6). More than 200 years before Jesus' birth, His life and works were predicted. He fulfilled these prophecies and performed many miracles. It is absurd for someone to call Jesus insane. To accept His claims is the only reasonable response.

The historical evidence shows that Jesus claimed to be God and proved it by raising Himself from the dead, performing miracles, and fulfilling numerous Old Testament prophecies. History shows these claims are not legends, and that He was not a liar, insane, or merely a great man. Therefore, Jesus of Nazareth is God.

Therefore, Jesus is God

The following ancient creed was formulated and proclaimed by the first generation church. It declares Jesus to be God and Savior, and instructs all creation to surrender to His Lordship:

> Have this attitude in yourselves which was also in Christ Jesus, who, although He existed in the form of God, did not regard equality with God a thing to be grasped, but emptied Himself, taking the form of a bond-servant, and being made in the likeness of men. And being found in appearance as a man, He humbled Himself by becoming obedient to the point of death, even death on a cross. Therefore also God highly exalted Him, and bestowed on Him the name which is above every name, that at the name of Jesus every knee should bow, of those who are in heaven, and on earth, and under the earth, and that every tongue should confess that Jesus Christ is Lord, to the glory of God the Father (Philippians 2:5-11).

This ancient creed states that the day will come when all creation will bow down before Christ and confess that He is Lord. One can bow to Jesus now, or one can bow to Jesus later; but, the fact remains, that the day will come when all will bow before Christ, both the saved and the unsaved. The saved will bow before Jesus to worship Him as their Savior and King. The lost will bow before Him, due to their fear of His power and authority. The question is not: "Will you bow?" Instead, the question is: "When will you bow?"

Chapter Seventeen
The Main Themes of Jesus' Teachings

We have made a strong case that the New Testament is a historically reliable witness to the true Jesus of history, and that Jesus claimed to be God and rose from the dead to prove His claims to be true. Now we will examine the main themes of Jesus' teachings. They are: the Kingdom of God, true spirituality (i.e., Spirit-filled living), He is God, He is Savior, He is Messiah, and He will return. Jesus also taught that the Old Testament is God's inerrant Word, and He promised that there would also be an inspired, inerrant New Testament as well.

The Kingdom of God

Most New Testament scholars, liberal and conservative alike, believe the main theme of Jesus' teachings is the Kingdom of God (also called the Kingdom of Heaven). Both John the Baptist and Jesus proclaimed, "The Kingdom of God is at hand" (Matthew 3:2; 4:17). But, what exactly is the Kingdom of God? First, a kingdom is the domain (or sphere of rule) of a king. Second, since God is the King of His Kingdom, then the Kingdom of God is wherever God rules.

To be more specific, we need to look at what Jesus said about God's Kingdom. Jesus often taught in parables. Parables are true to life stories that teach spiritual truth. In Matthew, chapter thirteen, Jesus taught the people parables about the Kingdom of God, telling them what the Kingdom would be like. In the parable of the sower, Jesus said that people could accept or reject the word of the Kingdom. Those who accept the word of the Kingdom would bear much fruit (Matthew 13:18-23). In the parables of the mustard seed and the leaven, Jesus explained that the Kingdom of God would start out small but would grow to the point of filling the earth (Matthew 13:31-33). In the parables of the tares and the net of fish, Jesus preached that, in God's Kingdom, the unsaved would mingle with the saved until the harvest on the last day when the Son of Man would send God's angels to separate them, sending the unsaved into a "furnace of fire" (Matthew 13:36-43; 47-50). In the parables of the pearl of great price and the hidden treasure, Jesus proclaimed that the Kingdom of God was worth more than everything a person owned (Matthew 13:44-46).

These parables teach us that the Kingdom of God has two distinct phases or stages. First, the Kingdom of God apparently has a present stage in which God's Kingdom (the church) is growing throughout the world. During this stage, God's Kingdom grows until it fills the earth. Still, nonbelievers live side by side with believers during this stage. Second, the Kingdom of God has a future stage in which the Son of Man will come and send His angels to separate the unsaved from the saved, sending the unsaved into eternal torment.

The Apostle Paul spoke of the present stage of God's Kingdom when he wrote, "For the Kingdom of God is not eating and drinking, but righteousness and peace and joy in the Holy Spirit" (Romans 14:17). Hence, the present stage of God's Kingdom is a spiritual stage—God ruling in the hearts of believers.

The future stage of God's Kingdom is spoken of in the following manner: "And the seventh angel sounded [his trumpet]; and there arose loud voices in heaven, saying, 'The kingdom of the world has become the kingdom of our Lord and of His Christ; and He will reign forever and ever'" (Revelation 11:15). Revelation, chapters nineteen and twenty, tell us that Jesus will bring God's kingdom to earth by reigning on the earth and shepherding the nations with an iron rod for one-thousand years (Revelation 19:11-20:15). Hence, the future stage of God's Kingdom is when God's Kingdom physically comes to earth when Jesus returns to rule on earth (Matthew 24:29-31; 25:31-32).

Jesus taught the apostles that they would sit on twleve thrones judging the twelve tribes of Israel in the coming Kingdom (Matthew 19:28), and that many Jews would not make it into God's Kingdom, whereas some Gentiles would sit and feast with the Jewish patriarch Abraham (Matthew 8:10-12). Jesus told Nicodemus that "unless one is born again, he cannot see the Kingdom of God" (John 3:3). To be born again, a person has to believe in Jesus for salvation (John 3:16-18).

From these passages we can gain insight into God's Kingdom. In its present stage, God rules in the hearts of believers—those who trust in Jesus alone for salvation. But, in the future, Jesus will return and bring God's Kingdom to earth, and He will reign on the earth for one-thousand years. The Kingdom of God coming in all its fullness was prophesied in the Old Testament and will be fulfilled by Jesus at His return when He conquers the enemies of Israel and establishes God's Kingdom on earth (Zechariah 14:1-5, 9-21; Isaiah 2:1-4; 9:6-7; 11:4-9; Zechariah 9:9-10). Jesus instructed believers to pray for God's Kingdom to come to earth (Matthew 6:10).

True Spirituality (Spirit-Filled Living)

In the Sermon on the Mount (Matthew chapters 5, 6, and 7), Jesus gave His own infallible interpretation of the Old Testament Law. In contrast to the Jewish rabbis (i.e., the Pharisees) of His day, Jesus did not teach mere outward obedience to God's laws, nor did He add man-made technicalities to God's law. Instead, He taught that His followers should obey the spirit of the Law from the heart. However, man cannot do this in his own strength. If a person wants to please God, he must first acknowledge that he is "poor in spirit" (Matthew 5:3). Without humbly admitting our sinfulness, we cannot be saved. This means that we must admit we are sinners; we are spiritually bankrupt and in desperate need of God's salvation. Apart from Jesus, we can do nothing that would please God (John 15:5).

Once Jesus saves us, we are indwelt by the Holy Spirit who gives us the new birth (John 3:3-8). The Holy Spirit then empowers us, for the first time in our lives, to obey God's laws from the heart. God only accepts Spirit led and empowered works. We need to be cleansed from the inside, not just on the outside (Matthew 23:25-26). We can be guilty of breaking God's laws in our thoughts and desires, not just in our deeds (Matthew 5:21-22, 27-28). God demands obedience from the heart, not mere outward obedience.

Though Jesus fulfilled the Old Testament ceremonial laws (i.e., animal sacrifices, feast days, temple furniture, etc.) and the Jewish civil laws do not always apply to Gentile nations, Jesus does not absolve His followers from obeying His Old Testament moral commands. Instead, Jesus taught that, now that believers are under grace, we must obey God from the heart, not just outwardly. Only the Holy Spirit can inwardly cleanse us to empower us to obey God from the heart (Matthew 5:8, 17-18).

Jesus also taught that His true followers, empowered by His Spirit, will be willing to suffer persecution for His name (Matthew 5:10-12). True followers of Jesus will also be willing to forgive those who sin against them, turn the other cheek, and love their enemies (Matthew 6:14-15; 5:38-48). True spirituality involves Spirit-filled living—it can only be experienced by those who, through faith in Jesus, have been born again (John 3:3).

Jesus is God

Jesus taught that He is God both explicitly and implicitly. Explicitly, Jesus called Himself the Son of God, claiming God was His own Father in a unique way. The Jews understood this to mean that Jesus was claiming to be equal with God (John 5:17-18). Jesus said that we should give Him the same honor that we give the Father (John 5:22-23). In other words, Jesus said we should worship Him, since worship is the ultimate honor. Jesus called Himself the "I Am" (Yahweh) who spoke to Moses from the burning bush (John 8:23-24; Exodus 3:14), the ertnal self-existent God who was in a covenant relationship with the nation of Israel. Jesus said that "Before Abraham was, I Am" (John 8:58-59), again claiming to be eternal. Jesus said "I and the Father are one" (John 10:30)., and that He perfectly represents the Father—"He who has seen Me has seen the Father" (John 14:9). And as Jesus prayed the night He was betrayed, He asked the Father to return to Him the glory He shared with the Father before the world was created (John 17:5). God does not share His glory with another and only the Creator existed before the world was created. Therefore, Jesus was unambiguously claiming to be God. The Jews often attempted to stone Jesus for blasphemy after He made these direct, explicit claims to be God.

Jesus claimed to be the Lord of the Sabbath (the Sabbath Law was given by God—Exodus 20:1, 8) and greater than the prophet Jonah, King Solomon, and the temple itself (Matthew 12:6-8; 41-42). Since the temple was an incarnation of God (it enclosed the special presence of Yahweh among His people), Jesus was claiming to be a fuller incarnation of God than that of the temple. Jesus claimed to be greater than the Jewish prophets and kings; He claimed to be greater than the temple. Hence, He considered His covenant (the New Covenant) to be superior to that of the Old Covenant. These are just a few ways Jesus explicitly claimed to be God. His Jewish audiences had no doubt about His claims to be God.

Many liberal critics of God's Word reject these explicit claims of Jesus to be God. However, Jesus not only explicitly claimed to be God, but He also implied that He is God by His words and actions. Many of these words and actions are accepted by liberal critics as authentic words and deeds of Jesus. Hence, a case can be made that Jesus claimed to be God on what even liberal scholars accept as authentic from God's Word.

Jesus claimed to have the power to forgive sin, a power only God has (Mark 2:5-7). He could forgive strangers immediately—there was no need for them to go through the temple sacrifices. Jesus claimed He had the authority to forgive sin—a power only possessed by God. The Jewish religious leaders understood His claim to be able to forgive sins as a claim to be God Himself.

Jesus called God His "Abba," a very intimate way to say "Father." Jesus implied that He was the unique Son of God by nature. The Jews understood this to be tantamount to claiming equality with God (Mark 14:36; John 5:17-18).

Jesus' "truly, truly" statements (John 6:47) show that Jesus believed His teachings about the Old Testament held as much authority as the Old Testament itself. Since the Old Testament is God's Word, Jesus was claiming to be as authoritative as God Himself.

Jesus' favorite title for Himself was "the Son of Man." In His Son of Man sayings Jesus gave Himself the characteristics of God. In these sayings, He claimed to be Savior (Mark 10:45) and claimed to be able to forgive sin, something only God can do (Mark 2:5-7). He also claimed He would return amidst the clouds to judge the world (Mark 14:61-64). Only the God of Israel will judge the world (Psalm 9:8; Isaiah 2:4; 33:22).

Jesus believed He had authority over the temple. Twice He cleansed the temple by casting money changers from the outer court. Since the temple was the embodiment of God's special presence on earth, Jesus was claiming to be a greater incarnation of God than the temple was (Matthew 12:6).

Jesus chose twelve apostles and seventy disciples. God had chosen the nation of Israel to be His nation. Israel had twelve tribes and seventy judges on the Sanhedrin (i.e., the Jewish ruling council). By choosing twelve apostles and seventy elders Jesus showed He was creating a new Israel, a spiritual Israel. Since God produced the first

Israel, Jesus was claiming to be God, the Creator of the new Israel (i.e., all true believers).

Jesus believed He would usher in the Kingdom of God, and that faithfulness to Him determined one's entrance into the Kingdom (Matthew 7:24-27). Jesus believed that a person's eternal destiny rested on Him (John 3:16-18;14:6; Matthew 11:28). Yet, the Old Testament said salvation only comes from Yahweh (Psalm 18:46; 25:5; 27:1, 9; 62:2, 6; Isaiah 12:2; Jeremiah 3:23). Hence, by claiming to be Savior, Jesus was claiming to be God. Whether explicitly or implicitly, it is clear that Jesus claimed to be God. His claims to be God were so clear that the Sanhedrin (the Jewish ruling council) sentenced Him to death for blasphemy, because He was claiming to be God (Mark 14:60-64; John 10:30-33).

Jesus is Savior

Jesus taught that He alone is Savior. He said that it is impossible for man to save Himself (Matthew 19:25-26), but that He alone is the way to be saved, and the way to the Father (John 14:6). Jesus taught that man is sinful and in need of salvation (Matthew 19:17; Mark 10:45; Luke 19:10; John 7:19). He said that the only way to be saved was to trust in Him alone for salvation (John 3:16-18; 11:25-26; 14:6). In fact, it was for this reason He came to earth—to seek and save that which was lost (John 3:16-18, 36; Luke 19:10). Eternal life is found only in Him (John 3:16; 5:39-40). Jesus cried out for others to come to Him to find rest (Matthew 11:28). Only through believing in Him can man be saved (John 6:47); only Jesus can quench our thirst for God and satisfy our hunger for God (John 6:35).

Jesus taught that man is so depraved that he cannot enter the Kingdom of God without being born again by the Holy Spirit (John 3:1-8). Jesus said that we cannot be born again unless we trust in Him for salvation (John 3:16-18). Only through Jesus can we receive eternal life (John 14:6).

Jesus is Messiah

The Jews, at the time of Christ, were waiting for the coming of their Messiah, the one God anointed to rescue the nation of Israel. When Jesus performed many amazing miracles, many Jews suspected He was their Messiah. However, Jesus only admitted that He was the Messiah in private conversations with others.

He acknowledged that the Apostle Peter was correct when he said that Jesus was "the Christ, the Son of the living God" (Matthew 16:13-20). Jesus told the Samaritan woman that He was the Jewish Messiah (John 4:25-26). He also told the disciples of John the Baptist that Jesus' miracles proved that He was the Messiah; therefore, John and his disciples should not wait for another to come (Matthew 11:2-6). Finally, Jesus admitted to the Jewish High Priest (when Jesus was on trial the night before His death) that He was "the Christ, the Son of the Blessed One" (Mark 15:61-63).

Jesus chose to not publicly call Himself the Jewish Messiah because the Jews understood Messiah to be merely a political, military conqueror who would rescue them from the Romans. This is why the Jews wanted to make Jesus King by force of arms. Rather than reinforce their inadequate understanding of Messiah, Jesus chose to call Himself "the Son of Man" (Mark 10:45). This was His favorite title for Himself. The Jews did not understand what Jesus meant by this title. Hence, by calling Himself the Son of Man, Jesus was able to define His ministry on His own terms—He could stress His mission to spiritually save His people from their sins, and downplay the physical deliverance He would accomplish for the Jews at His second coming.

It should be noted that this shows that the Apostles did not fabricate Jesus' claims to be Messiah. For, if the New Testament authors lied by claiming that Jesus considered Himself the Jewish Messiah, they would have made it much clearer—they would have placed the word "Messiah" on Jesus' lips on numerous occassions so no one would miss it. The fact that He only admitted to being the Messiah in private encounters shows that the Apostles did not lie—Jesus did believe He was the Messiah.

Eventually, Jesus did publicly announce that He was the long-awaited Jewish Messiah. But, He made this announcement without words. He proclaimed Himself to be the Messiah by riding into Jerusalem on a donkey, thus fulfilling a prophecy concerning the Messiah (Zechariah 9:9). His triumphal entry into Jerusalem clearly showed the multitude that He considered Himself the Jewish Messiah.

Jesus Will Return

Jesus taught that He would return from heaven someday (immediately after the tribulation period) to establish His Kingdom on earth (Matthew 24:29-31; John 14:2-3; Matthew 13:40-43). When He returns amidst the clouds, he will judge mankind (Matthew 25:31-45; John 5:21-22, 27). He will gather His believers, but judge those who reject Him. Then Jesus will reign over the earth (Matthew 19:28-30; Luke 22:28-30).

Jesus warned His disciples about the signs that would precede His return to earth (Matthew 24:1-31). The earth would experience famines, earthquakes, wars and rumors of wars. False christs and fale prophets will deceive many. Christians will be persecuted in all nations for following Jesus. The "official" church will fall away from the true faith, but the Gospel (the good news of salvation through faith in Jesus) will preached to all nations. Finally, the sun and moon will cease to give light, and the stars will fall from the sky. The heavens will be shaken. Then Jesus will return amidst the clouds in power and glory. He will rescue His people and bring His judgment on the non-believing world (Matthew 24:29-31; 25:31-46).

In the Book of Revelation, the Apostle John is told that Jesus will return from Heaven riding a white stallion amidst the clouds. He will defeat His enemies (including the antichrist and false prophet), rescue His people, and shepherd the nations with an iron rod (Revelation 19:11-20:15; 11:15). He will rule over the nations for a thousand years (Revelation 20:1-6). Then, after one final revolt led by Satan, Jesus will judge the living and the dead (Revelation 20:7-15). After that, Jesus will rule over the universe forever.

Jesus Taught the Old Testament is God's Inerrant Word

Besides the six main themes of Jesus' teachings mentioned above, Jesus also taught His disciples His views concerning the Bible. New Testament scholar John W. Wenham discussed Christ's view of the Old Testament:

> Our Lord not only believed the truth of the Old Testament history and used the Scriptures as final authority in matters of faith and conduct, he also regarded the writings themselves as inspired. To Him, Moses, the prophets, David, and the other Scripture writers were given their messages by the Spirit of God (Geisler, ed., *Inerrancy* 16-17).

Some of Christ's teachings concerning the Old Testament were as follows:

> Do not think that I came to abolish the Law or the Prophets; I did not come to abolish, but to fulfill. For truly I say to you, until heaven and earth pass away, not the smallest letter or

> stroke shall pass away from the Law, until all has been accomplished (Matthew 5:17-18).
>
> And He answered and said to them, "And why do you yourselves transgress the commandment of God for the sake of your tradition? For God said, 'Honor your father and mother,' and, 'He who speaks evil of father or mother, let him be put to death'" (Matthew 15:3-4).
>
> But regarding the resurrection of the dead, have you not read that which was spoken to you by God, saying, "I am the God of Abraham, and the God of Isaac, and the God of Jacob"? (Matthew 22:31-32).
>
> He was also saying to them, "You nicely set aside the commandment of God in order to keep your tradition. For Moses said, 'Honor your father and your mother'; and, 'He who speaks evil of father or mother, let him be put to death'; but you say, 'If a man says to his father or mother, anything of mine you might have been helped by is Corban (that is to say, given to God),' you no longer permit him to do anything for his father or his mother; thus invalidating the word of God by your tradition which you have handed down. . ." (Mark 7:9-13).

It is abundantly clear that Jesus considered the entire Old Testament (what the Jews of His day called "the Law and the Prophets") to be the inspired Word of God. He referred to the Old Testament authors as prophets (Matthew 11:13; 12:39; 22:40; 23:31-35; 24:15; 26:56; Luke 16:16-17, 31; 18:31; 24:44; John 6:45), meaning those who proclaim God's truth. In fact, Jesus spoke of the prophets as beginning with Abel and ending with Zechariah (Luke

11:49-51). This covers the exact time period of the Old Testament, from creation to about 400 BC. Since Christ is God Himself, His view of the Old Testament must be correct. Therefore, the Old Testament is the written Word of God.

Jesus Promised the New Testament would also be the Inerrant Word of God

Christ ascended to heaven before the New Testament was recorded. However, the promises He made to his apostles guaranteed that the New Testament would be the inspired Word of God:

Go therefore and make disciples of all nations, baptizing them in the name of the Father and the Son and the Holy Spirit, teaching them to observe all that I commanded you; and lo, I am with you always, even to the end of the age (Matthew 28:19-20).

> Heaven and earth will pass away, but My words will not pass away (Mark 13:31).
>
> But the Helper, the Holy Spirit, whom the Father will send in My name, He will teach you all things, and bring to your remembrance all that I said to you (John 14:26).
>
> When the Helper comes, whom I will send to you from the Father, that is the Spirit of truth, who proceeds from the Father, He will bear witness of Me, and you will bear witness also, because you have been with Me from the beginning (John 15:26-27).
>
> But when He, the Spirit of truth, comes, He will guide you into all the truth; for He will not speak on His own initiative,

> but whatever He hears, He will speak; and He will disclose to you what is to come (John 16:13).
>
> But you shall receive power when the Holy Spirit has come upon you; and you shall be My witnesses both in Jerusalem, and in all Judea and Samaria, and even to the remotest part of the earth (Acts 1:8).

From these quotes of Christ, five conclusions can be drawn. First, Jesus promised that His teachings would be preserved. Second, He said that the Holy Spirit would remind the apostles of all that He told them. Third, the Holy Spirit would reveal future events to the apostles. Fourth, the Holy Spirit would guide the apostles into the truth (prevent them from promoting doctrinal errors). Fifth, the Holy Spirit would empower the apostles to be Christ's authoritative representatives to the world.

From the above conclusions it is clear that Christ promised to preserve His teachings through the apostles' writings. Obviously, these writings make up the New Testament. Since Jesus is the almighty God, His plan cannot be thwarted. Therefore, since He promised to preserve His words through the teachings of the apostles, then their teachings (which have been passed on to future generations) are the teachings of Christ. Hence, they are the Word of God.

It should also be noted that Jesus taught that only the Old Testament and the teachings of His apostles (the New Testament) were the Word of God. Jesus did not teach that His written revelation would be continuously revealed throughout the centuries. Jesus' teachings about the Old and New Testaments leave no room for the Muslim Koran or the Mormon scriptures to be part of God's Word. God's written word, according to Jesus, would be completed during the lives of the original apostles—His Spirit-empowered and authoritative witnesses.

The evidence declares Jesus to be God. Jesus taught that both the Old and New Testaments are the Word of God. Therefore, the Old and New Testaments are the Word of God. We need to submit our lives to what God has revealed to us in His Word.

Chapter Eighteen
Why Did Jesus Die?

The death of Jesus of Nazareth by crucifixion is one of the most firmly established historical events of ancient history. The world's leading New Testament scholars acknowledge that Jesus died by crucifixion nearly 2,000 years ago. We must now try to answer the question: why did Jesus die? Throughout history several different theories of Christ's death have been proposed. In this chapter we will discuss these views.

False Theories of Christ's Death

In the past, some scholars have argued that Jesus did not really die on the cross; instead, He merely passed out on the cross, only to be revived later in the tomb. He then departed the tomb and showed Himself alive to His disciples, and they mistakenly proclaimed Him to be risen. This is called the swoon theory.

The swoon theory has fallen from favor in scholarly circles for several reasons. First, John reported that when Jesus' side was pierced, blood and water flowed out. Modern medical science has shown this to be evidence that Jesus was already dead before His side was pierced. Had He still been alive, only blood would have flowed from His side. Second, a crucified victim needs to push up from his feet to breathe while on the cross. In the down position, the victim cannot breathe. Hence, if someone is in the down position, they are most likely dead, not passed out. Third, assuming Jesus was alive while in the tomb, He would not have had the strength to remove the stone, overpower the guards, travel for miles on feet with open wounds, and convince the apostles He had conquered death. The rigors of scourging and crucifixion would have left Him in a critical state. Rather than worshiping Jesus as the risen Lord, the apostles would have sought medical attention for their battered rabbi. For these reasons, the swoon theory is rarely held today.

Another false theory of Christ's death is the tragic accident theory. According to this view, Jesus had become very popular and suddenly, without expecting it, He was tragically condemned to death by the Romans. This view fails because it does not acknowledge that Jesus considered His death the focal point of His mission. Jesus' death was not unexpected to Him; He came to earth to die for the sins of mankind.

A third false theory of Jesus' death is called the ransom to Satan theory. This theory correctly teaches that Jesus died to pay the ransom price for our sins. However, this theory incorrectly has Jesus paying the ransom price to Satan. In reality, Jesus owes Satan nothing. Through Jesus' death and resurrection, Jesus defeated Satan. Jesus conquered Satan—He did not pay any ransom price to him. The only ransom price Jesus paid for our sins, He paid to the Father's justice and holiness.

Inadequate Theories of Christ's Death

Several theories of the atonement (the death of Christ for our sins) are not necessarily false, but they are inadequate. They do not fully explain the significance of Jesus' death. Three inadequate theories of Christ's death are the moral influence theory, the example theory, and the victory over Satan theory.

Proponents of the moral influence theory believe that the sole purpose of Jesus' death on the cross was to morally influence us to be better people. Though it is true that Christ's death should encourage us to live lives of obedience to the Lord, this is not the main reason why Jesus died. Those who hold to the moral influence theory teach a liberal, watered-down version of Christianity which contradicts true biblical Christianity by teaching salvation by works. In this false view, Jesus empowers us to earn our salvation through our own good works. This clearly contradicts the teachings of God's Word (Romans 3:10; 3:23; Matthew 19:25-26).

The second inadequate view of Christ's death is called the example theory. The example theory teaches that Jesus died on the cross to set the example for us so that we will be willing to die for what we believe in. Jesus' death motivates us to be willing to die for what is right and true. Though there is a sense in which Jesus, by dying on the cross, set an example for us of humble, selfless service (Philippians 2:5-11), still, this is not the main reason for Jesus' death.

The third inadequate view of Jesus' death is called the victory over Satan theory. This view claims that the only reason why Jesus died was to defeat Satan and his works. Though it is true that Jesus died on the cross to defeat Satan and His works (Colossians 2:13-15), there is more to His death than this—He died as a substitute sacrifice for the sins of mankind (1 Peter 2:24; 3:18; John 1:29). Certainly the Bible teaches that the crucifixion dealt Satan's kingdom a fatal blow (Genesis 3:15; John 12:31-33; 1 John 3:8); but, this alone does not exhaust the significance of Jesus' death.

The True Theory of Christ's Death—Substitution and Victory

The true theory of Jesus' death is twofold: 1) Jesus died in our place and took our punishment for us as a substitute sacrifice for our sins, and 2) Jesus conquered Satan and the forces of evil through His death.

The main significance of Jesus' death He is that He died as a substitutionary sacrifice for our sins (1 Peter 2:24; 3:18; 2 Corinthians 5:21). The bloodshed of animal sacrifices never took away the sins of man (Hebrews 10:1-4). Instead, these sacrifices pointed forward to the day when the ultimately worthy substitute sacrifice for our sins would come and die as the "Lamb od God who takes away the sins of the world" (John 1:29).

God created mankind in His image (Genesis 1:27). One aspect of the image of God in man is that we were morally perfect and in complete fellowship with God (Genesis 2:25). Since God is a loving God, He gave mankind free will—true love gives the recipient of that love the freedom to accept or reject that love. God did not create Adam and Eve as robots programed to obey. Because He loved them, He gave them the freedom to obey Him or disobey Him (Genesis 2:15-17). By choosing to sin (Genesis 3:1-8), Adam and Eve rebelled against God and perverted their perfect natures. Since they would reproduce offspring, their offspring would now inherit their corrupted (i.e., sinful) nature. Because we inherit a sin nature from our forebearers (Psalm 51:5), we naturally sin and join Adam and Eve in their rebellion against God. Because we inherit a sin nature, we are born separted from God and we cannot save ourselves.

All sin, even the smallest sin, separates us from God; for God is absolutely holy and He cannot fellowship with sin. God is so holy that cannot forgive sin unless it has been paid for in full—His justice demands no less. But, since all sin is rebellion against the ultimately worthy Being (i.e., God), the punishment for sin must be the ultimate punishment. This is what the Bible calls eternal torment (i.e., eternal separation from God—the only source of true, eternal joy). There is no greater punishment than the eternal lake of fire (Revelation 14:9-11; 19:20; 20:10; Matthew 25:41, 46; Mark 9:42-48).

Therefore, if there is going to be a substitute sacrifice for our sins, the substitute sacrifice must be ultimately worthy (i.e., God). This means that only God can be the substitute sacrifice for our sins. However, God as God cannot die. Hence, in order to represent man and to be able to die as our substitute sacrifice, God the Son had to become a man. This is called the incarnation. In order to be able to redeem mankind, the ultimately worthy sacrifice must be both fully-God and fully-man.

God the Son did not cease to be God by becoming a man. Instead, He added a human nature without subtracting from Himself His divine nature. Jesus always existed as God the second Person of the Trinity, but at a point in time He became a man by adding a human nature. This is called the hypostatic union—Jesus is one Person with two natures forever. He is fully-God and fully-man.

As we stated earlier, God cannot forgive sin unless it has been paid for in full. But Jesus, the God-man, has paid the full price for our sins by dying on the cross. God is satisfied with Jesus' death—the ultimate price. Therefore, we do not need to suffer in hell for our sins since Jesus took our punishment and paid the price to God's holiness and justice (Hebrews 1:3; 10:10-14). However, God is a God of love; He will not force us to accept His forgiveness and salvation—we are free to either accept or reject God's forgiveness and salvation by either accepting or rejecting Jesus as our Savior. Only those who trust in Jesus for salvation will be forgiven and will be regenerated by the Holy Spirit (John 3:3, 16-18; 6:47; 14:6; Titus 3:3-5; Ephesians 2:8-9; Romans 6:23).

Therefore, the primary reason for Jesus' death is that He became a substitute sacrifice for our sins. He paid the penalty for our sins and took our punishment for us. If we trust in Jesus alone for salvation, we receive the free gift of salvation and our sins are forgiven.

The second main reason why Jesus died on the cross is to defeat Satan, his demons, and his works (Colossians 2:13-15; 1 John 3:8). Satan is the adversary who opposes God and all that God stands for (Revelation 12:9). Satan led mankind astray by tempting him in the garden and continues to tempt mankind to do evil and resist God's salvation through Jesus. Though God gave dominion to man in the Garden of Eden, Satan deceived mankind and stole the earth from man. This is why Satan is called "the god of this world" (2

Corinthians 4:4). By dying on the cross, Jesus saves man from the loss of paradise due to Satan's deception. But, Jesus also redeems the planet earth from Satan's dominion (Revelation 11:15; 20:1-7). Through His death, Jesus has won the victory over Satan and his works. He has defeated Satan and sin; He has conquered the greatest enemy of God and man.

Hence, Jesus died on the cross to be a substitute sacrifice for our sins and to defeat Satan and his works. Because Jesus died and rose again, there is hope; for, by rising from the dead, Jesus has conquered death for mankind. Those who trust in Jesus for salvation will be saved. For Jesus is "the Way, the Truth, and the Life; no one comes to the Father except through Him" (John 14:6).

Is Christ's Death on the Cross Divine Child Abuse?

The radical "new atheist" Richard Dawkins believes that the biblical account of Jesus' death on the cross, if true, is a case of "Divine child abuse." Dawkins states:

> I have described atonement, the central doctrine of Christianity, as vicious, sado-masochistic, and repellent. We should also dismiss it as barking mad. . . . If God wanted to forgive sins, why not just forgive them, without having Himself tortured and executed in payment? (*New Statesman* 80).

To address Dawkins' attack on the atonement, several points need to be made. First, Jesus willingly suffered and died on the cross—God the Father did not force Him to die (John 10:15-18). Jesus was not a passive victim (Copan, *Is God a Moral Monster?* 52).

Second, Jesus was no child. Jesus was an adult—He made the choice to die for our sins in eternity as God the second Person of the Trinity. God the Son, in His divine nature, was never a child.

Third, Dawkins and other atheists ignore the fact that love drove Jesus to the cross. Jesus loved us so much that He voluntarily chose to die on the cross for our sins (Romans 5:8; John 3:16-17). Jesus loved us so much that He willingly joined with mankind and experienced suffering and death for the purpose of rescuing man from his sin (Copan, *Moral Monster* 51-53). "Greater love has no one than this, that a man lay down his life for his friends" (John 15:13).

Fourth, the new atheists do not see the need for the death of Jesus because they downplay sin. Atheists deny the fall of mankind into sin; hence, they see no need for atonement (Lennox, *Gunning for God* 146-151). They trivialize sin and, therefore, ignore the drastic measures needed to remedy it (154).

Even with the horrible evils of the twentieth century, the new atheists minimize man's sin problem. If one downplays sin, rejects the fall, and ignores the horrible evils in the world, then the atonement appears to be unnecessary.

Yet, the new atheists attempt to stand up for justice. But, one wonders if they even know what "justice" means. Justice demands that the punishment fit the crime. If God really exists and man has rebelled against Him, then we are guilty of crimes of cosmic proportions. We are deserving of the ultimate in punishment. Only an ultimately worthy substitute sacrifice can atone for man's sins. Hence, only God can offer Himself as a substitute sacrifice for our sins. But, the new atheists deny the incarnation—God the Son becoming a man. By rejecting the incarnation and deity of Jesus, the new atheists cannot make any sense of the atonement (Lennox, 145-162).

In the fullest sense of the word "forgive," only God can forgive sin since all sin is rebellion against Him. The incarnation and atonement are inseparable. There was no other way for man to be saved. Christ's death was not arbitrary; instead, it was necessary. Only Christ's death could satisfy the perfect justice of God. God the Son had to become a man and die as a sacrifice for our sins if man is to be saved (Galatians 2:21; 2 Corinthians 5:19; 1 Peter 2:24; 3:18). Rather than being "divine child abuse," Christ's death on the cross is the ultimate expression of God's love for mankind (Romans 5:8; John 15:13).

Chapter Nineteen
Is Jesus the Only Way to be Saved?

A Biblical Refutation of Universalism

Universalism is the false view that teaches that everyone is or will be saved. This clearly contradicts the New Testament, which we have shown to be historically reliable and the inerrant Word of God. Jesus clearly taught that many people choose the path that leads to destruction and would not find eternal life (Matthew 7:13-14). He said that many people would spend eternity in "everlasting fire prepared for the devil and his angels" (Matthew 25:41). Jesus called the place of eternal torment "Gehenna," and refered to it as a place where "their worm does not die and the fire is not quenched" (Mark 9:42-48). The Book of Revelation also speaks of a place of eternal torment called "the lake of fire" (Revelation 14:9-11; 19:20; 20:11-15). Those who die without accepting Jesus as their Savior will spend eternity apart from God in conscious torment.

Jesus taught that the only way to escape the coming wrath of eternal torment is to trust in Him alone for salvation (John 3:16-18). Jesus proclaimed, "I am the Way, the Truth, and the Life; no one comes to the Father except through Me" (John 14:6). Clearly, Jesus did not teach universalism; He did not teach that everyone will be saved.

A Biblical Refutation of Religious Pluralism

Religious pluralism is the view that all religions lead to God—that a person can be saved regardless of their religious beliefs. This view teaches that there are many different paths to the same God, and that the different world religions all worship the same God, though in different ways. This is the view espoused by many Hindus, the Bahai

Faith, and liberal "Christians." But, according to Jesus and the Bible, all religions do not teach the same thing and do not all lead to God.

The world religions do not teach the same things, nor do they worship the same God. The leading religions of the world disagree about God. Traditional Buddhism is agnostic towards God's existence, while Hinduism promotes a god that is a non-personal force. Secular Humanism denies the existence of God, while the New Age Movement agrees with Hindusim that god is a non-personal force. The Latter-Day Saints (i.e., Mormons) belive that there are many gods and that Mormon males can someday become gods. The Jehovah's Witnesses believe that God the Father is the all-powerful God, but Jesus is a lesser god. Though Judaism and Islam agree with Christianity that there exists only one God who is personal and the Creator of all else that exists, these two religions teach that God is only one person, whereas Christianity teaches that the one true God is three equal and eternal Persons—the Father, Son, and Holy Spirit. Hence, the world's religions do not teach the same thing about God. In fact, they all disagree with Christianity concerning God.

The world's religions also disagree regarding the identity of Jesus. Christianity teaches that Jesus is God the second Person of the Trinity; He is fully God and fully man; He died on the cross for our sins and bodily rose from the dead. Hinduism, the New Age Movement, and the Bahai Faith teach that Jesus is just one of many manfestations of God; whereas Christianity teaches that Jesus is "the only begotten Son" (John 3:16). Buddhists acknowledge Jesus as a great moral teacher, nothing more. Secular Humanists believe Jesus is merely a man. Contemporary Judaism teaches that Jesus is either merely a man, or a great teacher, or possibly a prophet; but, He is not God. Islam teaches that Jesus was a great prophet, but not as great as the prophet Muhammad. Jehovah's Witnesses instruct their adherents that Jesus is not fully God; instead, He is a lesser god who was created by God the Father. Mormonism proclaims a Jesus who is one of many gods; He was not always god; He became god and is now progressing in godhood.

The world's religions also differ on the issue of salvation. Christianity teaches that salvation is by God's grace alone, through faith alone, in Jesus alone. Orthodox Judaism teaches salvation through devotion to the God of Israel and obedience to His commands as proclaimed in the Old Testament, while Islam adheres to salvation through devotion to Allah (the Muslim name for God) and obedience to His commands as spelled out in the Koran. Hinduism and the New Age Movement proclaim salvation through Eastern meditation, reincarnation, self-deification (believing that man is god), and devotion to a guru (a teacher of Eastern religious thought). Buddhism teaches that salvation is the cessation of desire (one of the four noble truths) and that it can be attained through what they call the eight-fold path. Secular Humanism rejects the idea of life after death altogether. Salvation, according to the Bahai Faith, can be reached through devotion to God and faithfulness to any one of the world's religions. Mormon salvation is through faith in the Mormon Jesus, receiving Mormon baptism, obeying Mormon ordinances, and eternal progression—a process whereby Mormon males can someday become a god of their own planet. Jehovah's Witnesses teach that salvation comes through faith in the Jehovah's Witnesses' Jesus (a false Jesus who is not fully God) and obedience to God's laws. Since all the world's religions teach a different way of salvation, they cannot all be right. If the Christian doctrine of salvation is true (as we have argued in this book), then all other religions do not save. Only Christianity saves because only the true Jesus of the Bible saves.

Jesus clearly taught that salvation comes only through Him. He said He is the only way for us to be saved (John 14:6; see also Acts 4:12 and 1 Timothy 2:5). He proclaimed that those who believe in Him for salvation receive the free gift of eternal life (John 3:16-17; 6:29, 47); but, those who do not trust in Him for salvation remain condemned (John 3:18). Jesus taught that we remain lost if we do not worship Him as God (John 5:22-23; 8:23-24). The Apostle Peter taught that salvation is only found in Jesus, not in other religions as well (Acts 4:12).

The Apostle Paul clearly states: "I do not nullify the grace of God; for, if righteousness comes through the works of the law, then Christ died needlessly" (Galatians 2:21). If man could earn his own salvation (which is basically what all other world religions teach), then Jesus was being foolish when He died on the cross. For, He believed He was dying for our sins. If we can earn our salvation through good works, then Jesus wasted His time on the cross—His death was entirely unnecessary. Of course, the truth of the matter is this: we cannot save ourselves by our works; we can only be saved through faith in Jesus, the one who died on the cross for our sins (Ephesians 2:8-9; 1 Petyer 2:24; 3:18; Romans 5:8; John 1:29).

Many people claim that they are heavenbound because they believe in God the Father, but they do not believe in Jesus. Jesus disagreed. Jesus said, "he who rejects Me rejects the One who sent Me" (Luke 10:16). A person cannot have the Father if they reject the Son (1 John 2:23); the only way to receive the Father is to accept the One whom He has sent. Jesus proclaimed:

> Therefore everyone who confesses Me before men, I will also confess him before My Father who is in heaven. But whoever denies Me before men, I will also deny him before My Father who is in heaven" (Matthew 10:32-33).

The Bible clearly teaches that all religions do not lead to God; only Christianity is salvific (i.e., has the power to save). The Bible consistently condemns false religion (Joshua 24:14-15; 1 Kings 18:21; Isaiah 45:22; Jeremiah 16:19; Acts 17:11). Any other view of salvation is condemned as false by the Scriptures (Galatians 1:8-9).

Anyone who believes they can save themselves without Jesus, in essence, is claiming that Jesus died needlessly (Galatians 2:21) and is boasting before God (Ephesians 2:8-9).

A Biblical Refutation of Inclusivism

Some professing Christians believe that even though salvation comes only through Jesus, a person does not have to believe in Jesus as Savior to be saved. This view is called Inclusivism. A moderate form of Inclusivism would say that those who never heard the Gospel (i.e., those who never heard about Jesus) can be saved by Jesus, without them actually knowing it, if they love God with all their heart and their neighbor as themselves. The more extreme type of Inclusivism teaches that even people of other religions who have heard about Jesus and knowingly reject Him can still be saved by Him if they love God and their neighbors.

The extreme form of Inclusivism is easy to refute with Scripture. Anyone who denies the Son does not have the Father (1 John 2:23; Luke 10:16; Matthew 10:32-33). If you reject the Son, you are not saved.

However, even the moderate form of Inclusivism is unbiblical as well (except possibly in cases of infants who die before they reach the age of accountability, or people who are permanently and severely handicapped in their mental abilities). For the Bible declares that he who does not believe in Jesus remains condemned (John 3:18). The only was for a person to be saved is by trusting in the true Jesus of the Bible alone for salvation (John 3:16-18; 6:37-40, 47; 11:25-26).

A Biblical Defense of Christian Exclusivism

The true, biblical view of salvation is called Exclusivism. This means that, with the possible exceptions of infants and people who are severely mentally handicapped, only those who trust in Jesus for salvation will be saved (John 14:6; 3:16-18). All who do not trust in Jesus alone for salvation are excluded from salvation; they remain lost.

But, this raises the question, "What about those who never heard the Gospel message of salvation through Jesus?" I believe the Bible provides the answer to this important question.

The Bible teaches that God draws all people to Himself (John 12:32; 16:7-11; 1:9). He does this through the lesser lights of creation and conscience. Through creation God reveals to us that the Creator exists (Romans 1:18-22). Through our consciences God reveals His laws to us and shows us that we are sinners in need of His salvation (Romans 2:14-15). If a person responds to the lesser lights of creation and conscience, God will reveal Jesus to him. From creation, we learn the Creator exists. From our conscience, we learn that we stand condemned before Him and in need of salvation. If a person anywhere on earth is seeking the true God, that person will find Him (Jeremiah 29:13; Psalm 145:18-19; Acts 17:22-31; 16:6-10; James 4:8). The Holy Spirit will reveal the greatest Light, the Lord Jesus, to the person who practices the truth revealed to him through nature (John 3:19-21). God usually reveals Jesus to people by sending missionaries (Romans 10:13-15), but has at times revealed Jesus to people through visions or an appearance of Jesus Himself (Acts 9:1-9).

My point is this: God sits enthroned—He is in control. He draws people to Himself through the Holy Spirit and testifies of Himself through nature. Those who accept God's witness of Himself in nature receive greater revelation. In short, if anyone would freely accept Christ if given the opportunity, will, by the grace of God, receive the opportunity. A biblical example of this is Cornelius (Acts 10, 11). He was a Gentile who acknowledged that the God of Israel was the true God. But he did not yet know Jesus as Savior. God gave visions to both Cornelius and Peter, and guided Peter to preach the Gospel message to Cornelius. The Bible is clear that Cornelius the God-seeker was not saved until the moment he accepted Jesus while Peter preached (Acts 11:13-14). If Inclusivism is true, Cornelius was already saved before he met Peter. Hence, the Bible teaches exclusivism—Cornelius was not saved until he actually believed in Jesus for salvation.

The Gospel message is exclusive—only those who knowingly trust in Jesus for salvation will receive eternal life. Yet, God's love is unlimited (Matthew 5:43-48). He loves all mankind and desires that all mankind be saved (John 3:16-18; 1 Timothy 2:1-6; 2 Peter 3:9; 1 John 2:2). Jesus even died on the cross for false teachers (2 Peter 2:1). The Bible teaches that we are all sinners and we cannot save ourselves (Romans 3:10, 23; 6:23). But, God loves us so much that He sent His Son to die for our sins. However, as a God of love, He will not force us to trust in Jesus. He will not force us to worship Him. Through the power of the Holy Spirit, God draws all people to Himself; but, in the end, we must make the choice to accept or reject Jesus as our personal Savior. God will not force us into heaven. Yet, He cries out to us, "Turn to Me and be saved, all the ends of the earth; for I am God, and there is no other" (Isaiah 45:22; see also Matthew 11:28).

Postscript: A Rational Defense of Salvation Only Through Jesus

We have already provided a biblical defense of salvation only through Jesus. But, a rational case for salvation through Jesus alone can also be made. This case begins with the justice of God. For, if God is just, then His justice demands that He punish all sin. To excuse or ignore sin would be an act of injustice, compromising with sin. Hence, if God is to remain just, He must punish all sin.

Only Christianity proclaims a substitute sacrifice for our sins. Yet, without a substitute sacrifice for our sins, a just God cannot forgive us—our sins remain. The Apostle Paul realized this—that only through Jesus' death could God remain just and yet justify the unrighteous (Romans 3:21-26). Hence, the God of Christianity is more just than the Gods of other religions. For, He cannot tolerate sin but must punish it in full. All other religions offer a cheap salvation—a salvation without a ransom price, a salvation without a substitute sacrifice.

Not only is the Christian God more just than any other concept of God, but the Christian God is also more loving. No other God is so loving that He sacrificed Himself in our place and took our punishment for us. Only the God of the Bible is so loving that He became a man to suffer and die for us (Romans 5:8).

If we acknowledge that evil is real—if we acknowledge that none of us are perfect—then it seems, if we are to be saved, there must be a substitute sacrifice for our sins. There was no other way for us to be saved. Jesus is the only hope for mankind—He is the only way for us to be saved.

Chapter Twenty
Conclusion—The Biblical Jesus is the True Jesus of History

The Historical Jesus

This book has made a strong case that the Jesus of the Bible is the true Jesus of history. Wild speculation by liberal scholars is no substitute for the historical evidence found in the writings of the early church fathers and the New Testament texts themselves. Liberal scholars analyze and criticize the New Testament like no other book. They claim to have a "higher knowledge" which allows them to reconstruct the texts, and Jesus Himself, two-thousand years after the fact! When they disagree with the Apostle Paul, they tell us to trust them and reject Paul as an "innovator." But, as for me, I think I'll side with Paul, the ancient creeds, the ancient sermons, the New Testament texts, and the writings of the Apostolic Fathers and the early church fathers.

The evidence is clear: the Jesus of the New Testament is the true Jesus of history. Liberal scholars have hijacked Jesus and replaced Him with a watered-down Jesus created in their own image. And this they have done without any historical or rational justification. These scholars merely presuppose that miracles are impossible—in other words, they assume the Jesus of the Bible is not the Jesus of history; they have not proven this. All the evidence is against their wild theories.

Our Response to the True Jesus of History

Since the Jesus of the Bible is in fact the true Jesus of history, we are called to make a decision—the most important decision we will ever make. We must decide if we will ignore this fact, pushing Jesus aside and living our lives as if He never lived, or acknowledge that He is Savior, Lord, God, and Messiah. We must choose to reject the Lord Jesus or accept Him—we must decide. Eternity is at stake.

We are all sinners and we cannot save ourselves (Romans 3:10, 23; Isaiah 64:6). Only through Jesus can we be saved. If you have not done so already, I beseech you to accept the Lord Jesus Christ as your Savior—commit your life to Him. Trust in Him alone for salvation. Then find a church that preaches God's Word, a church whose people live in accordance with the teachings of Christ through the power of the indwelling Holy Spirit. Jesus of Nazareth is who He claimed to be. As the Apostle Paul said, Jesus is "our great God and Savior" (Titus 2:13). May He receive all the glory.

Appendix 1
A Refutation Of Marcus Borg's View of the Resurrection

In this paper, I will discuss and critique Dr. Marcus Borg's view of Jesus' resurrection. Borg is the Distinguished Professor of Religion at Oregon State University and one of the leading members of the Jesus Seminar.[1] He is considered one of the world's formost New Testament scholars. Before examining Borg's view of the resurrection, we must briefly discuss his view of Christianity, for this dictates his approach to Jesus' resurrection.

Borg's View of Christianity

Borg believes and argues that Christianity needs to be reinterpreted in light of our culture.[2] He views the older paradigm (traditional Christianity) as outdated and in need of transformation, and proposes what he calls the "emerging paradigm." This new paradigm rejects the Bible as being inspired by God; rather it is a human product.[3] Borg denies that the Bible is "absolute truth" or "God's revealed truth." Rather, he views the Bible as "relative and culturally conditioned."[4] In other words, the Bible is not an infallible authority from which to interpret culture; instead, culture becomes the authoritative principle through which we reinterpret the Bible.

The miraculous events of the Bible, says Borg, are to be interpreted metaphorically, not literally. In his view, the miracles of the Bible should be interpreted as stories or parables—the important thing is not whether or not these miracles really happened, but the spiritual truth being taught through figurative language.[5] Borg views the Christian Faith as our experience with God, yet rejects the traditional idea that Christianity also entails a set of doctrinal truths.[6]

Though Borg rejects the reality of miracles, he believes that Jesus was some how in touch with a spiritual reality in a special way. Jesus was able to, in some mysterious way, bring healing to people's lives. This transcends a mere psychological explanation, but Borg still falls short of acknowledging the reality of miracles—supernatural works of God.[7] Borg also acknowledges that this mysterious ability is common to mystics of other world religions as well.

Borg is pluralistic in his thought. He believes that "God is also known in other ways in other religions."[8] He rejects the idea that Jesus is the only way for man to be saved and he insists that we do not have to believe that Jesus literally died for our sins to be saved.[9] It appears that Borg's religion is determined by his politically correct view of tolerance. He detests the idea that there is only one way to heaven. Concerning Jesus' death, Borg states, "I have trouble imagining that Jesus saw His own death as salvific."[10] Therefore, Borg denies the substitutionary atonement of Jesus; according to him, Jesus did not literally die for our sins.

Borg rejects the literal, bodily resurrection of Jesus. Instead, he views Christ's resurrection metaphorically; the message is that Jesus is alive to us—His message of love still lives.[11] Still, in his written dialogue with conservative scholar N. T. Wright, Borg had a difficult time explaining away the post-resurrection appearances of Christ. Knowing that the past alternative/naturalistic explanations of the resurrection have failed, Borg does not claim that the apostles hallucinated. Rather, he acknowledges that the apostles had "visions" or "apparitions" of Jesus after His death.[12] Borg does not explain what he means by this; however, it is clear that, while he rejects the bodily resurrection of Jesus, he offers no plausible alternative explanation of the New Testament data.

Borg draws a clear distinction between what he calls the "pre-Easter Jesus" and the "post-Easter Jesus."[13] The pre-Easter Jesus is the true Jesus of history—the first century Jew who was crucified and died and is no more. The post-Easter Jesus is the Jesus of faith—the Jesus of Christian experience and tradition.[14] The post-Easter

Jesus is the experience within the hearts of Christians of the divine reality; but, there is no real continuity between the pre-Easter Jesus (the historical Jesus) and the post-Easter Jesus (the Christian's experience of God). Like Bultmann before him, Borg draws a clear distinction between the Christ of Faith and the true Jesus of history.

Borg denies what he calls "supernatural theism" (the traditional view of God), and expouses the world view called panentheism.[15] In this view, the "universe is not separate from God, but in God."[16] Panentheism is the view of God espoused by process theologians; it is a rejection of traditional theism. Evangelical scholar Ben Witherington III describes Borg's non-traditional view of God as follows: "he wishes to deny the sense of God as 'Holy Other' and affirm a God who is around and within us all, apparently without regard to our belief or behavior."[17]

Borg does not accept the true deity of Christ. In his view, Jesus showed us what God is like. It is only in this sense that deity can be figuratively asserted of Jesus.[18] While denying Jesus' literal deity, Borg is honest enough to admit that, before the Gospels were written, "prayers were addressed to Jesus as if to God."[19]

Within the context of Borg's reinterpretation of Christianity, we now need to examine more closely Borg's view of the resurrection. There are two aspects of Borg's view concerning Christ's resurrection: the resurrection as metaphor or parable and the post-resurrection appearances as "visions" or apparitions."

Borg's View of Christ's Resurrection as Metaphor or Parable

Borg admits that, as a child, he believed that Jesus literally rose from the dead.[20] However, Borg no longer accepts Christ's bodily resurrection from the dead. As stated above, Borg re-interprets the miraculous aspects of Christianity as metaphors rather than actual historical occurrences. In his 1999 dialogue with conservative New Testament scholar N. T. Wright, Borg stated:

> I now see Easter very differently. For me, it is irrelevant whether or not the tomb was empty. Whether Easter involved something remarkable happening to the physical body of Jesus is irrelevant. . . it doesn't matter.[21]

> The truth of the Emmaus story . . . and the truth of Easter itself, does not depend upon their being literally and historically factual. It does not depend upon the tomb being empty or on something happening to the corpse of Jesus. . . The truth of Easter is grounded in these experiences [the visions the apostles received], not in what happened (or didn't happen) on a particular Sunday almost two thousand years ago.[22]

Borg rejects the importance of a historical, bodily resurrection of Jesus of Nazareth from the dead. Instead, he believes that what is important is the metaphorical meaning of the resurrection. The historical dimension is not the important factor. Borg acknowledges that many Christians consider the "historical factuality of the Easter stories" central to Christianity, so that if Jesus did not literally and historically rise from the dead, the truth of Christianity would "disappear."[23] Borg disagrees—he believes the resurrection should be viewed as a metaphor or a parable. Borg states:

> For me, the historical ground of Easter is very simple: the followers of Jesus, both then and now, continued to experience Jesus as a living reality after his death. In the early Christian

> community, these experiences included visions or apparitions of Jesus.[24]

> I see the empty tomb and whatever happened to the corpse of Jesus to be ultimately irrelevant to the truth of Easter. . . I see them as the product of a developing tradition and as powerfully true metaphorical narratives.[25]

Borg believes that the significance of the resurrection has nothing to do with history. The important thing is that, after His death by crucifixion, Jesus became alive to His disciples—His message of love still lives despite His horrible death.[26] The historical status of the empty tomb is of no importance to Borg; all that matters is the message of Jesus being reborn within the hearts of His disciples after His execution at the hands of the Roman authorities.

Borg's View of Christ's Post-Resurrection Appearances as Visions or Apparitions

Though Borg considers the resurrection of Jesus to be primarily a metaphor or a parable, he realizes that something had to occur to transform the lives of the apostles from despairing individuals void of hope into courageous proclaimers of Jesus' message of love. Since Borg denies the bodily resurrection of Jesus, he is forced to suggest an alternative explanation. He knows that the hallucination theory[27] has failed to explain the historical data; hence, he proposes the idea that the apostles experienced "visions" or "apparitions" of Jesus. Borg makes this clear in the following quotes:

> Paul saw a great light and heard the voice of Jesus. Those travelling with Paul did not share the experience, indicating that it was a private and not a public experience. It was what is

> commonly called a vision. It is possible, perhaps even likely, that Paul thought of the appearances of the risen Jesus to others as also visions.[28]

But not all visions are hallucinations. They can be disclosures of reality.[29]

> The story of the empty tomb may be a metaphor of the resurrection rather than a historical report. . . the story of the empty tomb is really true, even though it may not be literally true; the story of the Emmaus Road is really true, even though it may not be literally true, and so on. Stories can be true without being literally and factually true.[30]

> I find these stories powerfully true as parables of the resurrection. It does not matter to me as a Christian whether any of them describe events that you or I could have witnessed. It does not matter to me whether the tomb was empty. But I am aware that a historical question can be asked: what happened? What I am confident of is this. The followers of Jesus had experiences of him after his death that convinced them that he continued to be a figure of the present. Almost certainly some of these experiences were visions; it would be suprising if there weren't any. . . If the risen Jesus exists as a body, it is a body radically different from any meaning we give to the word "body" that it seems misleading to use the term.[31]

Borg assumes that Paul's reference to the "spiritual body" (soma pneumatikon) in First Corinthians, chapter fifteen, indicates that Paul did not believe that Jesus' resurrection was bodily.[32] It should be noted that Borg, one of the world's leading liberal New Testament scholars, comes very close at this point to accepting a spiritual resurrection of Jesus, though he does deny Christ's bodily resurrection.

Critique of Borg's Metaphorical View of Christ's Resurrection

The evidence clearly demonstrates the deficiencies of Borg's view of the resurrection as a metaphor or parable. Also, Borg's belief that the post-resurrection appearances were visions does not stand up to the evidence.

Resurrection scholar Gary R. Habermas has developed a strong case for Jesus' bodily resurrection based on a list of twelve historical facts accepted by virtually all New Testament scholars. The evidence for these facts is so overwhelming that nearly all New Testament scholars feel compelled to acknowledge them as historical. This list includes: 1)Jesus died by crucifixion, 2) He was buried in a private tomb, 3) because of Jesus' death, His disciples began to depair, 4) Jesus' tomb was found empty a few days after His death, 5) the disciples had experiences in which they believed Jesus actually appeared to them, 6) due to these experiences, the disciples' lives were greatly transformed to the point that they were willing to suffer and die for their faith, 7) the resurrection was proclaimed very early in the history of the chruch, 8) the early preaching of the disciples concerning the resurrection took place in Jerusalem, the city where Jesus was crucified in the recent past, 9) the Gospel message, from the start, focused on Jesus' death and resurrection, 10) Sunday became the primary day of worship for the early church, 11) James, Jesus' brother, was a skeptic but became a Christian—and a leader in the early church—when he believed he saw the risen Jesus, and 12) within a few years of Jesus' death, the apostle Paul became a Christian when he believed he saw the risen Jesus.[33] Nearly all New Testament scholars accept eleven of these historical facts. Only the empty tomb has been called into question, though over seventy percent of leading New Testament scholars do accept the empty tomb.[34]

In a work on the resurrection co-authored with his former student Michael Licona,

Habermas narrows his resurrection apologetic by using only five of the twelve historical facts. These five facts are: 1) Jesus' death by crucifixion, 2) the disciples' belief that He rose and appeared to them, 3) Paul's conversion, 4) James' conversion, and 5) the empty tomb.[35] Using these five historical facts, we can refute both Borg's view that the resurrection was a metaphor and his assertion that the post-resurrection appearances were merely visions—not bodily appearances.

Borg's thesis that Paul and the New Testament authors were reporting the resurrection of Jesus as a metaphor or parble has numerous problems. First, if the resurrection was just a parable or metaphor, then this probably would not have led Paul and James to convert to Christianity. James was a skeptic concerning Jesus and Paul persecuted the early church. Anything less than a real resurrection cannot adequately explain their conversion experiences. Second, it is extremely doubtful that the disciples (who were orthodox Jews) would have faced persecution and possible death for a parable. It is widely recognized that James and Paul died martyrs' deaths for their faith. It is unlikely that they, as Jews, would have been willing to die for a parable. Third, the metaphor view does not explain the empty tomb.[36] Fourth, the New Testament resurrection accounts were not written in the genre of metaphor. The authors wrote as if they were recording historical events of the recent past.[37]

It seems that Borg is aware that his view of the resurrection accounts as metaphor or parable does not adequately explain the New Testament data concerning the resurrection. He apparently recognizes the need for an explanation of the report of the early church concerning the post-resurrection appearances of Christ. At this point Borg suggests that the experiences the apostles had may have been "apparitions" or "visions."

Critique of Borg's Apparition View of Christ's Resurrection

Marcus Borg admits that the post-resurrection appearances of Jesus were not hallucinations. Instead, he refers to them as "visions" or "apparitions."[38] If I understand him correctly, Borg acknowledges that the apostles saw something objective, though he rejects a bodily resurrection. On this point, though he is extremely vague, Borg comes very close to acknolwedging a spiritual resurrection of Jesus. Hence, to refute Borg's view, evidence for Jesus' bodily resurrection must be provided. If Jesus bodily rose from the dead and bodily appeared to His followers, then the post-resurrection appearances were obviously not mere "apparitions" or "visions."

There are several reasons for believing that Jesus bodily rose from the dead. First, New Testament scholar N. T. Wright pointed out that the first century AD Jewish concept of resurrection always entailed the raising of a dead body and bringing it back to life—life reentering a corpse.[39] If Christ's corpse remained in the tomb, according to the Jewish concept of resurrection, no resurrection would have occurred. Wright's research shows that the Greek words for resurrection or rising from the dead (i.e., anastasis, anistemi, egeiro, etc.), when used in a literal fashion, always mean a physical resurrection. Even those who rejected the idea of a future physical resurrection (i.e., the Sadduccess, pagans, Platonic philosophers, etc.) nonetheless understood these Greek words to signify a physical resurrection, not mere spiritual life after death.[40]

Second, the Apostle Paul's view of resurrection was bodily. It is important to remember that Borg is not calling the Apostle Paul a liar when he reports that he saw several post-resurrection appearances of

Jesus. However, Borg contends that Paul did not view these appearances as bodily appearances, but as spiritual "visions" or "apparitions." But this cannot be the case, for if we examine the writings of Paul that are accepted even by liberal New Testament critics like Borg, we find that Paul viewed resurrection as a bodily event. Paul spoke of resurrection as "resurrection out of the dead" (Philippians 3:11; exanastasin ton nekron). Paul wrote that he was a Pharisee (Philippians 3:5), and Pharisees believed in a future physical resurrection of God's people (Acts 23:6-10). They developed their belief in the future resurrection from Old Testament passages such as Daniel 12:2 and Isaiah 26:19. Paul, as a Pharisee, believed in a future physical resurrection of the children of God. Since Paul taught that our bodies will be transformed so that they will be like Jesus' "glorious body," it is evident that he believed Jesus' resurrection was bodily (Philippiand 3:21). Paul speaks in terms of physical resurrection when he said, "He who raised Christ from the dead will also give life to your mortal bodies through His Spirit, who lives in you" (Romans 8:11). In the same passage, Paul stated that "we eagerly await our adoption as sons, the redemption of our bodies" (Romans 8:23). Paul taught that believers' bodies will someday be raised just as Jesus' body was raised on the third day. Paul taught that Jesus rose from the dead—by this he means a bodily resurrection—despite Borg's protest.

Paul believed in life after death. He taught that when a child of God dies they immediately are ushered into the Lord's presence (2 Corinthians 5:8; Philippians 1:21-23). But, Paul taught that Jesus was raised "the third day" after His death (1 Corinthians 15:4). In other words, Paul believed that Jesus' resurrection occurred on the third day after Jesus' life after death began. This is what N. T. Wright refers to as "a new life after a period of life after death" and "life after life after death."[41]

Third, Paul's instruction on the state of the spiritual body in 1 Corinthians 15 strongly implies an empty tomb and a physical resurrection. First, Paul mentions that Jesus died, was buried, rose, and appeared (vs 3-8). There is no reason to mention the burial unless Jesus was bodily raised. He implies that what was buried (Jesus' body) was that which was raised. Second, verses 42 to 44 tell us that whatever was sown (or buried) was raised. Since Jesus' body was buried, it was His body that was raised. Third, Paul says of the resurrection body—our resurrection bodies will be patterned afterJesus' resurrection body—that it was sown a "natural body" (soma psuchikon), but it will be raised a "spiritual body" (soma pneumatichon). If Paul meant to say that a resurrection is a spiritual event and not a bodily event, then it is rather odd that he described both the pre-death state and the resurrected state as a "soma" (body). If Paul wanted to teach a spiritual resurrection, then why not say: "it is sown a soma (body), but it is raised a pneuma (spirit)?" Apparently, Paul is teaching that the same body that dies is raised, but it is changed and it receives new powers. It was buried a soulish/natural body (soma psuchikon), but it will be raised a spiritual/supernatural body (soma pneumatikon).

Fourth, the apostolic father Ignatius, Bishop of Antioch, clearly taught, as early as 107 AD, that Jesus bodily rose from the dead. Ignatius had been trained by leaders of the early church who were contemporaries of the apostles (if not by the apostles themselves); yet, he was adamant that Jesus' resurrection was bodily. He wrote that Jesus was:

> . . . truly nailed in the flesh for us under Pontius Pilate and Herod the tetrarch . . . and he truly suffered just as he truly raised himself—not, as certain unbelievers say, that he suffered in appearance only. . . For I know and believe that he was in the flesh even after the resurrection.[42]

Fifth, even Borg admits the four cannonical Gospels (Matthew, Mark, Luke, and John) are first century AD documents.[43] Yet, these first century documents do not speak of a spiritual resurrection, but a physical resurrection. Jesus said He would raise His body (John 2:21). After He rose, Jesus invited Thomas to touch His wounds (John 20:26-29). The risen Jesus told the apostles He had "flesh and bones," He showed them His hands and His feet, He invited them to touch His wounds, and He ate some fish in their presence (Luke 24:36-43). Mark's Gospel tells us that the risen Jesus left His tomb empty (Mark 16:1-8; see also Matthew 28:1-6). In Matthew's Gospel, the women held the feet of the risen Christ and worshiped Him (Matthew 28:9). In John's Gospel, Jesus had to tell Mary Magdalene to stop clinging to Him (John 20:17).

All the first century evidence (Paul and the four Gospels) teaches a bodily resurrection. There is no early evidence to support Borg's "apparition" or "vision" theory of Christ's post-resurrection appearances. In fact, the first writers to use the words for resurrection in an entirely different way—a spiritual resurrection rather than a physical one—were the Gnostic heretics of the late second century.[44]

Conclusion

We have shown that Marcus Borg of the Jesus Seminar believes that what really occurred two-thousnad years ago is not important. He believes that the metaphorical meaning of the resurrection is all that matters. Borg also believes the post-resurrection appearances of Jesus were not bodily appearances—they were "visions" or "apparitions." But we have shown that Paul taught and believed that Jesus had bodily risen from the dead and bodily appeared numerous times to different people, including himself.

Paul believed the bodily resurrection of Jesus in history is of the utmost importance. Paul, while proclaiming the physical resurrection of Jesus, wrote, "And if Christ is not risen, then our preaching is vain and your faith is also vain. . . . And if Christ is not risen, your faith is futile; you are still in your sins!" (1 Corinthians 15:14, 17). It is clear that Paul, contrary to the conclusions drawn by Borg, believed that the bodily resurrection of Jesus is a true historical event that has eternal consequences. In Paul's view, Christianity stands or falls on whether Jesus of Nazareth bodily rose from the dead two-thousand years ago. In Paul's thought, there is no salvation in Christ's death if Jesus did not truly, and bodily, rise from the dead.

For Paul, the resurrection was a true historical event; it was no mere metaphor or parable. And, for Paul, the post-resurrection appearances were not merely "visions." Jesus actually appeared to him and to others in the body in which He was crucified. Jesus' body, though the same body in which He had died, had been glorified and given new powers—it was an immortal body, a spiritual body. When Paul saw the risen Christ, he knew that "death had been swallowed up in victory" and that the victory over death had been won. He knew that our work for the Lord would never be in vain. He knew that the future resurrection of God's children was guaranteed by the bodily resurrection of the Jewish Messiah, the Lord Jesus Christ. This conviction, based on Jesus' bodily resurrection, enabled Paul to suffer and die proclaiming the same message uttered by the angel at the tomb, a message rejected by Marcus Borg: "He is not here: He has risen, just as He said. Come and see the place where He lay" (Matthew 28:6).

Endnotes

[1]The Jesus Seminar is a group of New Testament scholars and their associates who began to meet in 1985 to vote on which sayings of Jesus, recorded in the New Testament, are authentic. They were led by recognized New Testament scholars such as Marcus Borg, John Dominic Crossan, Robert Funk, and Burton Mack. Due to the fact that the Jesus Seminar continues to receive much media attention, many now believe that this radical group of scholars represents mainstream New Testament scholarship. However, this is not the case. The Jesus Seminar goes against the thrust of Jesus research as embodied in the scholarly work being done in the third quest for the historical Jesus. The Jesus Seminar dates the four Gospels found in the New Testament to have been written in the late first century AD. Supposedly, they were not authored by eyewitnesses who knew Jesus or by people who knew eyewitnesses. The Seminar also believes *The Gospel of Thomas* to be as reliable (or as unreliable) as the four traditional Gospels (i.e., Matthew, Mark, Luke, and John). The Jesus Seminar published the resuls of their research in their book *The Five Gospels* in 1993. It contains the four traditional Gospels and *The Gospel of Thomas. The Five Gospels* is color-coded based upon the votes taken by by the Seminar members: words in red contain statements that, according to the Jesus Seminar, Jesus definitely said. Words in pink were probably spoken by Jesus, while gray-lettered words were only possibly spoken by Jesus. Finally, words in black were statements that Jesus definitely did not say. *The Five Gospels* contain some startling conclusions. A few examples will suffice. The Gospel of John has only one statement of Jesus in red, just one in pink, and only a few statements in gray. Over 82% of Jesus' sayings recorded in the four Gospels combined are rejected, whereas only 15 sayings of Jesus are red-lettered. According to the the Jesus Seminar,

Jesus never claimed to be God, Messiah, or Savior. Hence, the Jesus Seminar rejects the Jesus found in the New Testament and presents the public with an alternative, non-supernatural Jesus.

[2]Marcus J. Borg, *The Heart of Christianity* (San Francisco: HarperSanFrancisco, 2003), 18-19.

[3]Ibid., 45.

[4]Ibid.

[5]Ibid., 12-15.

[6]Ibid., 40-41.

[7]Marcus J. Borg, *Jesus: A New Vision* (San Francisco: HarperSanFrancisco, 1987), 33-34.

[8]*The Heart of Christianity*, 43.

[9]Ibid., 44.

[10]N. T. Wright and Marcus J. Borg, *The Meaning of Jesus: Two Visions* (San Francisco: HarperSanFrancisco, 1999), 81.

[11]*The Heart of Christianity*, 54.

[12]Wright and Borg, 132-133.

[13]*The Heart of Christianity*, 82.

[14]Ibid.

[15]Ibid., 65-70.

[16]Ibid., 66.

[17]Ben Witherington III, *The Jesus Quest* (Downers Grove: InterVarsity Press, 1997), 106.

[18]Wright and Borg, 150.

[19]Ibid., 153.

[20]Ibid., 131.

[21]Ibid.

[22]Ibid., 135.

[23]Marcus J. Borg, *Jesus* (San Francisco: HarperSanFrancisco, 2006), 276.

[24]Wright and Borg, 135.

[25]Ibid., 130.

[26]*The Heart of Christianity*, 54.

[27]See Gary R. Habermas and Michael R. Licona, *The Case for the Resurrection of* Jesus (Grand Rapids: Kregel Publications, 2004), 106-109, 113. The hallucination theory fails to explain the post-resurrection appearances of Jesus for several reasons. First, modern psychology has shown that hallucinations occur in someone's mind.

Therefore, no two people can have the same hallucination. But, the New Testament reports that Jesus appeared to groups of people, not just to individuals. Second, the hallucination theory cannot account for the empty tomb. Third, hallucinations cannot account for the conversions of Paul or James. People who have hallucinated are often easily convinced by others they are mistaken. Paul and James believed they had seen the resurrected Christ and were willing to die martyr's deaths for that belief. Fourth, there exist too many personal variations (believers and non-believers, individuals and groups, men and women, outdoors and indoors, etc.) in the accounts of the post-resurrection appearances to be explained by the hallucination theory.

[28]*Jesus*, 277.

[29]Ibid., 278.

[30]*The Heart of Christianity*, 55.

[31]*Jesus*, 287-289.

[32]Ibid.

[33]Gary R. Habermas, *The Risen Jesus and Future Hope* (Lanahm, Maryland: Rowan & Littlefield Publishers, Inc., 2003), 9-10. Many New Testament scholars start their research on the historical Jesus assuming that passages in the Gospels are not authentic data concerning Jesus. Basically, they start their research in a state of skepticism towards the historical Jesus. It is as if the New Testament data concerning Jesus is considered false until proven true. These New Testament scholars have proposed several principles that help them to determine which passages of the Gospels are probably historically authentic. These principles do not disprove Gospel or

New Testament passages, but they can show that there is good reason to accept certain passages as authentic (even after starting with a skepticism towards the Jesus of the Bible). Dr. Habermas identified some of these principles used by New Testament scholars in a course on the resurrection he taught at Southern Evangelical Seminary, North Carolina, in 2004. These principles or rules are as follows. 1) *Multiple attestation* says that two ancient sources are better than one. There are 5 sources for Jesus material: Mark, "Q," special Matthew (i.e., material unique to Matthew), special Luke (material unique to Luke), and John. Mark is Mark's Gospel. "Q" contains the passages found in Matthew and Luke, but that are not in Mark. Special Matthew contains the information found in Matthew that is not found in Mark or Luke. Special Luke includes the information found in Luke that is not in Matthew or Mark. The John source is basically the information found in the Gospel of John. If an event or saying of Jesus is attested by two or more of these sources the likelihood of it being true greatly increases. The importance of this principle becomes obvious when we note that much of what we know from ancient times comes from only one source. 2) The principle of *discontinuity or dissimilarity* says that if a saying of Jesus can't be traced back to first century Jewish culture or to the teachings of the early church, then Jesus must have said it. This is because, in this case, there would be no possibility of the early church putting their words on Jesus' lips or taking something from the Jewish culture and projecting it onto Jesus. 3) The principle of *embarrassment* informs us that passages should be considered authentic if they would bring embarrassment to the author—the author would have had no insentive to fabricate the passage. Some examples of these include: Jesus' brothers were skeptics until His resurrection, Jesus did not know the day or the hour of His return, ladies (not the apostles themselves) were the first witnesses of the empty tomb and the risen Christ, Peter denied Jesus three times, and the apostles fled when Jesus was arrested. 4) The principle of *enemy attestation* occurs when enemies admit something that hurts their case or when you receive praise from your opposition. There would be no reason for your opposition to praise you if it were not true. An example of this is the alternative explanation of Jesus' resurrection given by the Jewish religious leaders—they claimed that the disciples stole the body. The principle of embarrassment shows the apostles did not fabricate this story. Yet, the response of the Jewish religious leaders shows that they admitted the tomb was empty. 5) The principle of *coherence* tells us that if there is a saying that you are unsure is historically accurate but it fits well with certain well-attested statements, it's probably an authentic statement. 6) The principle of *Aramaic substrata* tells the New Testament scholar that if he or she finds evidence that the Greek New Testament passage appears to have been translated from an Aramaic creed or hymn, then the scholar would be justified in accepting the passage as early and authentic. These 6 rules or prinicples were used by Habermas to arrive at the twelve core historical facts mentioned above. This is why these twelve facts are accepted by virtually all the world's leading New Testament scholars.

[34]Ibid., 35. This author received the figure of "over seventy percent" from Dr. Gary Habermas in a personal conversation with him at an apologetics conference in Spring of 2005 in the Seattle area. See also Habermas and Licona, *The Case for ther Resurrection of Jesus*, 70.

[35]Gary R. Habermas and Michael R. Licona, *The Case for the Resurrection of Jesus* (Grand rapids: Kregel Publications, 2004), 48-75.

[36]Habermas, *Future Hope*, 23-24. See also Habermas and Licona, 69-74. As Habermas' research has shown, most New

Testament scholars ("roughly 75 percent") acknowledge the historicity of the empty tomb. We know the tomb was empty for several reasons. First, the resurrection was proclaimed in Jerusalem shortly after Jesus died—it would have been easy and advantageous for the Jewish religious leaders to produce the rotting corpse of Jesus had the tomb not been empty. This would have stifled the spread of early Christianity and killed the new religious movement. Second, even the enemies of early Christianity admitted the tomb was empty—they claimed the body had been stolen (Matthew 28:12-13). Scholars believe it is unlikely that the early church would have fabricated this. Third, the account of the women being the first to find the empty tomb was not a fabrication because of the low view of a woman's testimony in the first-century AD—their testimony held no evidential value. Had the apostles lied, they probably would have credited themselves with finding the empty tomb. There was no reason to say that women found the tomb empty unless that was actually the case. Fourth, the empty tomb is mutiply attested by several early sources: Mark, Matthew, John, and probably Luke. Most ancient historical events are attested by only one or two sources. Finally, early traditional texts (i.e., ancient creeds, hymns, or sermons) found in the New Testament affirm or imply the empty tomb (see 1 Corinthians 15:3-4; Acts 13:29-31, 36-37).

[37]Habermas and Licona, 87-88. The Gospels include parables, and they are easy to identify. But, the resurrection accounts do not read like parables. In fact, the early preaching of the Gospel clearly indicates that Peter and Paul believed that Jesus' body had literally been raised (Acts 2:22-32; 13:34-37).

[38]Borg and Wright, 133.

[39]N. T. Wright, *TheResurrection of the Son of God* (Minneapolis: Fortress Press, 2003), 201-206.

[40]Ibid., 31, 83-84. See also Borg and Wright, 111-119.

[41]Wright, *Resurrection*, 215, 218.

[42]Ignatius, *Letter to the Smyrneans*, 1-3.

[43]Borg, *Jesus*, 32.

[44]Wright, *Resurrection*, 547-551.

Appendix 2
Is the Shroud of Turin the Burial Cloth of Jesus?

Is the Shroud of Turin the burial cloth of Jesus? This question has often divided Christians. Before we examine the evidence for and against the Shroud, it should be noted that the historical evidence for Jesus' resurrection is strong enough without the Shroud. The historical case for Jesus' resurrection spelled out in this book is sufficient without the Shroud of Turin. Hence, if the Shroud of Turin is proven to be a hoax, it would not do any damage to the historical case for Jesus' resurrection. However, if the Shroud can be shown to be the burial cloth of Jesus, then this would corroborate the historical case for Jesus' resurrection.

Two Extremes to Avoid

Also, we must be careful to avoid two extremes when dealing with the Shroud of Turin. First, we must avoid idolatry. The Bible tells us we are to worship God alone (Exodus 20:4-6); we are not to worship objects or relics. Even if a Christian believes the Shroud is authentic, he must not worship or venerate the cloth. If authentic, the Shroud is an important piece of evidence for the historical Jesus and His resurrection. Still, it is not to be worshiped.

The second extreme to avoid is uninformed skepticism. If you examine the evidence for the Shroud and still conclude it is a forgery, that's fine. What must be avoided is the tendency of some to dismiss the Shroud as a fraud without examining the evidence in its favor. We should examine the evidence and then make up our minds. As Christians, we should examine all things in the light of God's Word, and in the light of the evidence, and then determine whether or not we are to accept a certain belief. Sometimes skepticism (suspending judgment) is justified. But, uninformed skepticism is never justified. Therefore, we need to avoid these two extremes and evaluate the evidence for and against the Shroud.

Details Found on the Shroud

The Shroud is currently kept in Turin, Italy. It is an ancient linen cloth that many believe to be the burial cloth of Jesus of Nazareth. It is 14'3" long and 3'7" wide. On the cloth is a head to head image of a crucified man, showing both sides of his body. The crucifixion victim was approximately 5'10" to 6' tall and weighed about 175 pounds (Wilson, 41). The man in the Shroud has Semitic or Middle-Eastern features (Stevenson and Habermas, *Verdict on the Shroud* 44). The victim's body appeared to be in a state of rigor mortis (43).

Evidence of the victim's suffering is clearly depicted on the cloth. This suffering is consistent not only with death by crucifixion, but, more specifically, with Christ's death (45-51). The blood on the Shroud reveals severe puncture wounds on the wrists and the feet. The side of the corpse had been pierced, after death, leaving blood and water stains on the chest area of the image (56). Numerous puncture wounds are found on the scalp of the man in the cloth. Over 120 scourge wounds (dumbell-shaped markings consistent with wounds caused by the ancient Roman flagrum) are visible on the body (45, 51, 54, 154, 159). Shoulder abrasions, that may have been caused by the carrying of a heavy object, are also visible. Knee contusions are present (indicating that the victim had several significant falls); yet, there is no evidence of broken ankles—something that would be common with most crucifixion victims, but not with Christ (49). Finally, the beard of the victim had been violently torn. These wounds precisely match the details of Christ's suffering and death given in Scripture.

Though the victim is in the state of rigor mortis and therefore obviously dead, there is no evidence of decomposition on the cloth. Yet the blood stains are in tact—they would have been disrupted had the body been removed from the Shroud before decay set in (203-204). Hence, it is as if the corpse somehow disappeared from the cloth, thus leaving the blood clots undisturbed!

The blood on the cloth is human blood. In fact, it is the blood of a male human of the AB blood-type. This blood group is rare; still it is much more common among present-day Jews living in the Near East (Wilson ans Schwortz, 76).

It is interesting to note that the image on the Shroud displays very little detail to the naked eye. However, a photographic negative of the Shroud exhibits incredible detail. This was discovered when an Italian photographer named Secondo Pia was the first to photograph the Shroud in 1898 (Stevenson and Habermas, *Verdict* 39). Yet, the concept of negativity was not known until the nineteenth century. How could the supposed medieval forger of the Shroud check the details of his work since these details were not evident on the Shroud itself and would not be discovered until the invention of photography?

The image on the shroud is extremely superficial—it is only found on the very surface of the cloth (84-85). Yet, the bloodstains had soaked completely through the cloth and can be seen on both sides of the Shroud. If the image of the corpse on the Shroud had been painted, it (like the bloodstains) would have soaked completely through the cloth. This is strong evidence that the image is not a painting.

The image of the body on the cloth is three-dimensional and nondirectional. Modern scientific investigation has proven that the image was caused by a three-dimensional object (like a body). If the image was a painting, it would only have two-dimensional properties. Also, if the image was painted, the brush strokes would reveal directionality; but, the image is nondirectional (83-85).

There is no sign of paint, dye, powder, or any other substance that could have caused the image. However the image was formed, it was not painted (Wilson, 74-83). In fact, even with modern scientific technology, scientists have been unable to reproduce the image with all its details. The cause of the image remains unknown at this time. Most scientists who have examined the Shroud agree that painting, heat scorch, or light scorch have been ruled out as possible causes of the image. Some suggest that something like modern X-Ray technology is needed to explain the image with all its details (Stevenson and Habermas, *The Shroud and the Controversy* 136). Obviously, this would not have been available to a medieval forger.

The abdomen of the Shroud victim appears severely distended (Stevenson and Habermas, *Verdict* 49-50). This would be expected on the corpse of a crucifixion victim since asphyxiation would be the most likely cause of death.

The known, recent history of the Shroud places it in France and Italy. Yet, criminologist Max Frei identified pollens from Turkey and Israel on the Shroud (33, 79). This reveals that the Shroud had spent significant time in those countries, and that there is an unknown history of the Shroud that precedes its known history.

Due to the work of textile expert Dr. Mechthild Flury-Lemberg, it is now known that the weave and type of the cloth is consistent with first-century Palestine (Wilson and Schwortz, 41). The owner of the cloth would have had to have been wealthy in order to be able to afford it. This is consistent with the biblical statement that the grave clothes were donated by Joseph of Arimathea, a wealthy member of the Jewish Ruling Council (Mark 15:46).

Another amazing detail found on the Shroud is what appear to be coins from Pilate's reign over the eyes of the man in the Shroud (Stevenson and Habermas, *Verdict* 34-35). Pontius Pilate reigned as Governor over Judea from 26 to 36 AD—Jesus was crucified around

30 to 33 AD. The coins would have prevented the eyes of the corpse from opening.

Many of these details point to Jesus of Nazareth as the man in the Shroud. Yet, much of the data on the Shroud would have been impossible for a medieval forger to produce.

Known History of the Shroud (Since 1354 ad)

The known history of the Shroud of Turin goes back to 1354 AD. At that time, it was owned by Geoffrey de Charny of France. Geoffrey de Charney had close ties to the Knights Templar which was a secret religious order founded by former crusaders. The Knights Templar were notorious for collecting religious relics. Since 1354 AD, the Shroud of Turin has only been in France, Italy, and Western Europe (Wilson, 277).

In 1452 AD, Geoffrey's granddaughter, Margaret de Charny, traded the Shroud for a castle. The new owner, Anna de Lusignano, was the wife of the Duke of Savoy, Italy. At this point, the Shroud began to be kept in a silver basket. In 1532, the Shroud was in a fire. The fire melted some of the silver container, causing it to burn the edges of the Shroud (Wilson, 289).

In 1578, the Shroud was moved to Turin, Italy (292). In 1898 it was photographed for the first time. The photographer was an Italian named Secundo Pia. When he noticed the amazing detail of the image in the photographic negative, interest in the Shroud greatly increased throughout the world (298-299).

During World Wars I and II, the Shroud was hidden in order to protect it. In 1946, after World War II, the Shroud was returned to Turin, Italy. In 1978, the Shroud of Turin Research Project (i.e., STURP) was conducted by some of the world's leading scientists. For the first time, a thorough examination of the Shroud by scientific experts was allowed. The results of the research pointed in the direction of the authenticity of the Shroud (301-305).

From 1452 to 1983, the Shroud was owned by the House of Savoy. However, King Umberto II of Savoy willed it to Pope John Paul II in 1983. From then on, the Roman Catholic Church has been the official owner of the Shroud (305-306).

In 1988, the Vatican allowed a piece to be cut from the Shroud. This piece was divided into smaller pieces and then sent to several labs throughout the world to be scientifically tested for age. The shroud was Carbon 14 dated from 1260 to 1390 AD (307-311). For many people, the Shroud had been proven a medieval forgery; any further study of the Shroud was thought to be somewhat of a waste of time. But, since 1988 much data has been produced which has called into question the accuracy of the Carbon 14 dating of the Shroud.

On April 11, 1997, the Shroud was rescued by Italian firemen from a fire that consumed its chapel. The Shroud was not harmed from the fire. Since then, the Roman Catholic Church has taken more extreme means to ensure the protection of the Shroud (313).

Possible Ancient History of the Shroud (Before 1354 AD)

Ian Wilson has done extensive historical research into the Shroud of Turin. He has proposed a plausible history of the Shroud from Christ's death up until 1354 AD, the point at which the known history of the Shroud begins (Wilson, 263-277).Wilson has managed to string together reports throughout history of a cloth bearing Jesus' image. Is it possible that these reports could be describing what we now call the Shroud of Turin? Wilson argues that this is probably the case.

If the Shroud of Turin existed before 1354 AD, we would expect to find some mention of it throughout history, going back to the death of Christ. Ian Wilson believes he has found a paper trail about the

Shroud from Christ's death to 1354. The paper trail begins in a place called Edessa.

Early church tradition reports an interesting story. King Abgar V of Edessa (now Turkey) was very ill. Hearing that Jesus of Nazareth had the miraculous power to heal, he sent for Jesus. But, Jesus was unable to travel to Edessa. After Jesus' death, resurrection, and ascension, the Apostle Thaddaeus visited King Abgar. Thaddaeus brought with him a cloth bearing an image of Jesus' face. The cloth was called "archeiropoitos," the Greek word for "not made with human hands." Wilson's research led him to the conclusion that the cloth of Edessa was the Shroud of Turin folded in such a way that only the face was visible (263-264).

A hymn, dating to 569 AD, refers to the cloth of Edessa by saying "the image not made with human hands" (Wilson, 158, 266). A pre-600 AD document entitled the *Acts of Thaddeus* refers to the cloth of Edessa as "tetradiplion," meaning "doubled in four." This may indicate that the Shroud was normally folded in fours, thus showing only the face. This would explain why much of the early history of the Shroud speaks of it as an image of the face, not the entire body (266-267).

In 692 AD, Byzantine Emperor Justinian II had gold coins made bearing Christ's image. The image is thought to have been based on the cloth of Edessa. Yet, the image shows a striking resemblence to the image of the face on the Shroud of Turin (267).

Pope Stephen III, who reigned as Pope from 768-772 AD, wrote a sermon about the Shroud that he preached shortly after he was elected Pope. Pope Stephen III spoke of Christ's body being stretched on a white cloth, leaving "the glorious image of the Lord's face and the length of His whole body" on the cloth (Guerrera, *The Shroud of Turin* 24). It is easy to see that this Pope was referring to the Shroud of Turin. Hence, the Shroud did exist as far back as the eigth century AD.

In 787 AD, Leo, Lector of Constantinople, stated that he travelled to Edessa and saw what he called "the holy image made without hands" (Wilson, 267). In the Spring of 943, the Byzantine Emperor Romanus promised not to invade Edessa, which had by this time been populated by Moslems. The Emperor paid 12,000 pieces of silver and released 200 Moslem prisoners in exchange for the cloth of Edessa. The Emperor then brought the cloth to Constantinople (267).

In 944 AD, an archdeacon named Gregory preached a sermon describing the cloth of Edessa in such a way that he implied the image on the cloth displayed more than Jesus' face, but His body as well. Gregory noted that the cloth displayed "blood and water from His very side." This would make no sense if only Jesus' face was visible on the cloth of Edessa (268).

In 958 AD, Constantine Porphyrogenitus wrote a letter mentioning holy relics. Included in his list was "the God-bearing shroud and other signs of His undefiled Passion" (268-269). The Greek word he used for shroud was "sindon," the same Greek word used in the Gospels for Jesus' grave cloths (Mark 15:46).

In 977 AD, the cloth is referred to as "a blood-stained image of the Lord not made by hands." In 990 AD, the cloth with Christ's image is referred to, for the first time, as the "Mandylion." In Constantinople in 1036 AD, the cloth of Edessa is carried in a procession (269).

In 1130 AD, a sermon described the cloth of Edessa as displaying the entire body of Christ, not just His face (270). Wilson argues that the cloth of Edessa, the Mandylion, and the Shroud of Turin are one and the same cloth. In fact, Wilson makes the case that the Roman Catholic legend of "Veronica's Veil" was probably, originally, a reference to the Shroud. Veronica means "true image." Veronica was probably not an actual lady, but a legendary character who was invented as the story was told and changed with time (269).

In 1204 AD, the Knights Templar, a secret order made up of former crusaders, apparently stole the Mandylion from Turkey and delivered it to the Charny family of France (272-273). Twelfth and thirteenth century documents state that the image on the Mandylion was that of Christ's entire body, not merely His face. From the eleventh century on, many paintings were produced with full-length, head-to-head representations of Christ's body on cloth.

Finally, in 1354 AD, we find the Shroud of Turin in the hands of Geoffrey de Charny of France. He had close ties to the Knights Templar. Historians agree that he owned the Shroud of Turin at that time. Wilson connects the historical dots for us by showing the cloth of Edessa is the Mandylion, and that this cloth displayed an image of the entire body of Jesus, not just His face. The Knights Templar brought the Mandylion to the Charny family of France in 1204, whereas Geoffrey de Charny of France is the first known owner of the Shroud of Turin by 1354 AD (277-278). Apparently, Ian Wilson has built a plausible history of the Shroud of Turin from the death of Jesus to the present day. Hence, the Shroud of Turin could possibly be the burial cloth of Jesus of Nazareth.

Wilson's conclusion that the Shroud of Turin has a history going back to the time of Christ is confirmed by art expert named Paul Vignon. Vignon researched ancient Byzantine paintings of Jesus. These paintings date back to the sixth century AD. Yet, they bear striking similarities to the image on the Shroud. In fact, a strange "V" can be found between the eyes of the face of Christ in 80% of ancient Byzantine depictions of Christ. This "V" can also be seen on the face of the man in the Shroud. Other similarities between the Shroud image and these ancient paintings include the absence of a neck, a raised eyebrow, an enlarged left nostril, a heavy line below the lower lip, a line across the throat, and the presence of a forked beard. Vignon argues that this is evidence that these ancient and medieval painters were looking at the Shroud when painting a likeness of Jesus

(Wilson, 159). This is circumstantial evidence that the Shroud of Turin existed centuries before its known history.

Though Wilson and Vignon's research point to the antiquity of the Shroud of Turin, and the possibility of it actually being the burial cloth of Christ, everything changed in 1988. In that year, the Shroud of Turin was Carbon 14 dated to between 1260 to 1390 AD (310-311). For many, the authenticity of the Shroud of Turin was refuted. The Shroud was nothing more than a medieval forgery. Still others had a hard time accepting the results of the Carbon 14 dating, especailly since the image could not be reproduced with modern scientific technology. Is is possible that the Carbon 14 dating of the Shroud was mistaken?

Refutation of the Carbon 14 Dating of the Shroud

Since 1988, several reasons for doubting the results of the Carbon 14 dating of the Shroud have been proposed. However, the final death blow to the Carbon 14 dating of the Shroud came at the hands of the former Shroud skeptic, the scientist Ray Rodgers (Wilcox, 214-222). Ray Rodgers was a well-known retired scientist who had worked at the Los Alamos National Laboratory in New Mexico. He had served as part of the 1978 Shroud of Turin Research Project (STURP), but was very skeptical about the Shroud's authenticity. In fact, Rodgers accepted the results of the 1988 Carbon 14 dating results (215).

Rodgers became angry when his friend Barry Schwortz, the former photographer of the 1978 STURP team and founder of www.shroud.com, posted an article (on his website) written by non-scientists Sue Benford and Joseph Marino. The article argued that the Carbon 14 dating of the Shroud was inaccurate because the portion of the Shroud that was tested was actually a medieval repair to the Shroud. Rodgers told Schwortz he could disprove Benford and

Marino's work. Schwortz encouraged him to do so, and Rodgers accepted the challenge (214-215).

Rodgers studied a sample of the Shroud that had been in close proximity to and intertwined with the sample that was tested in 1988. He examined the sample with a high-powered microscope. Rodgers was schocked by what he saw. He found cotton fibers that had been spliced into the linen fibers of the Shroud (215). Due to his 1978 research on the Shroud, Rodgers knew that the rest of the Shroud had no cotton interwoven with the linen. The portion of the Shroud that had been Carbon 14 tested was not representative of the rest of the Shroud. It was the product of a medieval repair done to the Shroud. Cotton threads had been interwoven with the linen threads of the Shroud to repair a torn edge of the Shroud. The cotton threads would distort any Carbon 14 dating of that portion of the Shroud (216-219).

Though Rodgers died in 2005, his research was corroborated by Dr. John L. Brown, a forensic scientist who had worked at the Georgia Tech Research Institute's Energy and Materials Science Lab, and by Robert Villarreal, a retired nuclear chemist who had worked for the Department of Defense at Los Alamos (217-221). Before he died, Rodgers published the results of his research in the peer-reviewed science journal *Thermochimica Acta*. In the article, Rodgers stated:

> The combined evidence proves that. . . the material from the radiocarbon area of the shroud is significantly different from that of the main cloth. The radiocarbon sample was thus not part of the original cloth and is invalid for determining the age of the shroud (219).

Rodgers was a true scientist. Though he was skeptical at first, he was willing to examine the evidence. He found that the portion of the Shroud that had been Carbon 14 dated was not representative of the rest of the Shroud. Also, Brown's research showed that whoever repaired the damaged Shroud (probably in the sixteenth century) had also added dye to the newly repaired area in an attempt to duplicate the aged appearance of the rest of the Shroud (218). Before Rodgers had died, he re-examined the 1978 ultraviolet and X-ray photos of the Shroud. These photos showed that the sample area that was to be Carbon 14 dated was darker and a different color than the rest of the cloth. Hence, though unnoticed until Rodgers re-examination, these photos show the Shroud sample that was dated in 1988 was in fact chemically different from the rest of the Shroud (216).

Rodger's conclusions were also verified by Mechthild Flury-Lemberg, one of the world's leading textile experts. Her research concluded that the Shroud's weave was consistent with a style commonly used in the Jerusalem area during the time of Christ (227). The Vignon markings (mentioned earlier) also validate the work of Rodgers. Hence, the 1988 Carbon 14 dating of the Shroud of Turin should no longer count against the antiquity of the Shroud. The presence of cotton threads from medieval times in the sample portion of the Shroud distorted the date given by the Carbon 14 testing.

Evidence for the Antiquity and Authenticity of the Shroud

I believe the evidence strongly favors the antiquity and the authenticity of the Shroud of Turin. Enough evidence has been presented to dismiss the 1988 Carbon 14 dating results. There are numerous levels of support for the authenticity and antiquity of the Shroud.

In 1999, the Sudarium (also known as the Cloth of Oviedo, Spain) was compared with the Shroud of Turin. This cloth is thought to be the face cloth of Christ which covered His bloody face when He was taken down from the cross until He was placed in the tomb (John 20:6-7). The history of the Sudarium was recorded in the twelfth century by Bishop Pelayo of Oviedo. He wrote that the Sudarium, as well as other relics, was brought to Spain in 614 AD for protection. During that time, a Persian King named Chosroes II was invading Jerusalem (Zugibe, 292). According to Pelayo, up until 614 AD, the cloth had been in Jerusalm for almost five-hundred years.

The Sudarium shares several features with the Shroud. First, the blood on both cloths has been identified as type AB. This blood type is rare in Europe, but is common in the Middle East (Guerrera, 49). Second, Dr. Alan Whanger of Duke University developed and utilized the polarized image overlay technique to show that there are well over one-hundred congruent blood stains on the Shroud and the Sudarium, thus proving both cloths covered the same victim (47). And third, Professor Avinoam Danin, a world-renowned botanist from Hebrew University, confirmed that the Middle-Eastern pollen grains on the Sudarium match the Middle-Eastern pollen grains on the Shroud (47). Since the Sudarium's known history can be traced back into ancient times, this strongly argues for the antiquity of the Shroud as well.

As mentioned above, world-renowned textile expert Mechthild Flury-Lemberg, after closely examining the Shroud of Turin, confirmed that it has a "three-to-one herringbone pattern" that was almost exclusive to the area of ancient Jerusalem around the first century AD. She found the weave to be "surprisingly similar to one found on a cloth in the Jewish fortress of Masada in the Dead Sea area outside Jerusalem. That particular cloth dates back to between 40 BC and 73 AD" (Wilcox, 227). This argues for an early date of the Shroud.

The Vignon markings (mentioned above) show parallels between unusual features found on the Shroud and the same features found on ancient paintings of Jesus. These features seem to indicate that these ancient artists painted their portraits of Jesus while looking at the Shroud.

Again, it should be noted that most of the details of the Shroud are found in a photographic negative of the Shroud. The Shroud image itself is rather cloudy and not easy to decipher. The numerous details that can be studied and examined are found in photographic negatives of the Shroud. A medieval forger, long before the invention of photography, would have no way to check his work. This would seem to indicate that the Shroud of Turin is not a medieval fraud.

The Shroud presents an accurate depiction of a crucifixion victim. The nail wounds through the wrists (not the palms), the hidden thumbs, and the stretching of the fingers are all consistent with crucifixion. These features of crucifixion were unknown to modern researchers until they examined the Shroud and than confirmed its accuracy concerning the rigors of crucifixion by experimenting on cadavers (Zugibe, 211-227). The wounds from the Roman flagrum have also given modern researchers insight into the brutality of Roman scourging. Much of what we now know concerning ancient cricifixion comes from detailed, scientific studies done on the Shroud. This would not be the case if the Shroud was a medieval fraud.

A further piece of evidence for the authenticity of the Shroud is the fact that, even with modern twenty-first century scientific advances, we cannot reproduce the image on the Shroud with all its details. In order to disprove the authenticity of the Shroud, if someone were to attempt to replicate the image of the Shroud (with all its unique details), they would have to use medieval technology to prove it was a medieval forgery. This is very unlikely since, as noted above, even with our current scientific knowledge, no one has been able to reproduce all the data found on the Shroud.

The fibers and pollen found on the Shroud by the late Swiss criminologist and botanist Max Frei also support the authenticity and antiquity of the Shroud. His research shows that the Shroud was, at one time, exposed to the open air of both Israel and Turkey. Yet, the Shroud resided in Europe (i.e., France and Italy) since the mid fourteenth century. Hence, the Shroud existed before that century and had to have spent some time in Israel and Turkey (Stevenson and Habermas, *Verdict* 33).

The three-dimensional qualities of the Shroud image provide further support for its authenticity. John Jackson and Eric Jumper were two physicists and Air Force officers who worked on the 1978 Shroud of Turin Research Project. Using a VP-8 Image Analyzer, they were able to generate a three-dimensional image from the two-dimensional Shroud. This is not possible when working with photographs or paintings (80-82). The fact that the Shroud of Turin contains three-dimensional information strongly counts against the medieval forgery hypothesis.

Jackson and Jumper's research also indicated that coins from Ponius Pilate's reign had been placed over the eyes of the crucified victim whose image is found on the Shroud (82). Pilate reigned as governor over Judea from 26 to 36 AD. Jesus was crucified around 30 to 33 AD.

The image on the Shroud could not possibly be a painting for several reasons. First, the image is superficial—it does not bleed through the cloth as the blood stains do or as paint would do. Second, the Shroud lacks the amount of paint pigment needed to account for the image if it were a painting. And third, the image shows absolutely no directionality; whereas paint strokes would reveal the direction of the painter's strokes (83-85). To this day, scientists have failed to reproduce the image found on the Shroud.

The X-ray effects found on the Shroud also lend support to its authenticity. Giles Carter, a professor of chemistry at Eastern Michigan University, detected X-ray information on the Shroud of Turin. He believed he identified the bone structure of the knuckles, some of the backbone, and some of the teeth on the image found on the Shroud (Stevenson and Habermas, *Controversy* 131). A medieval forger would have no reason to display skeletal structures of the crucified man.

The intact blood clots found on the Shroud not only support the authenticity of the shroud. These blood clots may also provide empirical evidence for Jesus'resurrection. If the corpse had been removed from the cloth using natural means, the blood clots would have been disrupted (Stevenson and Habermas, *Verdict* 203-204). But, this is not the case. It is as if the body miraculously disappeared from the cloth!

Conclusion

The historical case for Jesus' bodily resurrection is incredibly strong regardless of the status of the Shroud of Turin. Still, when all the available evidence is examined, it appears that the Shroud of Turin may in fact be the actual burial cloth of Jesus of Nazareth. Since no one knows exactly how the image was formed, it is possible that the Shroud of Turin offers corroborating empirical evidence that Jesus of Nazareth bodily rose from the dead.

The interesting point is not that modern science has failed to prove the Shroud of Turin authentic. The interesting point is this: modern science has failed to *disprove* the authenticity of the Shroud. It seems highly unlikely that a medieval artist could outsmart modern scientists by producing effects that modern science would be unable to replicate.

After decades of scientific investigation, the Shroud has yet to be proven a fraud, nor can it be duplicated. Modern science can land a man on the moon. It can heal many diseases. But, it cannot reproduce the image on the Shroud. It has also failed to prove it to be a hoax. At this point, there appears to be no natural explanation for the formation of the image on the Shroud. Since no adequate natural explanation exists, the possibility of a supernatural explanation remains a viable option.

We do not know what kind of chemical exchanges may occur when God reanimates and transfigures a corpse. And, we do not know what effect a resurrection would have on a cloth in close proximity to the body being raised. But, we do know the image on the cloth depicts the biblical description of Christ's suffering and death. And, we cannot explain the origin of the image. Is it possible God chose to give mankind a photographic negative of the corpse of Christ at the exact moment it was reanimated with life? Regardless of how someone answers this question, at this point in history, the evidence does seem to favor both the authenticity and antiquity of the Shroud of Turin.

Appendix 3
The Opening Statement from the Phil Fernandes-Doug Krueger Debate

Is Belief in the Bodily Resurrection of Jesus Reasonable?
By Phil Fernandes

I would like to thank Pastor Zachary Neyhard for promoting this debate, and Professor Doug Krueger for debating me. I would also like to express my appreciation to the State University of New York for hosting this debate.

This debate asks the question: is belief in the bodily resurrection of Jesus reasonable? I will argue that, based on the oldest and best historical evidence, it is reasonable to believe that Jesus bodily rose from the dead. It is my contention that, if we refrain from an unwarranted bias against the possibility of miracles, the early evidence is clear: Jesus bodily rose from the dead.

For purposes of this debate, I do not have to prove with absolute certainty that Jesus rose from the dead. I merely have to prove that, after examining the earliest historical evidence we have, it is reasonable to conclude that Jesus of Nazareth bodily rose from the dead. My opponent, to win this debate, must refute my case for the resurrection and show that it is not reasonable to believe that Jesus rose from the dead. If he believes that it is unreasonable to believe that Jesus rose from the dead, he needs to present an alternative theory of the resurrection data. This alternative theory must be more reasonable to believe than it is to believe that Jesus did rise from the dead.

This debate is not about whether or not the Bible is inerrant—this debate is not about Bible contradictions. Hence, supposed Bible contradictions that do not touch on the basic core teachings of the death, burial, resurrection, and appearances of Christ are irrelevant to this debate. Peripheral discrepancies often appear when there are multiple accounts of a single historical event; but, this does not wipe out the core data of the event itself.

My argument is as follows. We have ancient first-century AD accounts stating that Jesus bodily rose from the dead. Either these accounts are legends, lies, misunderstandings by the apostles, or true accounts. I will argue that the apostles told the truth and that Jesus did, in fact, bodily rise from the dead.

The First-Century Evidence

Ample first-century AD evidence exists to support Jesus' bodily resurrection from the dead. Since Jesus was crucified around 30 AD, all first-century evidence would be within the lifetime of eyewitnesses.

First, seven of Paul's letters (i.e., Romans, 1 & 2 Corinthians, Galatians, Philippians, 1 Thessalonians, and Philemon) are almost universally accepted as authentic letters of Paul by the world's leading New Testament scholars today. Even the liberal Jesus Seminar accepts the authenticity of these seven letters. The dates of these letters fall between 49 and 64 AD, and Paul proclaims Jesus as bodily risen from the dead (Philippians 3:21). Paul's writings give us strong evidence for the resurrection since they take us to within twenty years from the death of Christ. Paul also tells us that the Gospel he preached was the same Gospel that Peter, James, and the original Apostles preached (1 Corinthians 15:1-11; Galatians 1 & 2). Paul taught that Jesus bodily rose from the dead, and Paul was not an innovator—he preached the same Gospel the original Apostles preached.

Second, there is the ancient creed or hymn of 1 Corinthians 15:3-8 quoted by the Apostle Paul. This creed reads as follows:

> "For I delivered to you as of first importance what I also received, that Christ died for our sins according to the Scriptures, and that He was buried, and that He was raised on the third day according to the Scriptures, and that He appeared to Cephas, then to the twelve. After that He appeared to more than five hundred brethren at one time, most of whom remain until now, but some have fallen asleep; then He appeared to James, then to all the apostles; and last of all, as it were to one untimely born, He appeared to me also" (1 Corinthians 15:3-8).

The vast majority of New Testament scholars date the origin of this creed to within one to five years of Jesus' crucifixion. Even skeptical scholars such as Gerd Luedemann, Marcus Borg, and the Jesus Seminar accept this early date for the creed. Yet the creed states that Christ died for our sins, was buried, rose on the third day, and appeared to Peter, to the Apostles twice, to over 500 people at one time, and to James. Paul adds to this creed Jesus' appearance to Paul himself. Paul also adds that many of the 500 witnesses were still alive when he wrote 1 Corinthians, implying that they could be interrogated to verify Christ's resurrection. This creed is early and based on eyewitness testimony—it is not the "stuff" of which legend is made.

Third, many scholars accept the sermons found in Acts, chapters one through twelve, as representing the earliest preaching of the Christian church, going back to the early 30's AD. There are several reasons for dating these sermons so early: these sermons translate well into Aramaic, whereas the sermons after Acts 12 do not. These sermons have their own unique vocabulary and style that differ from the rest of Acts. And, the theology of these sermons is also primitive and undeveloped, showing them to represent the earliest preaching of the church. These sermons proclaim Jesus as bodily risen from the dead, stating things like, "This Jesus God raised up again, to which we are all witnesses" (Acts 2:32).

Fourth, most New Testament scholars and historians, despite their hyper-critical training, date the four Gospels to between 60 and 110 AD. (Skeptical New Testament scholar Marcus Borg of the Jesus Seminar even concedes that John, the last Gospel, was written about 90 AD.) Even if we assume that Matthew and Luke borrowed material from Mark, scholars still agree that Matthew and Luke used material other than Mark when they recorded their accounts of the post-resurrection appearances. Also, the Gospel of John includes its own distinct accounts of Christ's appearances. Leading New Testament scholars such as Richard Bauckham, N. T. Wright, John Wenham, Craig Blomberg, and Larry Hurtado consider the sources of these resurrection accounts in the Gospels to be very early since they are theologically undeveloped. In fact, Bauckham and Blomberg persuasively argue that the Gospels themselves are based on eyewitness testimony.

And fifth, the first century AD Jewish historian Josephus, though he was not a Christian, mentions Jesus in his *Antiquities*. Though the standard reading of this passage is usually rejected by most scholars, an alternative shorter reading in an Arabic translation has gained wide acceptance as authentic. This alternative reading was presented in 1972 by Professor Schlomo Pines of the Hebrew University in Jerusalem. This shorter reading states that, after Jesus was crucified by Pontius Pilate, His followers reported that He appeared to them alive three days later, and that they considered Him to be the Christ. Josephus also mentions that many Jews and Gentiles were becoming Christians by the latter part of the first century AD.

There exists no independent first century AD account that denies Jesus' death, burial, and bodily resurrection. All the available first century evidence proclaims Jesus as risen.

The Core Historical Facts

Most New Testament scholars today utilize the "historical-critical method" when they study the New Testament documents. This method, influenced greatly by enlightenment rationalism, presupposes that miracles are impossible; therefore, only natural causes are allowed in history—the supernatural is dismissed without any serious consideration of the evidence. The historical-critical method assumes that the miracle-working Jesus of the Bible cannot be the true Jesus of History. The approach of these scholars is so biased against the New Testament documents that these scholars usually will only accept the latest possible dates for each New Testament book; they also view New Testament passages as false until proven true. However, despite these unwarranted biases against the New Testament, many New Testament scholars have reached a consensus on several core historically established facts concerning the resurrection accounts.

Due to the strong first century AD evidence for Jesus' bodily resurrection, the vast majority (between 95 and 97%) of the world's leading New Testament scholars agree on several core historical facts. First, Jesus died by crucifixion. Second, He was hastily buried in a tomb. Third, His followers had experiences in which they believed they had seen Him risen from the dead. Fourth, the lives of the original Apostles, Paul, and James (the brother of Jesus) were radically transformed by these experiences, so that they were willing to suffer and die for their cause. Fifth, the primary worship day was changed from Saturday to Sunday by the early church, which was comprised of traditional Jews. Sixth, the earliest preaching of the church proclaimed Jesus as risen. Seventh, the early church grew rapidly as the resurrection was preached in Jerusalem.

Also, an eighth core fact should be added since over 70% of critical New Testament scholars accept the historicity of the empty tomb. This is confirmed by the Gospels recording women as the first witnesses of the empty tomb, at a time when a woman's testimony was not respected. The Gospel authors had no incentive to invent these accounts since, in their ancient culture, a woman's testimony held no evidential value. Also, the earliest Jewish rebuttal of the resurrection presupposes that the tomb was empty—the Jewish religious leaders claimed that the Apostles stole the body.

The Resurrection Accounts are not Legends

There are several reasons why the ancient resurrection accounts cannot be legends. First, though this explanation was popular in the late nineteenth century (i.e., F. C. Bauer), since then the legend hypothesis has fallen out of favor in scholarly circles. Second, the Gospels were not written in the genre of mythology—they list real historical people and places. Third, the supposed parallels and similarities between Christianity and the pagan myths have been greatly exaggerated. Usually, the pagan so-called "resurrection" myths were based on the seasonal crop cycles, not on historical data. In the case of Osiris, he did not return to this world but to the nether realm of the departed. Any real parallels with Christ's resurrection actually post-date Christianity by at least one-hundred years. If borrowing occurred, it was the pagan myths that borrowed from Christianity. Fourth, New Testament scholars now recognize that Jesus must be understood in His Jewish cultural background. Fifth, ancient Jews were very exclusive; they were totally opposed to borrowing views from pagan religions. And sixth, legends take several generations to wipe out core historical data. But, in the case of the resurrection, we do not have generations—from the beginning, the Apostles proclaimed Jesus as risen from the dead. Hence, the legend hypothesis fails.

The Resurrection Accounts are not Lies

What if the resurrection accounts were lies? Maybe the Apostles stole the body and fabricated the resurrection accounts? But, this does not explain the early data that we have. Early evidence indicates that James the son of Zebedee was martyred for his faith, as were Peter, Paul, and James the brother of Jesus. Men do not die for what they know to be a hoax. The Apostles were not lying—they sincerely believed they had seen Jesus alive after His death, and were willing to die for this claim.

The Resurrection Accounts are not Misunderstandings

If the resurrection accounts were not legends or lies, maybe the Apostles misunderstood the data? Maybe they hallucinated, or went to the wrong tomb? Maybe someone else stole the body, leaving the Apostles to find the tomb empty? Maybe Jesus only swooned on the cross, and did not actually die?

None of these naturalistic, alternative explanations of the resurrection suffice. The hallucination theory fails for several reasons. First, hallucinations are not group events—no two people have the same one. But, the evidence indicates Jesus appeared to numerous groups of people. Second, the Apostles were not in the proper state of mind to experience hallucinations. Third, the different places, times, and people speak against hallucinations. Fourth, hallucinations do not produce life-long changes. Fifth, hallucinations do not explain the empty tomb. Sixth, hallucinations do not stop suddenly—why did the appearances stop after Paul? Seventh, the New Testament clearly differentiates between the resurrection appearances and visions. And, eighth, Paul and James, since they were originally opposed to Jesus, were unlikely candidates to hallucinate an appearance of the risen Jesus.

If the Apostles went to the wrong tomb or someone else stole the body, this would explain the empty tomb, but not the appearances. Since virtually all New Testament scholars accept the fact that the early church had experiences in which they believed they saw the risen Christ, the wrong tomb theory and the stolen body theory both fail as adequate explanations for the resurrection accounts.

The swoon theory also fails because a battered, scourged, and crucified Jesus, though still alive in this scenario, would not be able to convince the Apostles He had truly conquered death. Instead, the Apostles would have rushed Jesus off to a doctor for life-saving measures. Also, the flow of blood and water from Jesus' side confirmed that Jesus was dead before being removed from the cross.

Leading resurrection expert Gary Habermas stated in his first resurrection debate with philosopher and then atheist Antony Flew, "Although nineteenth-century liberals decimated each others' views individually, twentieth-century critical scholars have generally rejected naturalistic theories as a whole, judging that they are incapable of explaining the known data."

The Apostles Told the Truth: Jesus Bodily Rose

Since I have shown that the earliest evidence for Christ's bodily resurrection is not legend, lies, or misunderstandings, the only option we have is to admit that the first century evidence shows that the early church told the truth—Jesus bodily rose from the dead.

My opponent has chosen to reject all the first-century historical data merely because it does not match up with his atheistic philosophy—he presupposes that miracles are impossible, or at least unverifiable by historical methods. But there is no justification for this biased dismissing of the historical evidence. If the early and reliable historical evidence points to an empty tomb and the post-death appearances of Christ, then a strong historical case for Jesus' resurrection can be made.

Conclusion: It is Reasonable to Believe Jesus Bodily Rose from the Dead

In conclusion, we have shown that all the early evidence points to Jesus bodily rising from the dead. If we do not dismiss the evidence due to an unwarranted bias against miracles, we must go where the evidence leads. Since all alternative, naturalistic explanations have failed to explain the first-century data, it is reasonable to believe that Jesus bodily rose from the dead.

Appendix Four: Paul: The Disciple of the Historical Jesus

Matthew J. Coombe

German higher criticism has been a thorn in the side of the conservative plight since the turn of the 19th century. Within the vein of this criticism are questions concerning the motivations or authenticity of the writings of the Apostle Paul. For some time Paul's earlier works were never called into question, but critics and skeptics, such as Robert Price, have recently called into question the overall credibility of Paul, claiming that he was something of an avant-garde to Christianity and that either Jesus never existed or that He did not exist in the sense that the evangelicals think he did.

The critics hold to this view because they believe the writings of Paul pre-date the writing of the Gospels and, as Robert Price has often argued, there are no quotations of Jesus in the epistles (which of course is not true). Critics often claim that Paul, for whatever reason, created the foundations of Christianity by expounding on a Jesus that either never existed or was greatly embellished.

This treatise is aimed at defending an historical account of Jesus by the writings of Paul and showing that Paul was in all actuality a disciple of Jesus. This will be accomplished through several key premises. Before these premises are posited and argued for, I wish to state several key points that will be presupposed for the purposes of this paper because I lack the space to warrant such thoughts being fully argued.

The first premise is that, since this paper is concerned with the writings of Paul and because of the Socratic method of ancient manuscript analysis, I will posit the Gospels were written by those who have been classically assigned by them. The second premise is that the dates of the origin of the Gospels and Epistles are relatively an un-important issue. This is because the critics themselves acknowledge that the writings of Paul predate the Gospels. And, since the writings of the apostolic fathers are in the early first century, we should presuppose the Gospels (specifically John) were written no later than before the turn of the first century. The final presupposition is that I will not call into question the authenticity of the Pastoral Epistles or any other debated Pauline epistles. I will assume Paul wrote them.

This paper will be segmented into several sections, each in the hopes of bolstering a classical evangelical view of Jesus from the writings of Paul. This process entails a survey of the writings of Paul, an evaluation of the writings of Paul and the Gospels (specifically the most crucial teachings of Jesus), and answers to commonly raised objections to the authenticity of Paul's writings in general.

The credible and authoritative Paul

In preparing to write this paper, it became evident that this essay must also be centered on the authenticity of Paul. For if even a cogent historical Jesus could be gleaned from his writing, it would not matter at all if Paul was in fact part of a fringe segment of Christianity and did not represent the true Christian voice (or Jesus for that matter). This first section will be comprised of establishing Paul as a creditable source. Once this is accomplished, I will deal with common objections to key Pauline texts as well as common objections to Paul. After that, we can begin to formulate our historical model (though in arguing these things a historical Jesus will begin to be formed).

Critics will often claim that Paul's writing is not as credible as the Gospels because he never spent time with Jesus or the apostles. However from a historiography standpoint his writing is considered especially valid because it represents the earliest history of

Christianity (Barnett, *Jesus and the Logic of History* 41). Examining these texts will then be our first goal.

A key hermeneutic tool is recognition of patterns: patterns of thought, an author's tendencies, writing systems, and so on. Patterns are helpful because when a pattern is broken it tends to be evident. In his letters, Paul has a standard greeting. His greeting usually contains an introduction of himself, a statement of credentials (usually a reference to receiving his apostleship from God), a note to the church he is writing, a blessing to the church, and a note of thanksgiving for the church. This pattern is seen in virtually all of the Apostle Paul's writings. The only letter missing a key aspect of this introduction is his letter to the Galatian church—the thanksgiving is absent. Paul neglects the thanksgiving because he is quite upset with the church, "I am amazed that you are so quickly turning away from Him who called you by the grace of Christ and turning to a different Gospel."

There are a few crucial aspects of a historical Jesus that can be gleaned from the short letter to the Galatians. First of all, Paul is definitely claiming to have knowledge of the gospel of Christ. I am not equivocating on the word "gospel" since it merely means "good news." It is in reference to a lower case "g" gospel, and not the upper case "G" Gospel as recorded by the apostles. My second point is this: in Galatians 2:11, Paul states that he admonished Peter to his face for refusing to fellowship with Gentiles while other Jews were present. This second point has several key aspects to its significance. First, this passage without a doubt seals the authority of Paul. If Peter did not consider Paul as an authoritative source to rebuke him, would he have let the admonishment continue uncontested? Peter is not known for being silent. In fact, he seems to always put his foot in his mouth. Yet, when he is called out by a wretched Pharisee (nonetheless), he accepts his admonishment. It is evident he accepts the admonishment because there is not only no record of him fighting against it from Paul, but also nothing in the writing of Peter himself, or of any of the other apostles or apostolic fathers. Further, the opposite is true, (which is a perfect segue into my second point) not only does Peter accept his criticism from Paul, but goes so far as to say that Paul's writing is Scripture (2 Peter 3:15-16). So not only does Peter accept rebuke, but even goes on to claim that Paul's writing is on the same level as the cherished Old Testament Scriptures.

The third point is within the same vein as the first two. It would be very easy for Peter to argue something like, "Who do you think you are talking to, did you eat and sleep with Christ? Did He say that you are the Rock of the Church? Did Jesus give you the keys to heaven?" It would have been very easy for Peter to claim such things, or even "you never even knew Christ." So not only does Peter not attempt to resist the rebuke against him, but he considers the correction to be sound and from an authoritative source. Thus, it would seem that Paul had the same knowledge (or quite similar) to that of Peter. Further evidence of this is when Paul met with James, Peter, and John.

The three men who knew Jesus best were arguably James (his half-brother), and the Apostles Peter, and John. When they met, as recorded in Galatians 2:9, they fellowshipped. Though Paul had never spent any time with the pre-resurrected Jesus, the three men who knew Jesus best felt confident with Paul's ministry and encouraged him to continue to preach what he had been preaching. Now if Paul really was the creator of Christianity or had so perverted it, would not these three forbid him from preaching this false gospel? Barnett, in his book *Jesus and the Logic of History*, writes that during this time of fellowship it is likely the Paul was able to learn even more about the historical Jesus (Barnett 21). Also, this encounter is significant because it showed that, although these apostles had never met before, they had each received their gospel message and authority from Jesus (Barnett 126).

Let us return to the Galatian aspect. Because of the confrontation with Peter, Paul's claim that the Galatian church was following a different gospel, and the blessing Paul received from the three biggest leaders in the early church, it seems that Paul indeed had knowledge of a Gospel that not only coincided with that of James, Peter, and John, but that they even encouraged him to continue preaching. This is all evidence that Paul was not preaching a new Gospel, but the same one that was given by Jesus to the apostles to preach to the ends of the earth.

Now, it might be charged that while it is profitable for me to present this first point for the purposes of bolstering Paul's authority, it is still not proof that Paul actually says something concerning a living and breathing Christ. To some extent this criticism holds, but now I will present more substantive verses that actually mention Jesus (though my focal point is still with the credibility of Paul).

The majority of the verses are short and quite subtle. Because of this, not only are many of the verses overlooked, but likewise, the significance of them is overlooked. A quick note to anticipate criticism: while many of these passages are short and are charged with insignificance, there are three primary factors that we need to consider before expounding on what Paul writes concerning a historical Jesus. The first is that the death and the life of Christ have four distinct works dedicated to them. Each of the Gospels is not only written by different men with different backgrounds, but each seems concerned with focusing on various aspects of Jesus' life. One would think that four works would be sufficient.

The second is that Paul is writing letters to specific churches for specific reasons, or as Barnett put it, "The Letters are a literary vehicle used by Paul to address issues current at the time of writing in the life of a church..." (Barnett 42). If no issues concerning a historical Jesus ever arose, why would he feel compelled to address them? There is one point of criticism, however, I feel is quite noteworthy. If Paul was familiar with the historical Jesus, then why did not Paul quote Jesus more often? Indeed Paul quotes Jesus a few times and a few times discusses his humanity, but the majority of Paul's work never quotes him. In response, I have no problem with Paul failing to quote Jesus because everything that Paul wrote not only corresponded to what was being taught by the other apostles, but also because all of Jesus' main themes are written about in Paul's epistles. I will focus on this point in the final section of the paper.

However, since general themes are not enough for critics, there are quotations and references. 1 Corinthians 7:10-12 is evidence that Paul did have knowledge of specific doctrine taught by Jesus. Further, he even knew enough concerning Jesus' doctrine of marriage that he is able to delineate what Jesus taught about marriage and what he himself was arguing. We should note that Paul is merely making a distinction between his teaching on marriage and that of Jesus; he is not contradicting Jesus' teaching.

The third point is explained in Eddy and Boyd's book *The Jesus Legend* that "…it cannot be regarded as a coincidence that Paul's own thought, attitude, and conduct paralleled closely what we find in the Jesus of the Gospels" (Paul Rhodes Eddy and Gregory A. Boyd, *The Jesus Legend: a Case For the Historical Reliability of the Synoptic Jesus Tradition* 209). The authors go on to give examples of similarity between Jesus and Paul: the healing ministry, the welcoming of sinners (especially Gentiles), the lives of poverty, and the humble service to others (Eddy and Boyd 209).

The fourth factor we must consider is that, according to Paul, he had a vast knowledge that no one else had. He stated, "And lest I should be exalted above measure through the abundance of the revelations, there was given to me a thorn in the flesh, the messenger of Satan to buffet me, lest I should be exalted above measure" (2 Corinthians 12:7). This verse arguably implies that Paul had greater knowledge of revelation than any other living person. In fact, as this verse points out, his knowledge was so great that he had to have a "thorn" given to him so that he would not become too proud of his knowledge. Now, whether this knowledge contains information of a historical Jesus or not is moot, for whatever the case may be, Paul had greater knowledge than any other living person. If it were necessary, this revelation would contain information concerning Jesus. If not, then it would be absent.

Hurtado, in *LORD Jesus Christ*, utilizes this verse for another purpose, however. Since Corinthians is such an early book, Hurtado notes it is significant that this displays a very early High Christology because Paul prays to Jesus (Hurtado, 141).

The Damascus Road and Paul's Credibility

Historical analysis is unique because it mixes metaphysical reality (the event) with epistemological limitations. The epistemological limitations are vast and include subjective bias, limited records of events or persons, conflicted reports, and much more. For the purposes of this paper, we must consider the general validity of Paul as a source. Gary Habermas, in a debate with Antony Flew, notes some of the criticism posited by Jack Kent in his book *The Psychological Origins of the Resurrection Myth*. He states namely that Paul experienced conversion disorder while on the road to Damascus, and did not have an experience with the risen Jesus. If this is true, and Paul never had an interaction with the resurrected Jesus, then it would follow that he did not have the authority he claimed. Therefore, this objection warrants attention if I am going to maintain my thesis that Paul was a disciple of the historical Jesus.

Conversion disorder is commonly known as hysteria, but Habermas explains away this misconception that Paul was afflicted with such a thing. If one is attempting to find a naturalistic explanation, conversion disorder alone will not get one there because the symptoms of conversion disorder do not usually include hallucinations. Further, Paul did not merely have normal visual hallucinations, but also auditory hallucinations. On top of this, Paul would also have something similar to a "God-Complex" where one feels as if God has spoken to him and told him to change his life and to preach this message to others (Gary R. Habermas and Antony G.N. Flew, *Resurrected?:An Atheist and Theist Dialogue*, ed. John Ankerberg).

Occam's Razor is an epistemological tool utilized in maintaining that explanations should not be multiplied beyond necessity. So if one is confronted with two competing answers that both can fully explain whatever is in question, whichever answer has fewest components would be preferable. For this inquiry, we have the possibility that either Paul had a form of conversion disorder, two different types of hallucinations and a God-complex, or he had an interaction with the risen LORD. Occam's Razor would suggest that the supernatural explanation is to be preferred.

Despite as unlikely the naturalistic explanation is, it loses even further credibility when one examines the aspects of conversion disorder. Habermas explains, "Conversion disorder occurs chiefly to women (up to five times more than men), adolescents, people of low economic status, persons with low IQ, and to military persons in battle. That's the five common circumstances. Not a single category applies to Paul" (Habermas 95).

If the naturalistic explanation fails, then only the supernatural explanation should be considered acceptable. If the supernatural explanation is the case, and Paul did indeed have an interaction with Jesus, this would be an important piece of evidence for the authenticity of Paul.

The conversion experience is also significant for the credibility of Paul for several other reasons. Larry Hurtado notes in his book *How on Earth Did Jesus Become a God*, that this conversion was a major turning point because "Paul refers to his own conversion as primarily focused on his realization of Jesus' glorious significance.

Furthermore, after his conversion, he quickly associated himself with the religious movement and faith in Jesus that he had been seeking to destroy" (*How On Earth Did Jesus Become a God?: Historical Questions About Earliest Devotion to Jesus* 35). Something significant happened to Paul for the power of his encounter completely transformed him and his desires.

The fact that Paul's desire had changed is the other significant aspect of his conversion. In Richard's Bauckham's book *Jesus and the God of Israel* he notes that the strict monotheism of the second temple Judaism was her defining characteristic. Because of this it is quite unusual that one of these Jews (especially one who was a Pharisee) would worship or serve anyone else other than God, "...worship in the Jewish tradition is precisely recognition of the unique identity." (25). The fact that Paul suddenly became devoted to Jesus as LORD is further evidence of a genuine and powerful conversion.

Besides Paul being a credible source, there are other problems with reliability concerning him. An often utilized verse of Paul quoting Jesus is Acts 20:35, "In all things I have shown you that by so toiling one must help the weak, remembering the words of the Lord Jesus, how he said, 'It is more blessed to give than to receive.'" It is often raised that Jesus never said this, and therefore Paul either fabricated this, or it is merely something someone told Paul and they themselves were mistaken. James Dunn writes that it is not fair to dismiss the probability of various allusions to Jesus in Paul's writing (James K. Beilby and Paul R. Eddy, eds., *The Historical Jesus: Five Views* 97). John wrote in his Gospel that Jesus performed many miracles that were not written about in the gospels (John 20:30). If this is true, it is not unlikely that there also existed sayings and teachings that were not contained in the gospels as well. Further, it seems from the context of the verse that Paul was not teaching this concept, but rather reminding people of something Jesus had said that was commonly known.

Another highly contested verse is 1 Corinthians 9:5, "Do we not have a right to take along a believing wife, even as the rest of the apostles and the brothers of the Lord and Cephas?" Because of the increasing popularity of the Jesus-Myth view, this verse has fallen on recent scrutiny. The classical understanding of this verse is that Paul had knowledge that the apostles, as well as Cephas, had wives. Paul also has knowledge that Jesus' half-brothers James, Joseph, Judas, and Simeon had wives as well. Two common alternate interpretations are that there was a church in Jerusalem called "The brothers of Jesus" and the other is that the word "brother" is in reference to fellowship, that under the fictional Christ, all believers are "brothers." Both of these interpretations have the same ultimate problem in that they are examples of putting meaning into the text (eisegesis) instead of pulling meaning from the text (exegesis). Indeed believers, in the New Testament, are often referred to as "Brothers" but never as "brothers of Jesus." Further, no other church in the New Testament has such a name. The New Testament churches are referred to as "The church at Corinth, the church at Ephesus" and so on. "The Church at Jerusalem" in which James (Jesus' half-brother) was overseer is referred to as the "Church at Jerusalem", but never as "The brothers of Jesus Church." Considering the amount of space warranted to the actions of the early church in Jerusalem in "Acts," it seems that if this was a common name it would have been used there as well. James Dunn in response to Robert Price (who holds this view) writes that this… "indicates an argument that is scraping the barrel and has lost its self-respect" (Beilby and Eddy 97).

Since these two errant interpretations fail, we are left justified only in the classical interpretation; it grants us a clearer picture of Paul's Historical Jesus, namely that he had brothers, and Cephas was his disciple, both of which correspond with the Gospels.

The rest of the paper will directly examine the knowledge Paul had concerning Jesus. This examination is composed of two parts: the first are verses where Paul displays specific knowledge of Jesus' life and the second part deals with parallel teachings of Jesus and Paul. The parallel teaching is the most significant portion of evidence. This is because the teachings of Jesus that we will be examining are his most recognized and distinguished teachings. Because Paul does not waiver in any way from these crucial teachings, one becomes persuaded that Paul was the disciple of the historical Jesus.

The most commonly used examples of Paul's knowledge of Jesus will only be briefly mentioned. The Lord's Supper passage (1 Corinthians 11:23-26) and 1 Corinthians 15 are perhaps the most popular. In fact, Paul's first letter to the Corinthians gives us much insight into Jesus. Paul relates that the death of Jesus was at the hands of earthly rulers (2:8), Jesus' death was related to the Passover Celebration (5:7), Jesus initiated the Lord's Supper and referred to the bread and the cup as his broken body and spilled blood (11:23-25), and Jesus was betrayed on the night of the Lord's Supper (11:23-25). Darrell Bock writes that the Last Supper, "is assumed in practically all early Christian communities" (Beilby and Eddy 101). Therefore, Paul was merely writing about what was commonly known. Paul also had other knowledge of Jesus' death: Jesus underwent abuse and humiliation (Romans 15:3), Jewish authorities were involved with Jesus' death (1 Thessalonians 2:14-16), his trial was overseen by Pontius Pilate (1 Timothy 6:13), and Jesus died by crucifixion (2 Corinthians 13:4).

The fifteenth chapter of 1 Corinthians also contains a wealth of information about Jesus. Jesus was physically buried (verse 4), Paul refers to Peter in the same way that Jesus did ("Cephas," verse 4), Jesus had twelve disciples and the Risen LORD appeared to them (verse 4), and the risen LORD appeared to James the half-brother of Jesus as well (verse 7). Michael Grant, in his book *The Search for the*

Historical Jesus, claims that this is a very early and therefore reliable account of the resurrection; this account predates the Gospel accounts by 20 years (Michael Grant, Jesus: *An Historian's Review of the Gospels* 178).

Jesus' Humanity

It is debatable if Paul ever mentions the virgin birth. One could make a solid argument from Galatians 4:4 where Paul writes that Jesus is "born of woman." Two things are worth noting from this verse. It would quite redundant for Paul to write that someone is born from a woman, for could not this be said of anyone? Thus, would he not be saying something specific about Jesus? Or that he was only born of women? Further, the mention of Jesus being born of woman (and not man) is crucial because Paul is arguing that the sin of Adam, which is passed through man, therefore has not tainted Jesus. Therefore, Paul is claiming that Jesus was without sin. The second significant aspect is the very mention of Jesus' birth, for this would be the first step in establishing a historical account of someone.

What else does Paul write about Jesus' birth? Romans 1:3 refers to Jesus as being born of flesh and specifically, "of the seed of David." Being born of the seed of David is quite revealing. It tells us that Jesus was a child of Israel, which He was born of the tribe of Judah, and of course the tribe of Judah was known for being the lineage of the king.

Conceptual teachings of Paul and Jesus are also significant for our purposes. Any writing of Paul's that corresponds with a saying or teaching of Jesus is evidence of a connection between the Paul and the historical Jesus; namely a disciple should be well versed in the primary principles of his master. It is clear from Galatians that Paul argued that he received both his apostleship and teaching from Jesus directly. While one might argue the lack of direct quotations is troublesome, there are several key doctrines and teachings that both Paul and Jesus argue for and these bear a striking similarity. I have compiled what many would claim are the most well-known and popular teachings of Jesus and have compared them with similar teachings of his disciple, Paul.

Jesus is God

Jesus said and did many things that displayed his deity. He accepted worship, forgave sin, cast out demons with his own authority, claimed to be LORD of the Sabbath, claimed to have authority over the temple, and predicted his death and resurrection. Paul likewise taught the deity of Christ throughout his epistles and referred to Jesus as God. One of the best examples is found in Philippians 2:6: "who, being in the form of God, did not consider it robbery to be equal with God." Also Paul referred to Jesus as "Son of God" (1 Corinthians 1:9). In the Jewish mindset, "the Son of God" entails equality with God. This seems to follow, for a puppy has the same nature as his dog dad, a guppy has the same nature as a fully grown fish; likewise, the Son of God has the same nature of God Himself.

Live from the Gospel

Paul's note in1 Corinthians 9:14, "Even so the Lord has commanded that those who preach the gospel should live from the gospel," corresponds with Matthew 10:9. "Provide neither gold, nor silver, nor copper in your money belts, nor bag for your journey, nor two tunics, nor sandals, nor staffs; for a worker is worthy of his food." This is another clear example of Paul having knowledge of a disseminated teaching of Jesus.

Cleanliness

Another parallel teaching is on cleanliness. Paul in Romans 14:14 wrote, "I know and am convinced by the Lord Jesus that there is nothing unclean of itself; but to him who considers anything to be unclean, to him it is unclean." And Mark 7:15, "There is nothing that enters a man from outside which can defile him; but the things which come out of him, those are the things that defile a man."

Dedication to the Cause of Christ

Jesus said, "No man having put his hand to the plow and looking back is fit for the kingdom of heaven." (Luke 9:62). Paul wrote often and argued for full dedication to Christ. Paul, in his second letter to the Corinthians, mentions how dedicated he is. While arguing for his apostleship, he states that three times he received 40 stripes minus one, five times he was beaten with rods, that he has been ship wrecked, beaten and also constantly has various perils about him (11:25). Despite all these things Paul had an unwavering dedication to the cause of Christ and he urged others to follow his example.

Retaliation

One of Jesus' more famous teachings is to "turn the other cheek" (Matthew 5:39) and to avoid retaliation. Likewise Paul wrote to the Romans in 12:7 "Do not repay evil for evil." These two teachings are very similar and also give us a segue into Jesus' and Paul's view of Government.

Government

Jesus does not talk much about government, but two of the most significant mentions of it correspond to a few key passages from Paul. The most famous quotation concerning Government and Jesus is "Render to Caesar what is Caesar's and to God what is God's" (Matthew 22:20). This quotation is in response to the question of whether Jews should pay taxes. The two most important aspects gleaned from this are: first, government has a place within Christian worldview and, second, God obviously created all things, which includes human government. God instituted human government after the flood by saying, "whoever sheds man's blood, by man shall his blood be shed" (Genesis 9:6). Because government is a creation of God, it is He that has control over it. Jesus confirmed this when He was on trial and said to the procurator that the authority he had was given to him (John 19:11). Paul likewise echoes both of these ideas in his letter to the Romans. In fact, Paul almost sounds as if he is contradicting himself when he claims, in Romans 13:1, "Let every soul be subject to the governing authorities. For there is no authority except from God, and the authorities that exist are appointed by God." Paul argues that Christians should submit to governing authorities. However, in the very next breath, he maintains that the government only exists and has authority because of God.

Do Not Worry

Another very famous saying of Jesus is his urge for people not to worry: God sees to it that the flowers of field are adorned and the birds of the air have food of plenty (Matthew 6:28). One of the most quoted verses by Paul was on this very subject: "Be anxious for nothing, but in everything by prayer and supplication, with thanksgiving, let your requests be made known to God" (Philippians 4:3).

Judgment

The current most popular saying of Jesus is, "judge not lest you also be judged" (Matthew 7:1). This teaching is often misunderstood for several reasons. First of all, this was not a command to not judge, for as the following verses confirm, it is a warning to know when it is appropriate to judge and to what audience. Jesus judged the Pharisees for their hypocrisy, but did not judge the people who knew they needed Him. Therefore, this confirms the interpretation that one must judge wisely. Paul taught something very similar to this to the Corinthian church. He had written to them to not judge the people of the world, for they had no right to do so. Conversely, he told them it was their duty to judge willful, habitual sinners who were inside the church (1 Corinthians 5:12).

Christ Getting the Glory

Jesus taught, "I am the vine, you are the branches, He who abides in me and I in him will bear much fruit, but apart from me he can do nothing" (John 15:5). Paul taught something very similar, even using a similar analogy, "Who then is Paul, and who is Apollos, but ministers through whom you believed, as the Lord gave to each one? I planted, Apollos watered, but God gave the increase. So then neither he who plants is anything, nor he who waters, but God who gives the increase" (1 Corinthians 3:7). Also, Paul finishes the well-known creed of 1 Corinthians 15 by adding a few personal caveats, one of them being "But by the grace of God I am what I am, and His grace toward me was not in vain; but I labored more abundantly than they all, yet not I, but the grace of God which was with me." Paul confirms in both of these verses that all are ineffectual without the grace of God.

The Greatest Commandment

Jesus stated that the greatest commandment is "You shall love the LORD your God with all your heart, with all your soul, and with all your mind" (Matthew 22:37). Paul, of course, was a brilliant scholar and had no trouble loving God with his mind. It is also incumbent within those writings that he loved God with all of his heart and soul as well. The best example of this writing is his first letter to the Corinthians and the "love" chapter. He writes that all the effort in the world is useless if it is not based on love.

The Second Greatest Commandment

Jesus taught that the second greatest commandment was like the first, "You shall love your neighbor as yourself" (Matthew 22:37). Not only does Paul echo this teaching throughout his works, but he also quotes this passage in Romans 13:8, "Let no debt remain outstanding, except the continuing debt to love one another, for he who loves his fellowman has fulfilled the law… 'Love your neighbor as yourself.'"

Being a Servant

Jesus had much to illustrate and teach about being a servant. He claimed that if you want to be a leader of many, you must be a servant of many (Mark 9:35). He set an example of service by washing the disciples' feet (John 13). In Philippians 2:5-7, Paul tells his readers: "Let this mind be in you which was also in Christ Jesus, who, being in the form of God, did not consider it robbery to be equal with God, but made Himself of no reputation, taking the form of a bondservant, and coming in the likeness of men." He also urged other Christians to have this same mindset, "let men so consider us as servants and stewards of the mysteries of God, moreover it is required that a servant be found faithful" (1 Corinthians 4:1-2).

Gaining the World versus Losing Your Soul

One of the more offsetting and thought provoking teachings of Jesus was "For what profit is it to a man if he gains the whole world, and loses his own soul? Or what will a man give in exchange for his soul?" (Matthew 16:26). Paul took this idea very seriously, and his dedication to Jesus was unwavering. "Yet indeed I also count all things loss for the excellence of the knowledge of Christ Jesus my Lord, for whom I have suffered the loss of all things, and count them as rubbish, that I may gain Christ" (Philippians 3:8).

The Law

Jesus cleared up many misconceptions concerning the Law, as did Paul. They both mention the weakness of the human interpretation of the law, the profit of the law, and the completion of the Law as found within Christ. Jesus pointed out several times to the Pharisees that they did not quite understand the law; the law was meant to benefit man. Paul writes in Romans that the law is good because it shows man his need for a savior, but the law itself does not save (Romans 2-3). He put it quite bluntly to the Galatian church, "If salvation comes through the Law, then Christ died in vain."

Jesus also made the miraculous claim, "Do not think I came to destroy the law and the prophets, I did not come to destroy but to fulfill" (Matthew 5:17). The verse we already examined by Paul is profitable here as well: "... Love does no harm to its neighbor. Therefore love is the fulfillment of the Law" (Romans 13:8-10).

The Kingdom of God

One of Jesus' biggest themes is the Kingdom, both the present and the future. The forerunner of Jesus proclaimed, "Repent, for the kingdom of God is at hand" (Matthew 3:2). And Jesus taught that the Kingdom of God is now here and within people (Luke 17:21), and that He would be coming again to set up a future kingdom (Matthew 25). Paul wrote of both the present and the future kingdoms. Paul spoke of the present kingdom in these words: "He has delivered us from the power of darkness and conveyed us into the kingdom of the Son of His love, in whom we have redemption through His blood, the forgiveness of sins" (Colossians 1:13-14). Paul also wrote of the future aspect of God's Kingdom: "And the future for the Lord himself will come down from heaven, with a loud command, with the voice of the archangel and with the trumpet call of God, and the dead in Christ will rise first. After that, we who are still alive and are left will be caught up together with them in the clouds to meet the Lord in the air. And so we will be with the Lord forever" (1 Thessalonians 4:15-17).

Divine Retribution

Jesus taught more about hell than He did about Heaven. He referred to it as "outer darkness," a place of "weeping and gnashing of teeth . . . where the worm does not die, and the fire does not cease." He shocked those listening by teaching that human righteousness is insufficient for salvation ("unless your righteousness exceeds that of the Pharisees and Sadducees you will by no means enter the kingdom of heaven," Matthew 5:20). Paul likewise taught in 2 Thessalonians 1:9: "These shall be punished with everlasting destruction from the presence of the Lord and from the glory of His power…" And, he also taught it was only the declaration of righteousness by Jesus that could save someone (Romans 5:1).

God Loves Everyone

Before the advent of postmodernism, the most quoted verse was John 3:16. Many have summed up Jesus' teaching with this verse. Paul likewise argued for the love of God in Romans 8:37-39: "Yet in all these things we are more than conquerors through Him who loved us. For I am persuaded that neither death nor life, nor angels nor principalities nor powers, nor things present nor things to come, nor height nor depth, nor any other created thing, shall be able to separate us from the love of God which is in Christ Jesus our Lord."

In examining the account of the road to Damascus revelation, it is evident that the most likely interpretation is that Paul had a supernatural encounter with the risen Jesus Christ; that this encounter marked the beginning of the ministry of Paul and the beginning of the instruction he received from Christ. Paul was considered by Peter, John, and James to be an authoritative preacher of the same gospel they preached. Paul had basic knowledge of various facts of Jesus' life and quoted him several times in his teachings.

Bibliography for Appendix Four

Barnett, Paul W. *Jesus and the Logic of History (New Studies in Biblical Theology).* Chicago: IVP Academic, 2001.

Eddy, Paul Rhodes, and Gregory A. Boyd. *The Jesus Legend: a Case for the Historical Reliability of the Synoptic Jesus Tradition.* Grand Rapids, MI: Baker Academic, 2007.

Grant, Michael. *Jesus: An Historian's Review of the Gospels*. New York: Scribner, 1995.

Habermas, Gary R., and Antony G.N. Flew. *Resurrected?: An Atheist and Theist Dialogue.* Edited by John Ankerberg. Lanham, Md.: Rowman & Littlefield Publishers, Inc., 2005.

Hurtado, Larry W. *How On Earth Did Jesus Become a God?: Historical Questions About Earliest Devotion to Jesus*. Grand Rapids, Mich.: Wm. B. Eerdmans Publishing Company, 2005.

Hurtado, Larry W. *Lord Jesus Christ: Devotion to Jesus in Earliest Christianity*. Pbk. Ed ed. Grand Rapids: William B. Eerdmans Publishing Company, 2005.

Appendix Five: Proposed Timeline

By Phil Fernandes

Date	Events
27 BC-14 AD	reign of Caesar Augustus
6-2 BC	birth of Christ
4-2 BC	death of Herod the Great
14 AD-37 AD	reign of Emperor Tiberius
26-36 AD	Pontius Pilate—governor of Judea
29-33 AD (or, 27-30 AD)	Jesus' public ministry
33 AD (or, 30 AD)	Jesus death & resurrection
33-34 AD	Saul (i.e., Paul) persecutes the early church
34 AD	Paul converted on the Road to Damascus
35-42 AD	Matthew writes his Gospel in Hebrew; later he translates it into Greek

37 AD	Paul's first visit to Jerusalem after being saved
37-41 AD	reign of Emperor Caligula
41-54 AD	reign of Emperor Tiberius
42 AD	James son of Zebedee beheaded by Herod Agrippa I
42-44 AD	Peter flees Jerusalem; visits Rome & preaches there
44 AD	Herod Agrippa I dies
45 AD	James (Jesus' brother) writes his epistle? Peter returns to Jerusalem? Mark writes his Gospel after Peter departs Rome
45-50 AD	Luke researches and writes his Gospel
46-48 AD	Paul's first missionary journey
48 AD	Paul's second visit to Jerusalem Peter is in Jerusalem at the time After leaving Jerusalem, Paul writes Galatians
49 AD	Peter and Paul attend the Jerusalem Council

50-52 AD	Paul's second missionary journey
51-52 AD	Paul writes 1 and 2 Thessalonians
Early to mid-50's AD	John writes his Gospel
53-57 AD	Paul's third missionary journey
55-56 AD	Paul writes 1 and 2 Corinthians
57 AD	Paul writes Romans
54-68 AD	reign of Emperor Nero
58 AD	Paul's fourth trip to Jerusalem; Paul imprisoned
58-59 AD	Paul imprisoned in Caesarea
59-62 AD	Paul's first Roman imprisonment
61 AD	Paul writes prison epistles (Ephesians, Philippians, Colossians, Philemon) Luke writes Acts
62 AD	James (Jesus' brother) martyred in Jerusalem
63-65 AD	Paul's fourth missionary journey—he goes to Spain?

60's AD	the Didache is written (were 1, 2, 3 John, Jude, & Revelation written this early?)
66-67 AD	Paul's second Roman imprisonment Paul writes 1 and 2 Timothy, and Titus Peter writes 2 Peter while imprisoned in Rome
67 AD	Peter and Paul martyred in Rome by Nero
68-69 AD	Hebrews written by one of Paul's colleagues
Early 70 AD	Clement of Rome writes his letter Domitian begins his first (temporary) reign as Emperor
70 AD	Jerusalem destroyed by the Romans
Mid 70's AD	Epistle of Barnabas written
70's to 96 AD	1, 2, 3 John, Jude, and Revelation written?
81-96 AD	Domitian's second reign as emperor
90's AD	the Apostle John dies as an old man

107 AD	Ignatius writes his seven letters before his martyrdom Polycarp writes his letter
156 AD	Polycarp, the last of the Apostolic Fathers, is martyred at the age of 86

At least 22 New Testament books were written before 70 AD:

--the four Gospels
--Acts
--Paul's 13 letters
--Hebrews
--James
--Peter's 2 letters

5 New Testament books that were possibly written after 70 AD:

--1, 2, 3 John
--Jude
--Revelation

(But, if the *Didache*, the *Epistle of Clement to the Corinthians*, and the *Epistle of Barnabas* were written in the 60's and 70's AD, then all twenty-seven New Testament books were probably written before 70 AD.)

Works Consulted

Antonacci, Mark. *The Resurrection of the Shroud: New Scientific, Medical and Archeological Evidence*. New York: M. Evans and Company, 2000.

Barnett, Paul. *The Birth of Christianity: The First Twenty Years*. Grand Rapids: Eerdmans, 2005.

Barnett, Paul. *Finding the Historical Jesus*. Grand Rapids: Eerdmans Publishing House, 2009.

Barnett, Paul. *Jesus & the Logic of History*. Grand Rapids: Eerdmans, 1997.

Barnett, Paul. *Is the New Testament Reliable?* Downers Grove: InterVarsity Press, 2003.

Barnett, Paul *Messiah: Jesus—the Evidence of History*. Nottingham: Inter Varsity Press, 2009.

Bauckham, Richard. *The Testimony of the Beloved Disciple*. Grand Rapids: Baker Book House, 2007.

Bauckham, Richard. *Jesus and the Eyewitnesses*. Grand Rapids: Eerdmans, 2006.

Blomberg, Craig. *The Historical Reliability of the Gospels*. Downers Grove: Inter - Varsity Press, 1987.

Bock, Darrell and Daniel Wallace. *Dethroning Jesus: Exposing Popular Culture's Quest to Unseat the Biblical Christ.* Nashville: Thomas Nelson Publishers, 2007).

Borg, Marcus. *The Heart of Christianity*. San Francisco: Harper, 2003.

Borg, Marcus. *Jesus: The New Vision*. San Francisco: Harper, 1987.

Borg, Marcus and N. T. Wright. *The Meaning of Jesus: Two Visions*. Harper,1999.

Boyd, Gregory A. *Cynic Sage or Son of God?* Wheaton: Victor Books, 1995.

Boyd, Gregory A. and Paul Rhodes Eddy. *The Jesus Legend—A Case for the Historica Reliability of the Synoptic Tradition*. Grand Rapids: Baker Book House, 2007.

Boyd, Gregory A. and Paul Rhodes Eddy. *Lord or Legend: Wrestling with the Jesus Dilemma*. Grand Rapids: Baker Book House, 2007.

Brown, Raymond E. *An Introduction to New Testament Christology*. New York: Paulist Press, 1994.

Bruce, F. F. *The Canon of Scripture*. Downers Grove: InterVarsity Press, 1988.

Bruce, F. F. *The New Testament Documents: Are They Reliable?* Downers Grove: InterVarsity Press, 1960.

Bultmann, Rudolph. *Kerygma and Myth.* New York: Harper and Row, 1961.

Cairns, Earl E. *Christianity Through the Centuries*. Grand Rapids: Zondervan Publishing House, 1981.

Carson, D. A., Douglas J. Moo, and Leon Morris. *An Introduction to the New Testament*. Grand Rapids: Zondervan Publishing House, 1992.

Copan, Paul, ed., *Will the Real Jesus Please Stand Up? A Debate Between William Lane Craig and John Dominic Crossan*. Grand Rapids: Baker Book House, 1998.

Copan, Paul. *Is God a Moral Monster?* Grand Rapids: Baker Book House, 2011.

Copleston, Frederick. *A History of Philosophy*. 3 books. 9 vols. New York: DoubleDay, 1960.

Corduan, Winfried. *Reasonable Faith*. Nashville: Broadman and Holman Publishers, 1993.

Craig, William Lane. *Apologetics: An Introduction*. Chicago: Moody Press, 1984.

Craig, William Lane. *Reasonable Faith*. Wheaton: Crossway Books, 1994.

Craig, William Lane. *The Son Rises*. Eugene: Wipf and Stock Publishers, 1981.

Crossan, John Dominic. *Jesus: A Revolutionary Biography*. San Francisco: HarperSanFrancisco, 1994).

Crossan, John Dominic. *The Historical Jesus: The Life of a Mediterranean Jewish Peasant*. San Francisco: Harper Collins, 1991.

Dawkins, Richard, "Forgive Me, Spirit of Science," *New Statesman*. 20 December, 2010.

Dunn, James D. G. *Christianity in the Making*, vol. 1. Grand Rapids: William B. Eerdmans Publishing, 2003.

Dunn, James D. G. *A New Perspective on Jesus*. Grand Rapids: Baker Books, 2005.

Ehrman, Bart. *Misquoting Jesus:The Story Behind Who Changed the Bible and Why*. New York: Harper Collins, 2005.

Erickson, Millard J. *The Word Became Flesh*. Grand Rapids: Baker Book House, 1991.

Evans, Craig A. *Fabricating Jesus*. Downers Grove: InterVarsity Press, 2006.

Evans, C. Stephen. *The Historical Christ and the Jesus of Faith*. Oxford: OxfordUniversity Press, 1996.

Fernandes, Phil. *The God Who Sits Enthroned*. Fairfax: Xulon Press, 2002.

Fernandes, Phil. *No Other Gods*. Fairfax: Xulon Press, 2002.

Flew, Antony. *There is a God*. New York: Harper Collins Publishers, 2007.

Foxe, John. *Foxe's Book of Martyrs*. Springdale: Whitaker House, 1981.

Fuller, Reginald. *Christ and Christianity*. Valley Forge: Trinity Press, 1994.

Funk, Robert and Roy W. Hoover. *The Five Gospels: What Did Jesus Really Say?* NewYork: Macmillian, 1993.

Gandhi, Mohandas K. *Mahatma Gandhi Autobiography*. Washington, D. C.: Public Affairs, 1948.

Geisler, Norman L. *The Battle for the Resurrection*. Nashville: Thomas Nelson Publishers, 1989.

Geisler, Norman L. *Christian Apologetics*. Grand Rapids: Baker Book House, 1976.

Geisler, Norman L. *In Defense of the Resurrection*. Charlotte: Quest Publications, 1991.

Geisler, Norman L., ed. *Inerrancy*. Grand Rapids: Academic Books, 1980.

Geisler, Norman L. *Miracles and the Modern Mind*. Grand Rapids: Baker Book House, 1992.

Geisler, Norman L. and William E. Nix. *A General Introduction to the Bible*. Chicago: Moody Press, 1986.

Geisler, Norman L. and Frank Turek. *I Don't Have Enough Faith to be an Atheist*. Wheaton: Crossway Books, 2004.

Geivett, R. Douglas and Gary R. Habermas. Editors. *In Defense of Miracles*. Downers Grove: Inter Varsity, 1997.

Grenz, Stanley. *A Primer on Postmodernism*. Grand Rapids: Eerdmans Publishing Company, 1996.

Guerrera, Vittorio. *The Shroud of Turin: A Case for Authenticity*. Rockford, Illonois: Tan Books and Publishers, 2001.

Guscin, Mark. *The Oviedo Cloth*. Cambridge: The Lutterworth Press, 1998.

Habermas, Gary R. *Ancient Evidence for the Life of Jesus*. Nashville: Thomas Nelson Publishers, 1984.

Habermas, Gary R. *The Historical Jesus*. Joplin, Missouri: College Press, 1996.

Habermas, Gary R. *The Resurrection of Jesus*. Lanham: University Press of America, 1984.

Habermas, Gary R. *The Risen Jesus and Future Hope*. Lanham: Rowan and Littlefield, 2003.

Habermas, Gary R. and Michael R. Licona. *The Case for the Resurrection of Jesus*. Grand Rapids: Kregel Publications, 2004.

Habermas, Gary R. and Antony G. N. Flew. *Did Jesus Rise From the Dead?* Edited by Terry L. Miethe. New York: Harper and Row, 1987.

Habermas, Gary R. and Antony G. N. Flew. *Resurrected? An Atheist and Theist Dialogue*. Edited by John F. Ankerberg. Lanham: Rowan and Littlefield, 2005.

Harris, Murray. *Raised Immortal:Resurrection and Immortality in the New Testament*. Grand Rapids: William B. Eerdmans, 1985.

Hick, John. *The Center of Christianity*. New York: Harper and Row, 1978.

Hume, David. *An Inquiry Concerning Human Understanding*. New York: The Liberal Arts Press, 1955.

Hurtado, Larry W. *Lord Jesus Christ: Devotion to Jesus in Earliest Christianity*. Grand Rapids: William B. Eerdmans Publishing, 2003.

Josephus, Flavius. *The Works of Josephus*. Translated by William Whiston. Peabody: Hendrickson Publishers, 1987.

Keating, Karl. *What Catholics Really Believe*. Ann Arbor: Servant Publications, 1992.

Kee, Howard Clark. *Jesus in History: An Approach to the Study of the Gospels*. New York: Harcourt Brace Jovanovich Publishers, 1977.

Kenyon, Frederic. *The Bible and Archeology*. New York: Harper, 1940.

Kostenberger, Andreas J. and Michael J. Kruger. *The Heresy of Orthodoxy: How Contemporary Culture's Fascination with Diversity Has Reshaped Our Understanding of Early Christianity*. Wheaton, Illinois: Crossway Books, 2010.

Lavoie, Gilbert R. *Unlocking the Secrets of the Shroud*. Allen, Texas: Thomas More, 1998.

Lennox, John C. *Gunning for God: Why the New Atheists are Missing the Target*. Oxford: Lion Hudson, 2011.

Let God be True. Brooklyn: Watchtower Bible and Tract Society, 1946.

Lewis, C. S. *Mere Christianity*. New York: Collier Books, 1943.

Lewis, C. S. *Miracles*. New York: Collier Books, 1960.

Lightfoot, J. B. and J. R. Harmer. Translators. *The Apostolic Fathers*. Grand Rapids: Baker Book House, 1984.

Longenecker, Richard N., ed. *Contours of Christology in the New Testament*. Grand Rapids: William B. Eerdmans Publishing Company, 2005.

Luedemann, Gerd. *The Resurrection of Jesus*. Minneapolis: Fortress Press, 1994.

Ludlow, Daniel H. Editor. *Latter-Day Prophets Speak*. Salt Lake City: Bookcraft, 1948.

Marshall, I. Howard. *The Origins of New Testament Christology*. Downers Grove: InterVarsity Press, 1990.

Martin, Walter R. *The Kingdom of the Cults*. Minneapolis: Bethany House, 1977.

McConkie, Bruce R. *Mormon Doctrine*. Salt Lake City: Brookcraft, 1966.

McDowell, Josh. *The New Evidence that Demands a Verdict*. Nashville: Thomas Nelson Publishers, 1999.

McDowell, Josh. *Evidence that Demands a Verdict*. San Bernardino: Here's Life Publishers, 1974.

McDowell, Josh and Don Stewart. *Handbook of Today's Religions*. San Bernardino: Here's Life Publishers, 1983.

McDowell, Josh and Bill Wilson. *He Walked Among Us*. San Bernardino: Here's Life Publishers, 1988.

Metzger, Bruce M. *The Canon of the New Testament*. Oxford: Clarendon press, 1987.

Miethe, Terry L. and Gary R. Habermas. *Why Believe? God Exists!* Joplin: College Press, 1993.

Moo, Douglas J. *James*. Leicester, England: Inter Varsity Press, 1985.

Moore, John. "The Quest for the Historical Jesus." *The Conspiracy to Silence the Son of God*. Ed. Tal Brooke. Eugene: Harvest House Publishers, 1998, 171-188.

Moreland, J. P. *Scaling the Secular City*. Grand Rapids: Baker Book House, 1987.

Moreland, J. P. and Michael J. Wilkins. *Jesus Under Fire*. Grand Rapids: Zondervan Publishing House, 1995.

Morris, Henry M. *Many Infallible Proofs*. El Cajon: Master Books, 1974.

Morris, Leon. *1 Corinthians*. Leicester, England: Intervarsity Press, 1995.

Nash, Ronald. *The Gospel and the Greeks: Did the New Testament Borrow from Pagan Thought?* Phillipsburg: Presbyterian and Reformed, 1992.

Nicholi, JR. Armand M. *The Question of God: C. S. Lewis and Sigmund Freud Debate God, Love, Sex and the Meaning of Life*. New York: The Free press, 2002.

Pentecost, J. Dwight. *The Words and Works of Jesus Christ*. Grand Rapids: Academic Books, 1981.

Reymond, Robert L. *Jesus: Divine Messiah*. Phillipsburg: Presbyterian & Reformed Publishing, 1990.

Robertson, A. T. *Word Pictures in the New Testament*, vol. 4. Grand Rapids: Baker Book House, 1931.

Robinson, John A. T. *Redating the New Testament*. Eugene: Wipf and Stock Publishers, 1976.

Sanders, E. P. *The Historical Figure of Jesus*. London: Penguin Books, 1993.

Sanders, E. P. *Jesus and Judaism*. Philadelphia: Fortress Press, 1985.

Schweitzer, Albert. *The Quest for the Historical Jesus*. Trans. W. Montgomery, 2nd ed. London: Adam & Charles Black, 1945.

Sherwin-White, A. N. *Roman Society and Roman Law in the New Testament*. Oxford: Clarendon, 1963.

Stevenson, Kenneth E. *Image of the Risen Christ*. Toronto: Frontier Research Publications, 1999.

Stevenson, Kenneth E. and Gary R. Habermas. *The Shroud and the Controversy*. Nashville: Thomas Nelson Publishers, 1990.

Stevenson, Kenneth E. and Gary R. Habermas. *The Verdict on the Shroud*. Wayne: Banbury Books, 1981.

Strimple, Robert B. *The Modern Search for the Real Jesus*. Phillipsburg: P & R Publishing, 1995.

Strobel, Lee. *The Case for Christ*. Grand Rapids: Zondervan Publishing House, 1998.

Strobel, Lee. *The Case for the Real Jesus*. Grand Rapids: Zondervan Publishing House, 2007.

Tenney, Merrill C. *John, the Gospel of Belief*. Grand Rapids: William B. Eerdmans Publishing, 1948.

Thiede, Carsten P. *The Dead Sea Scrolls and the Jewish Origins of Christianity*. New York: Palgrave, 2000.

Thiede, Carsten P. *Rekindling the Word*. Valley Forge: Trinity Press, 1995.

Thiede, Carsten P. and Matthew D'Ancona. *Eyewitness to Jesus*. New York: Doubleday, 1996.

Thiessen, Henry C. *Introduction to the New Testament*. Grand Rapids: William B. Eerdmans Publishing Company, 1987.

Thomas, Robert L. and F. David Farnell, eds. *The Jesus Crisis*. Grand Rapids: Kregel Publications, 1998.

Thomas, Robert L., ed. *Three Views of the Origins of the Synoptic Gospels*. Grand Rapids: Kregel Publications, 2002.

Varghese, Roy Abraham. *The Intellectuals Speak Out About God*. Dallas: Lewis and Stanley Publishers, 1984.

Wenham, John. *Redating Matthew, Mark, and Luke*. Downers Grove: Inter Varsity Press, 1992.

Wilkins, Micheal J. and J. P. Moreland. Eds. *Jesus Under Fire*. Grand Rapids: Zondervan Publishing House, 1995.

Wilkox, Robert K. *The Truth about the Shroud of Turin*. Washington, DC: Regnery Publishing, 2010.

Wilson, Ian. *The Blood and the Shroud*. New York: The Free Press, 1998.

Wilson, Ian and Barrie Schwortz. *The Turin Shroud: The Illustrated Evidence*. New York: Barnes and Noble, 2000.

Witherington III, Ben. *The Gospel Code*. Downers Grove: InterVarsity Press, 2004.

Witherington III, Ben. *The Jesus Quest: The Third Search for the Jew of Nazareth*. Downers Grove, Illinois: InterVarsity Press, 1997.

Witherington III, Ben. *The Paul Quest: The Renewed Search for the Jew of Tarsus*. Downers Grove, Illinois: InterVarsity Press, 1998.

The World Book Encyclopedia, vol. 11. Chicago: World Book, Inc., 1985.

Wright, N. T. *The Contemporary Quest for Jesus*. Minneapolis: Fortress Press, 1996.

Wright, N. T. *The Resurrection of the Son of God*. Minneapolis: Fortress Press, 2003.

Zugibe, Frederick T. *The Crucifixion of Jesus: A Forensic Inquiry*. New York: M. Evans and Company, 2005.

Websites Consulted

http://jesusevidences.com/originntgospels/evidencefirstcenturypublishing.php

http://jesusevidences.com/originntgospels/originntgospels.php

ABOUT THE AUTHORS

Phil Fernandes is the senior pastor of Trinity Bible Fellowship and the founder and president of the Institute of Biblical Defense, an apologetics ministry which trains Christians in the defense of the faith. Both ministries are located in Bremerton, Washington. Fernandes also teaches Bible, philosophy, and world religions at Crosspoint Academy in Bremerton, Washington.

Dr. Fernandes has earned a Ph.D. in philosophy of religion from Greenwich University, a Doctor of Theological Studies from Columbia Evangelical Seminary, and a Master of Arts in Religion from Liberty University. Fernandes is currently finishing his Doctor of Ministry in Apologetics studies at Southern Evangelical Seminary, where he studied under Dr. Norman Geisler, Dr. Gary Habermas, and Dr. Richard Howe.

Fernandes has lectured and debated in defense of Christianity on college campuses (such as Princeton, University of North Carolina-Chapel Hill, Washington State University, Oregon State University, University of Washington, etc.) and in public schools. He has debated some of America's leading atheists: Dr. Michael Martin (Professor of Philosophy at Boston University), Jeff Lowder (founder of Atheist Infidels), Dan Barker, Edward Tabash, Doug Kruger, Reggie Findley, Robert Price, and Jim Corbet. He has also debated Rev. Farley Maxwell (former Washington State President of Parents and Friends of Lesbians and Gays).

Dr. Fernandes currently teaches philosophy and apologetics for Columbia Evangelical Seminary. He is a member of the following professional societies: the Evangelical Theological Society, the Evangelical Philosophical Society, the International Society of Christian Apologetics, and the Society of Christian Philosophers.

Dr. Fernandes is the author of several books: *The Atheist Delusion: A Christian Response to Christopher Hitchens and Richard Dawkins* (2009), *Contend Earnestly for the Faith: A Survey of Christian Apologetics* (2008), *The God Who Sits Enthroned: Evidence for God's Existence* (1997), *No Other Gods: A Defense of Biblical Christianity* (1998), *God, Government, and the Road to Tyranny: A Christian View of Government and Morality* (2003), and *Theism vs. Atheism: The Internet Debate* (co-authored with Dr. Michael Martin; 2000).

Dr. Fernandes formerly wrote a monthly religious column for *The Bremerton Sun*. Dr. Fernandes resides in Bremerton, Washington with his lovely wife Cathy. Over 1,000 of Dr. Fernandes' audio lectures, sermon, and debates can be downloaded for free from the Institute of Biblical Defense website. One year certificate programs in apologetics, philosophy, theology, and biblical studeies can be earned on-line through the Institute of Biblical Defense. Dr. Fernandes can be contacted through the address or phone number listed below:

The Institute of Biblical Defense
P. O. Box 3264
Bremerton, WA. 98310
(360) 698-7382
phil@biblicaldefense.org
www.instituteofbiblicaldefense.com
www.philfernandes.org

Kyle Larson is a researcher and writer for the Institute of Biblical Defense. He is a graduate of The King's College with a BA in English. He also has a paralegal certificate from Westchester Community College in New York State. He has taken online courses at Southern Evangelical Seminary with Dr. Norman Geisler.

Kyle has had to deal with the lifelong disability of Cerebral Palsy. Yet his personal faith in the Lord Jesus Christ has kept him going. Kyle came to Jesus for salvation at the age of ten. He was led to Christ through his school bus driver.

Kyle's interest in apologetics began in his late teens, and into his early twenties, while Kyle read Josh McDowell's book *Evidence That Demands A Verdict*. As he continued to study the evidences for Christianity, he found that his personal faith in Jesus was well grounded. His ongoing friendship with Dr. Gary Habermas (of Liberty University) has also helped encouraged him in his faith in Jesus.

Kyle has been very involved in apologetics ministry in the local churches he has attended through various newsletter and small group venues. His passion is to see fellow believers become more effective witnesses for Christ by knowing not only what they believe, but why they believe as well.

J. P. Moreland's Endorsement of the Institute of Biblical Defense

"It comes as no surprise to the reflective Christian that there is a great need for believers who are able to defend the faith intelligently. For that ability to be developed one first must have the right intellectual tools for the job. This is where IBD can help. The programs offered through IBD provide the student with a good foundation in apologetics and introduces him or her to the labor of reason. I recommend IBD for anyone wanting to gain fundamental skills for defending the faith or as a good first step for those wanting to pursue advanced studies in philosophy and theology."

Dr. J. P. Moreland
Professor of Apologetics
Talbot School of Theology, Biola University

24707932R00223

Made in the USA
Middletown, DE
04 October 2015